Basic Concepts
in SAP
Materials Management

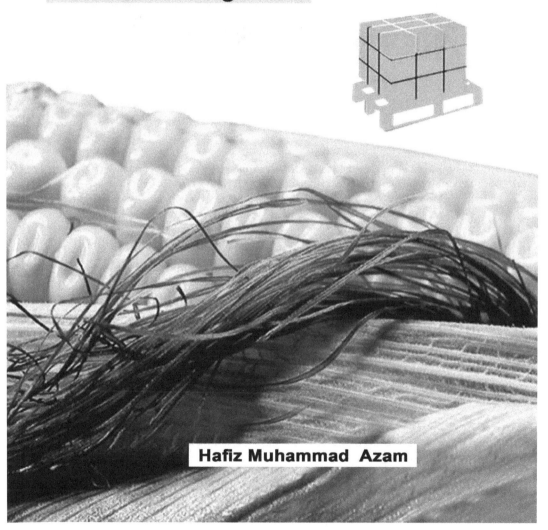

Hafiz Muhammad Azam

Copyrighted© Material

The purpose of this book is to guide you through the main functionality of SAP Materials Management (MM) while describing its important configuration and its integration with other functional areas within SAP. In reading this Book on "Basic Concepts in SAP Materials Management" you will also get a deeper knowledge and understanding of

- Enterprise structure
- Master data management and its important fields
- Components of purchasing
- Procurement processes
- Physical inventory and inventory management
- Logistics invoice verifications
- Material requirement planning (MRP)
- Automatic account determination in inventory posting
- Purchasing document release procedures
- Reporting in SAP MM

ISBN 978-1-9798-3336-3

9 781979 833363 >

Copyrighted© Material

The purpose of this book is to guide you through the main functionality of SAP Materials Management (MM) while describing its important configuration and its integration with other functional areas within SAP. In reading this Book on "Basic Concepts in SAP Materials Management" you will also get a deeper knowledge and understanding of

- Enterprise structure
- Master data management and its important fields
- Components of purchasing
- Procurement processes
- Physical inventory and inventory management
- Logistics invoice verifications
- Material requirement planning (MRP)
- Automatic account determination in inventory posting
- Purchasing document release procedures
- Reporting in SAP MM

ISBN 978-1-6798-3336-3

9 781979 833363

Basic Concepts in SAP Materials Management

(Hafiz Muhammad Azam)

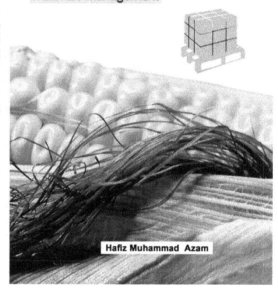

Basic Concepts
in **SAP**
Materials Management

Hafiz Muhammad Azam

Copyrighted© Material

1. Table of Contents

Chapter 1: Introduction 2

   1.1.   Introduction 3

   1.2.   Whom Do This Book Address? 3

   1.3.   ERP and Legacy systems 4

   1.4.   Need Recognition of ERP. 5

   1.5.   Operational Significance of Materials Management.............................. 6

   1.6.   SAP Industry Specific solutions 7

   1.7.   SAP Implementation (Standard) road map methodology 8

   1.8.   SAP S/4 HANA and Activate Road Map Methodology............................ 9

      3.1.1.   Transition to SAP S/4HANA with SAP Activate (Road Map) 10

   1.9.   SAP Solution Manager 12

   1.10.   SAP Modules 14

      1.10.1.   SAP Technical Modules: 14

      1.10.2.   SAP Functional Modules: 14

   1.11.   Introduction to SAP Functional Modules.. 16

      1.11.1.   SAP PP (Production Planning)... 16

      1.11.2.   SAP PM (Plant Maintenance) 16

      1.11.3.   SAP SD (Sales and Distribution) 16

      1.11.4.   SAP HCM (Human Capital Management).. 17

      1.11.5.   SAP MM (Materials Management) 17

      1.11.6.   SAP QM (Quality Management) 18

      1.11.7.   SAP PS (Project System) 18

      1.11.8.   SAP FI (Financial Accounting) 18

      1.11.9.   SAP CO (Managerial Accounting).. 19

Chapter 2: Enterprise Structure in SAP Materials Management...22

   2.1.   Enterprise Structure in SAP Materials Management 23

      2.1.1.   Client... 23

      2.1.2.   Company Code 24

      2.1.3.   Plant.. 24

      2.1.4.   Storage Location 28

      2.1.5.   Purchasing organization.. 30

Copyrighted© Material

2.1.6.   Enterprise Structure Assignments 32

2.1.7.   Purchase Group 34

Chapter 3: Basic Concepts of Material Master and Configuration 38

3.1.   Master Data in SAP Materials Management and Purchasing 39

3.2.   Material Master Data and Configuration 39

3.3.   Configuration aspects of Material types 40

3.3.1.   Material types 40

3.3.2.   Attributes of material types 40

3.3.3.   Assign number ranges 43

3.3.4.   Maintain field selection for data screen 45

3.3.5.   Define industry sector 48

3.3.6.   Lock Relevant Field in Material Master 48

3.4.   Mass maintenance of material master 49

3.5.   Bills of Material (BOM) 51

3.6.   Material Master Record 52

3.6.1.   Basic Data Screen 53

3.6.2.   Classification Data 56

3.6.3.   Sales and Distribution Data 57

3.6.4.   Purchasing Data Screen 58

3.6.5.   Forecasting Data 63

3.6.6.   General Plant Data 68

3.6.7.   Warehouse Management Data 72

3.6.8.   Quality Management Data 75

3.6.9.   Material Requirement Planning (MRP) Data 76

3.6.10.   Accounting Data 81

3.6.11.   Costing Data 85

3.5. External Services 88

Chapter 4: Basic Concepts of vendor Master Data and Configuration 92

4.1.   Vendor Master 93

4.2.   Vendor Master Configuration 93

4.2.1.   Account groups for vendor and field selection 93

4.2.2.   Vendor Number Ranges 96

4.3.   Vendor Master Record 97

Copyrighted© Material

4.3.1.   General Data Screen 98

4.3.2.   Accounting Information Data 99

4.3.3.   Purchasing Data.. 103

4.3.4.   Partner role for vendor master record 108

4.4.   Mass Maintenance of Vendor Master 112

Chapter 5: Master data in Purchasing...**116**

5.1.   Master data in Purchasing 117

5.1.1.   Purchase info Record 117

5.1.2.   Source list.. 122

5.1.3.   Conditions 125

5.1.4.   Quota arrangement 125

Chapter 6: Components of Purchasing...**132**

6.1.   External Procurement... 133

6.1.1.   External Procurement Activities 133

6.2.   Components of Purchasing 135

6.2.1.   Request for quotation.. 135

6.2.2.   Purchase Requisition.. 142

6.2.3.   Purchase Order 148

6.2.4.   Account assignment categories and Item Categories.................................. 151

6.2.5.   Outline Agreements... 157

6.2.6.   Scheduling Agreements 162

6.2.7.   Framework Order (FO)... 165

Chapter 7: Inventory Management with SAP Material Management...................................**168**

7.1.   Inventory Management in SAP 169

7.2.   Types of stock in Materials Management... 170

7.2.1.   Unrestricted stock: 170

7.2.2.   Restricted stock: 170

7.3.   Movement types in SAP.. 172

7.4.   Stock transfer and transfer posting.. 178

7.4.1.   Transfer Posting... 178

7.4.2.   Stock Transfer.. 180

7.5.   Stock Materials and Consumable Materials 183

7.5.1.   Difference between stock material and consumable material 183

Copyrighted© Material

7.5.2.   Financial Accounting impact in Stock and consumable materials.. 184

7.6.   Standard Price and Moving Average Price of Material... 185

7.6.1.   Standard Price 185

7.6.2.   Moving Average Price 188

7.7.   Variances in GR IR account 191

7.7.1.   Price Variance... 191

7.7.2.   Quantity Variance 191

7.7.3.   Price Quantity Variance 192

7.8.   Reservations and Goods issue... 193

7.8.1.   Reservations 193

7.8.2.   Goods Issues 196

7.9.   Automatic Create Purchase Order at the Time of Goods Receipt 198

7.10.   Consignment Stock 200

7.10.1.   Consignment Purchase Order... 201

7.10.2.   Reservation... 202

7.11.   Subcontracting 203

7.11.1.   SAP Process in Subcontracting 204

7.12.   Tolerances in Goods receipts 206

7.12.1.   Tolerance key B1 (Error Message).. 206

7.12.2.   Tolerance key B2 (Warning message)... 206

7.12.3.   Configuration aspects of tolerances 207

7.13.   Physical Inventory in SAP Materials Management.. 209

7.13.1.   Inventory Stock Management Unit.. 209

7.13.2.   Reasons of Accurate Physical Inventory 209

7.13.3.   Physical Inventory Procedures 210

7.13.4.   Physical inventory (P I) audit Process in SAP.. 211

Chapter 8: Logistics Invoice verification 218

8.1.   What is Logistics invoice verification?.. 219

8.2.   Subsequent Debit, Subsequent Credit and Credit Memos 220

8.2.1.   Subsequent Debit 220

8.2.2.   Subsequent Credit 220

8.2.3.   Credit Memo 221

8.3.   Planned and Unplanned delivery Cost in logistics invoice verification 222

Copyrighted© Material

8.3.1.   Standard and Moving Average Price Impact (unplanned delivery cost)... 223

8.4.   Logistics invoicing plan 224

8.4.1.   Partial Invoicing Plan.. 224

8.4.2.   Periodic Invoicing Plan 224

8.4.3.   Pre-Requisite for invoicing plan... 225

8.5.   Park and Hold Logistics Invoice document 228

8.5.1.   Hold Invoice Document... 228

8.5.2.   Park Invoice Document 228

8.6.   Invoice in foreign currency 231

8.7.   Stochastic Block and Manual Block of Invoice 233

8.8.   Invoice Reduction 236

8.9.   Cancelations in Materials Management 239

8.9.1.   Cancelation of logistics Invoice verification document 241

8.9.2.   Cancelation of Inventory Management Document 242

8.10.   Difference between Cancelations and Rejections (Movement types) 244

8.10.1.   Cancelation:.. 244

8.10.2.   Rejections: 245

8.11.   Delivery completion indicator in PO 246

Chapter 9: Release Strategies in Procurement Documents 250

9.1.   Release Strategies in Procurement Documents... 251

9.2.   Preparation of required objects for Release Strategy in SAP 252

9.2.1.   Configuration of Characteristics and Class for Release strategy 253

9.2.2.   Define Release Strategy for Purchase Order.. 260

Chapter 10: Material Requirement Planning 270

10.1.   Material Requirement Planning (MRP).. 271

10.1.1.   MRP Profile... 274

10.1.2.   Consumption based planning.. 275

10.1.3.   Planning calendar 275

10.1.4.   Planning Processes.. 276

10.1.5.   Planning Evaluation 277

10.1.6.   Lot Size Calculation 278

10.1.7.   Pre-requisites of Consumption Based Planning 282

10.1.8.   Material Requirement Planning Procedures... 285

Copyrighted© Material

10.1.9.   Reorder Point Planning 286

10.1.10.   Forecast Based Planning.. 291

10.1.11.   Time Phase Planning 300

Chapter 11: Automatic account determination 304

11.1.   Automatic account determination 305

11.1.1.   Valuation Area... 306

11.1.2.   Chart of accounts 306

11.1.3.   Valuation class... 306

11.1.4.   Transaction key... 307

11.1.5.   Material and Material Type.. 307

11.1.6.   Movement Type 307

11.1.7.   Valuation Grouping Code... 307

11.1.8.   Account Category Reference... 309

11.1.9.   Value String 310

11.1.10.   Process Steps for Automatic Account Determination 311

11.1.11.   Account determination with wizard 311

11.1.12.   Account determination without wizard 312

11.2.   Split Valuation 321

11.2.1.   Procurement Type 321

11.2.2.   Country of Origin 321

11.2.3.   Quality of material... 321

11.2.4.   Valuation category and valuation types 322

11.2.5.   Configuration of split valuation... 322

11.3.   Material Ledger in SAP... 324

11.3.1.   Material Price Analysis... 326

11.3.2.   Material Price Determination... 326

11.4.   Additional Topic... 327

11.4.1.   Reporting in SAP Materials Management... 327

Index

Copyrighted© Material

Copyrighted© Material

Copyright© 2017 "Basic Concepts in SAP Materials Management"

By Hafiz Muhammad Azam

Publishing Date: 11-11-2017

All rights reserved. Cover design, table of contents, texts and illustrations. No part of this book may be reproduced in any form or by any electronic or mechanical means, including information storage and retrieval systems, without permission in writing from the publisher, except by reviewers, who may quote brief passages in a review. The purchaser of this book is subject to the condition that he/she shall in no way resell it, nor any part of it, nor make copies of it to distribute freely.

ISBN-13: 978-1986294881

ISBN-10: 1986294889

A Note concerning the SAP copyright: SAP is a register trademark of SAP SE Germany and in several other countries. All Screenshots printed in this book are the copyright of SAP SE Germany. All rights are reserved by SAP SE. Copyrights pertains to all SAP images in this publication.

Printed by CreateSpace, an **Amazon**.com company, Charleston SC

Copyrighted© Material

DISCLAIMER

The following disclaimer must be included in the publication:

This publication contains references to the products of SAP AG. SAP, R/3, SAP NetWeaver, Duet, PartnerEdge, ByDesign, SAP BusinessObjects Explorer, StreamWork, and other SAP products and services mentioned herein as well as their respective logos are trademarks or registered trademarks of SAP AG in Germany and other countries.

Business Objects and the Business Objects logo, BusinessObjects, Crystal Reports, Crystal Decisions, Web Intelligence, Xcelsius, and other Business Objects products and services mentioned herein as well as their respective logos are trademarks or registered trademarks of Business Objects Software Ltd. Business Objects is an SAP company.

Sybase and Adaptive Server, iAnywhere, Sybase 365, SQL Anywhere, and other Sybase products and services mentioned herein as well as their respective logos are trademarks or registered trademarks of Sybase, Inc. Sybase is an SAP company.

SAP AG is neither the author nor the publisher of this publication and is not responsible for its content. SAP Group shall not be liable for errors or omissions with respect to the materials. The only warranties for SAP Group products and services are those that are set forth in the express warranty statements accompanying such products and services, if any. Nothing herein should be construed as constituting an additional warranty.

Copyrighted© Material

Acknowledgement

A Book "Basic Concepts in SAP Materials Management" of this segment would not have been possible without the continuous support of my family and friends. A very special thanks to my wife and especially to my parents for their continuous pray and follow-up to finish this book.

Furthermore, this book would not have been possible without the help and positive reception of SCIL-SAP team.

Finally, I would also like to thankful to **Amazon Createspace and Amazon Kindle** for enabling me to publish this book.

Copyrighted© Material

Preface

Dear readers, purpose of this book is to guide you through the main functionality of SAP Materials Management (MM) while describing its important configuration and describing its integration with other functional areas within SAP. In reading this Book on "Basic Concepts in SAP Materials Management" you will also get a deeper knowledge and understanding of enterprise structure, master data management and its important fields, components of purchasing, procurement processes, physical inventory and inventory management, logistics invoice verifications, material requirement planning (MRP), automatic account determination in inventory posting, purchasing document release procedures with front and back end functionalities, reporting in SAP MM and configuration aspects.

By Following the chapter in this book, you will find that SAP MM not as complex as it first may seem. The examples in this book are derived from practical and common scenarios that would normally arise in typical environment where SAP MM module is being used or implemented. These examples will serve to guide you to better understanding and feel more ease, logical ways and focuses on operations with SAP MM processes.

Lastly, I hope Book "Basic Concepts in SAP Materials Management" will good contribution to your knowledge, learning and extend your skills in SAP Materials Management.

Copyrighted© Material

Notes

Copyrighted© Material

Chapter 1:
Introduction

Copyrighted© Material

1. Chapter: Introduction

1.1.   Introduction

1.2.   Whom Do This Book Address?

1.3.   ERP and Legacy systems

1.4.   Need Recognition of ERP.

1.5.   Operational Significance of Materials Management

1.6.   SAP Industry Specific solutions

1.7.   SAP Implementation (Standard) road map methodology

1.8.   SAP S/4 HANA and Activate Road Map Methodology

    1.8.1.   Transition to SAP S/4HANA with SAP Activate (Road Map)

1.9.   SAP Solution Manager

1.10.   SAP Modules

    1.10.1.   SAP Technical Modules:

    1.10.2.   SAP Functional Modules:

1.11.   Introduction to SAP Functional Modules

    1.11.1.   SAP PP (Production Planning)

    1.11.2.   SAP PM (Plant Maintenance)

    1.11.3.   SAP SD (Sales and Distribution)

    1.11.4.   SAP HCM (Human Capital Management)

    1.11.5.   SAP MM (Materials Management)

    1.11.6.   SAP QM (Quality Management)

    1.11.7.   SAP PS (Project System)

    1.11.8.   SAP FI (Financial Accounting)

Copyrighted© Material

1.1. Introduction

The most crucial challenge facing a large number of Business Empires in recent era has been to regain lost share of market and secure and gain new competitive advantage. Globalization and intensification of international competition trend now a day's also significant impact on businesses. In fact several business empires need to recognize new and emerging value added processes to gain competitive edge in sale, procurement markets and production processes. So there is hardly business function that has grown in significance now a day as much as logistics.

Logistics is the part of supply chain management. Supply chain management is defining as

supply of material through induction of vendor to end customer. It is the administration and observation of process of logistics along with entire value creation chain, which includes all suppliers, consumers and customers.

This book is introducing and covering ERP (Enterprise Resource Planning) introduction, basic concepts in procurement, inventory management and planning, material requirement planning and logistics invoice verifications with SAP software and assist you in understanding the technological components, terminologies as well important configuration and integrations aspects.

1.2. Whom Do This Book Address?

The Book "Basic concepts in SAP Materials Management" cannot cover and answer all questions and every query, but hopefully provide and give you the tool with which to ask the right questions and understand the important and essential issues involved. Aim to provide concepts of this book to following target people

The book is dedicated to everyone looking for clear information about ERP as well want to know about SAP, materials management operations and logistics with SAP. Each chapter describes you in detail material management operations, configuration and important fields. It provides you the overview, importance and functionality of applications and its components in practical business scenarios. So in this regard, book is target to SAP beginners, SAP end users, power users, employees in departments where SAP is to be implemented and students who want to start

Copyrighted© Material

their career in SAP. It is target to SAP/IT staff and decision makers who are preparing for or considering the implementation of SAP system or its individual components. It is target to everyone who wants to obtain an overview of materials management processes with SAP.

1.3. ERP and Legacy systems

Now these days, word ERP's are most commonly used in business environment. In old Era of business environment, most of companies were used different applications in different functional areas. For example human resource management department was run their own application, similarly finance and accounts, warehouse management/ Store, purchase as well as sales and marketing etc. was also run own applications and was maintain own data. When every department was run own applications, then consequential problem arise at maturity level of business. Problems that were most commonly arise, hardware obsolescent, software customization as well as integration between functional departments. So these problems were eliminating the needs of single database where every department maintains data in single database and integrated with each other.

ERP systems are single information system for organization wide for co-ordination, communication as well as integration of real time key business processes. In ERP system, every functional area (Finance, Sales and Marketing, Accounts and Purchase etc.) maintain data in single data base, which helps functional departments for acquire relevant information. Single database helps different departments for integration (For example, PO is generated and goods receipts have been perform by store keeper and execute entry of goods receipts. In this case, system automatically performs an accounting entries e.g. Stock account debit and Goods receipts invoice receipts account credit that relevant to accounts department, system automatically generates notification for account department for relevant information). In short, I conclude, adoption of ERP directly impact on business process improvements, better productivity, Competitive edge over your competitors , meet business challenges, reduce labor and IT expenses, real time access of data, remove duplications and paperless environment, integration between departments and reduce waste and eliminate cost.

Copyrighted© Material

Most commonly known ERPs are SAP (System Applications and Products in data processing), Oracle, J D Edward and Microsoft dynamics etc. Every ERP has own advantages and disadvantages.

1.4.   Need Recognition of ERP.

These are problems were faced many of business empires, that directly cause and need for ERP systems

- Decentralize Applications: Individual applications of each department or functional areas
- Integration: No integration of one department data with another department
- Duplications: Inconsistency of data and duplication of records
- Lack of real time Info: Lack of timely information and records directly impact on CRM (Customer relationship management) and disrupt in supply and demand planning
- Monetary Value: Time and money consuming for different applications
- SCM Upstream: Large number of SRM (Supplier relationship management), for one application required one vendor and similarly for more applications required more vendors
- Inventory Management: Not proper planning of inventory which impact on high logistics cost as well as unable to forecast planning, capacity planning and demand planning of materials
- SAAS and Cloud: SAAS (software as a service) concept was not familiar and no concept of cloud
- Reporting: Inconsistency in reports due to real time data availability or limited information and also because of decentralize applications
- Software and hardware obsolescent: At specific time period software and hardware were outdated

Copyrighted© Material

1.5. Operational Significance of Materials Management

Logistics management is the management logistics operations and processes. These processes are relevant to materials management (e.g. procurement, inventory management, logistics invoices and inventory planning), warehouse management, production planning and control, sales and distributions etc. The operational significance of materials management for many business empires still fall in its rationalization potential. In general way of effective and efficiently reduction of logistics, procurement and inventory management cost should improve company success by achieving competitive edge.

Logistics management is the important part of supply chain management that plans, implements and control the efficient, effective forward and reverse flow of storage goods, services and relevant information between the point of origin and the point of consumption in order to meet requirement of your customers. (Source: Council of Supply Chain Management Professionals).

Materials management is the part of logistics management. One side of the procurement market is the task of procurement logistics to acquire raw materials and supplies mandatory for your production, manufacturing or distribution. Procurement is carried out with reference to stock situation and especially based on materials management planning.

Materials management includes all activities involved in supplying a company and its production processes with all necessary materials, spares and supplies with effective, efficient and optimal cost. It takes into account temporal and spatial gaps involved in supply processes not only with regard to material but also flow of information between buyer and suppliers. This is why to consider materials management is not only a part of logistics but its center, where the function of logistics are more comprehensive than those of materials management.

Copyrighted© Material

1.6. SAP Industry Specific solutions

SAP best practices, benchmarking and processes preconfigured for many industries to give business empires exact functionality according to needs and demand, when and where they want it. SAP standard and generic solution need to customize and cannot fulfill industry specific solution. Each of industry having own processes e.g. oil and gas industry having its own processes which are completely differ from hospitality. Similarly chemicals industry processes are completely differ from FMCG industry. SAP provides industry specific solutions according to industry type and industry specific processes along with proven values, techniques, tools and methodologies. SAP provides following industry specific solutions

- Aerospace and Defense
- Automotive
- Banking
- Chemicals
- Consumer Products
- Defense and Security
- Engineering, Construction, and Operations
- Healthcare
- High Tech
- Higher Education and Research
- Industrial Machinery and Components
- Insurance
- Life Sciences
- Media
- Mill Products
- Mining
- Oil and Gas
- Professional Services
- Public Sector
- Retail
- Sports and Entertainment
- Telecommunications
- Travel and Transportation
- Utilities
- Wholesale Distribution

Copyrighted© Material

1.7. SAP Implementation (Standard) road map methodology

SAP project implementation road map consist of the following phases

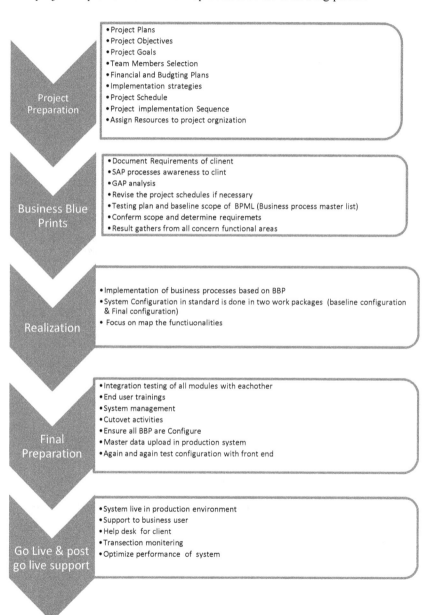

Project Preparation
- Project Plans
- Project Objectives
- Project Goals
- Team Members Selection
- Financial and Budgting Plans
- Implementation strategies
- Project Schedule
- Project implementation Sequence
- Assign Resources to project orgnization

Business Blue Prints
- Document Requirements of clinent
- SAP processes awareness to clint
- GAP analysis
- Revise the project schedules if necessary
- Testing plan and baseline scope of BPML (Business process master list)
- Conferm scope and determine requiremets
- Result gathers from all concern functional areas

Realization
- Implementation of business processes based on BBP
- System Configuration in standard is done in two work packages (baseline configuration & Final configuration)
- Focus on map the functiuonalities

Final Preparation
- Integration testing of all modules with eachother
- End user trainings
- System management
- Cutovet activities
- Ensure all BBP are Configure
- Master data upload in production system
- Again and again test configuration with front end

Go Live & post go live support
- System live in production environment
- Support to business user
- Help desk for client
- Transection monitering
- Optimize performance of system

Figure 1-1 (SAP Standard Implementation Road Map)

8

Copyrighted© Material

1.8. SAP S/4 HANA and Activate Road Map Methodology

SAP S/4 HANA is the next generation business tool. SAP S/4 HANA allows and helps you to digitize and realize end to end business, achieving digital transformation and combining the opportunities. It enables appropriate, contextual information and a personalized experience. SAP S/4 HANA having with the power of data with real time, scalable, innovative and predictive capabilities.

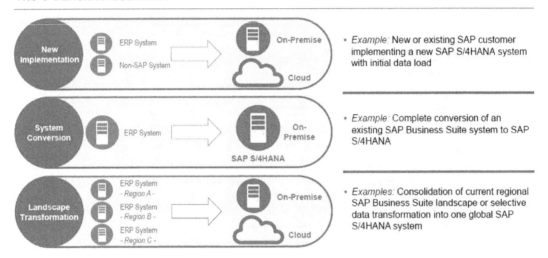

Figure 1-2 (Transition Scenarios to SAP S/4 HANA Implementation)
Source: www.open.sap.com

There are three transition scenarios for SAP S/4 HANA implementation. These three transition scenarios are new implementation, system conversion and landscape transformation. First scenario is to starting with new implementation. In this, you implement S/4 HANA on client premise edition or use S/4 HANA cloud solution of your choice. System conversion for your existing current system is the second scenario. In system conversion, if you are running ERP 6 on HANA or running on non-HANA data base, SAP facilitate to convert your system into S/4 HANA in one step, data base moving and installing the new code with the SAP software update manager. The third scenario is the landscape transformation, you can say system consolidation e.g. consolidate of your current regional SAP Business suit landscape into one Global SAP S/4 HANA system. You can implement landscape transformation both on premise or cloud edition as per your choice.

Copyrighted© Material

No meter you are choose which scenario from above, SAP Activate provide you best practices, guided configuration, and good proven methodologies to accelerate your time to value. It helps for SAP partners and consultants to implement S/4 HANA as a part of your digital transformation.

SAP activate is the innovation and adoption framework using for SAP S/4 HANA implementation. It is a standard way of implementation of SAP S/4 HANA. SAP S/4 HANA implementation edition can be on premise or can be cloud based. The goal of SAP activate is to provide customers faster and less service intensive initial implementation whether it is an on premise edition or cloud edition. SAP activate is rapid adoption of innovations throughout the entire product life cycle management. So resultant, reduce time to value and total cost of ownership. SAP activate includes best SAP implementation practices, road map for implementation methodology and guided configuration both for cloud edition as well as on premise edition. With SAP Activate, the cockpit of SAP S/4 HANA implementation is

❖ Configure your solution
❖ Test your processes
❖ View your solution scope
❖ Migrate your data into SAP
❖ Start training of client users and on boarding
❖ Manage your test processes

3.1.1. Transition to SAP S/4HANA with SAP Activate (Road Map)

Following are the phases of implementation

Figure 1-3 Transition to SAP S/4HANA with SAP Activate (Road Map)

1.8.1.1.   Prepare Phase

This phase tells you which innovation available in SAP S/4 HANA and you want which business processes in your implementation. In next step you start out Model Company. In this stage, initial planning and preparation start for the project. Project start up, project plans and teams are also assigns.

Copyrighted© Material

1.8.1.2.   Explore Phase

In explore phase perform fit gap analysis to validate the solution functionality included project scope and to confirm that the business requirements can be satisfied. Identify the gaps and configuration values are added to be backlog for use in the next phase.

1.8.1.3.   Realize

In realize phase incrementally build and test an integrated business and system environment that are based on the real time business scenario and identification of process requirements that are pointed in previous phase. Data adoption activities, data loading activities and operations are planned in this phase.

1.8.1.4.   Deploy

In deploy phase setup the production system, confirm customer organization readiness and switch the new business process and operations to the new system.

1.8.1.5.   Run

In this phase run the newly implemented system and apply SAP operation standards to optimize system operations.

Copyrighted© Material

1.9. SAP Solution Manager

SAP solution manager tool of software, gateway, content to create, operates, manage and monitoring business management solution along the application life cycle management. Solution manager is a central robust application management and administrative solution used to support implement of solution of SAP. It provide the contents that implement as well as up gradation of SAP solutions and theses contents includes configuration information and process driven approaches to convert BBP (Business Blue Prints), configuration of business processes and final preparation phase of SAP implementation roadmap. Solution manager support SAP implementation from end to end project life cycle. It directly enhances the reliability of SAP solution. Solution manager 7.1 was release on 2011.SAP Solution manager 7.1 provides features for use in IT support area for enhancing automating and improving the non-SAP and SAP system. Solution implementation and template management are

- Solution Documentation
- IT Services management
- Technical operations
- Custom code management
- Upgrade management
- Maintenance management
- Test management
- Change control management

The current version of SAP solution manager is 7.2. SAP Solution manager 7.2 focuses on outcome based delivery model and run only that infrastructure that manages both build and run. Before version 7.2, SAP solution manager could not run on SAP HANA. SAP Solution manager having fiori based interface as well as effective and efficient solution readiness dashboards. With SAP Solution manager 7.2 consultant and clients both build solution together, delta scoping and manage requirements with less time. It helps in S/4HANA implementation with SAP Activate methodology because it is structured according to SAP Activate methodology with entire phases including from beginning to planning to go live stage.

SAP solution manager's most important functions revolve around system health. Technical monitoring reports on system alerts and exceptions and also admin can see how availability, configuration and

Copyrighted© Material

performance are affected. You can create report to help resolve issues and easily assign task to service desk. SAP Early watch is another important and crucial solution manager tool that focusing on overall system health. Early watch checks system factors are includes,

- Consumption of resources
- Hardware utilization
- Load distribution
- Dialogue response time

Copyrighted© Material

1.10. SAP Modules

SAP Modules are categorize on two bases

1. **SAP Technical Modules**
2. **SAP Functional Modules**

1.10.1. SAP Technical Modules:

- SAP ABAP (Advance Business Application Programming)
- SAP BI (Business Intelligence)
- SAP BOBJ (Business Objects)
- SAP BW (Business Warehouse)
- SAP HANA
- SAP Basis

1.10.2. SAP Functional Modules:

- SAP PP (Production Planning and Control)
- SAP SD (Sales and distribution)
- SAP MM (Materials Management)
- SAP QM (Quality Management)
- SAP PM (Plant Maintenance)
- SAP HCM (Human Capital Management)
- SAP HS&E (Health Safety and Environment)
- SAP FSCM (Financial Supply Chain Management)
- SAP FI (Financials)
- SAP CO (SAP Controlling/ Management Accounting)
- SAP CRM (Customer Relationship Management)
- SAP SRM (Supplier Relationship Management)
- SAP Retailing
- SAP EWM (Extended Warehouse Management)
- SAP FM (Fund Management)
- SAP BPC (Budgeting, Planning and Consolidation)
- SAP SLCM (Student Life Cycle Management)

Copyrighted© Material

- Treasury (TR)
- Pay roll (PR)
- Enterprise Control (EC)
- Project System (PS)
- SAP CIM (Capital Investment Management)
- SAP CA (Cross Application Components)
- SAP CS (Customer Services)

- SAP GM (Grant Management)
- SAP RE (Real Estate)
- SAP SM (Services Management)
- Etc.

Copyrighted© Material

1.11. Introduction to SAP Functional Modules

1.11.1. SAP PP (Production Planning)

The production planning module covers the followings,

- Product cost plannings
- Capacity planning
- Materials requirement planning
- Distribution resource planning
- Shop floor control
- Production order processing
- Kanban
- Repetitive manufacturing
- Master data (BOM, routing, PRT, recipe, and work centers)
- Actual costing/ Material ledger
- Cost centers

1.11.2. SAP PM (Plant Maintenance)

The Plant maintenance module covers the following,

- Maintenance planning
- Predictive maintenance
- Breakdown maintenance
- Preventive maintenance
- Maintenance order management
- Services management
- Functional locations, equipment's, plant sections, work centers

1.11.3. SAP SD (Sales and Distribution)

SAP SD includes

- Sales support
- Shipping
- Transportation
- Billing
- Master data (Customers and Conditions)
- Reporting and Analysis
- Payment card processing
- Availability check and SD requirement of risk management
- Output determination
- Outbound deliveries
- Sales organization's and distribution channels
- Sales information system / logistics execution system

Copyrighted© Material

1.11.4. SAP HCM (Human Capital Management)

SAP HCM Includes

- Recruiting
- Hiring
- Personal development
- Maintain benefits and planning
- Change to pay
- Payroll
- Performance appraisals

- Leaves and overtime management
- Training and development
- Personal administration
- Master data and personal profiles
- Evaluation of time
- Travel and event management

1.11.5. SAP MM (Materials Management)

SAP MM Includes

- Procurement and supplier evaluations
- Inventory management
- Logistics invoice verifications
- Purchase requisitions, request for quotations, quota arrangement and source list
- Contracts and scheduling agreements
- Material requirement planning
- Inventory audits
- Master data (material master, vendor master, services master and purchasing info records)
- Purchasing information system
- Conditions and schemas
- Release strategies
- Split valuations

- Automatic account determination
- Enterprise structure
- Plants, storage locations, purchasing organizations and purchase groups
- Material types
- Stock types
- Transfer posting and stock transfer
- Subsequent debits, credits and credit memos
- Stock and consumable materials
- Subcontracting, pipeline and consignments
- Material ledgers
- Reservation and goods issuance
- Reporting in MM

Copyrighted© Material

1.11.6. SAP QM (Quality Management)

SAP QM Includes

- Quality planning
- Quality inspection
- Quality control
- Quality certifications and quality notifications
- Incoming, during process and final inspections

- Master inspection plans
- Lots clearances
- Test equipment management
- Quality reports
- Quality checks during Stock transfers

1.11.7. SAP PS (Project System)

SAP PS Module includes

- Project planning
- Project monitoring
- Project costing

- Milestones based costing
- Handling of work break down structure elements

1.11.8. SAP FI (Financial Accounting)

SAP FI Module includes

- Account receivables
- Account payables
- General ledgers
- Bank accounting
- Cash Management

- Fund management
- Monitoring and budgeting
- Financial statements
- Asset accounting
- Advances and Vendor management

Copyrighted© Material

1.11.9. SAP CO (Managerial Accounting)

SAP CO Module includes

- Cost center accounting
- Profit center accounting
- Product costing and actual costing
- Internal orders

- Costing and Profitability analysis (CO-PA)
- Cost element accounting
- Activity based accounting
- Overhead cost controlling

Copyrighted© Material

Copyrighted© Material

Chapter 2:

Enterprise Structure in SAP Materials Management

Copyrighted© Material

2. Chapter: Enterprise Structure in SAP Materials Management

In this lesson you will learn

2.1.   Enterprise Structure in SAP Materials Management

   2.1.1.   Client

   2.1.2.   Company Code

   2.1.3.   Plant

   2.1.4.   Storage Location

   2.1.5.   Purchasing organization

   2.1.6.   Enterprise Structure Assignments

   2.1.7.   Purchase Group

Copyrighted© Material

2.1. Enterprise Structure in SAP Materials Management

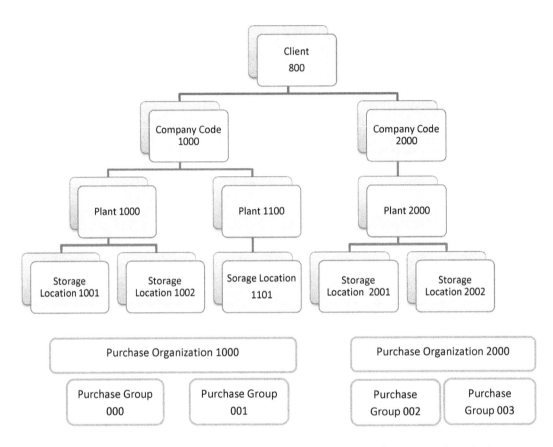

Figure 2-1 (Org. Structure in SAP MM)

2.1.1. Client

It is a highest level in SAP MM. A client is a self-contained unit in sap system with SAP separate master records and its own set of tables. Data is maintain at client level is valid for all organizational level. It also represents a corporate group and highest level in SAP system. It is define as 3 digit key (800).

Copyrighted© Material

When you buy SAP system, you install it on your servers and configure as per your particular needs. So it is called an instance. Client can have more than one instance and they will exist on different SAP system. In one instance, you can configure many clients. So client is a legal and organization entity in SAP system. The master data that belongs to client is valid only for this client and not valid for other clients. Each client has their own objective as well as environment. In standard SAP system deliver to customer with three clients 000, 001 and 066.

2.1.2. Company Code

Company code is an independent accounting entity under the client. It has a legal entity which have own balance sheet as well profit and loss statements with external accounting. In SAP system Company code define as four digit alphanumeric keys e.g. 1000, SC01 and DUST. A corporate group may have many companies' with different businesses and with different locations. These companies can be open in different codes in SAP system with different sets of configurations and which have their own balance sheets, profit and loss accounts and GL accounts etc.

Usually, company and company code creating with reference to another company and company code respectively. You can define company field in SAP system by transaction code OX15 or define by Menu path in customizing IMG-SPRO > Enterprise Structure > Definition > Financial Accounting > Maintain Company and you can create company code by transaction OX02 or by Menu path in customizing IMG-SPRO > Enterprise Structure > Definition > Financial Accounting > Define, Copy, Delete and Check Company Code

After creating of company code in SAP system, you must assign it with different objects. These objects are credit control area, company and financial management area.

2.1.3. Plant

Plant is separate organization unit under the company code where production facility/ branch located. Plant is produces goods and services that available for company for sale. It may also be distribution center, sale center, head quarter, services center and also maintenance facility. In SAP system plant define as four digit alphanumeric keys e.g. 1000, SC01 and TPQW.

Copyrighted© Material

For configuration of Plant, you go to transaction code OX10 or go to SAP easy access IMG-SPRO > Enterprise structure > Definition > Logistics- general > Define, copy, delete and check Plant

Before creating of Plant in SAP system you must need to configure country key if it is not exist in system. Factory calendar explain work days, public holidays and your company holidays. In standard SAP system some factory calendars exist but you need to configure factory calendar and must be assigned to plant. Your region key and country code are also mandatory objects for assignment to plant. So you need to configure both of them before creating a plant.

Note

In SAP system, for accuracy of configuration you must copy or adopt existing plant or any other object with reference to already existing one.

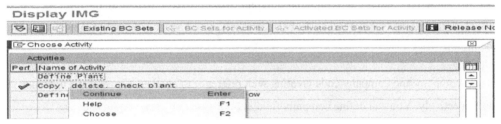

Figure 2-2 (Define Plant)

Right click on copy, delete, and check Plant and click on continue and then click on copy organization object button mention on below screen

Organizational object Plant

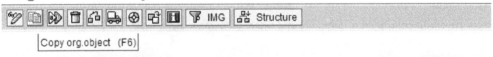

Figure 2-3 (Copy Org. Object)

1000 (Plant) is an existing organization object and TP01 (Plant) is newly created with reference to Plant 1000. However choose continue. Next window ask you transport number ranges and addresses from existing object to new object, you can click on continue button. New plant created in SAP system with Plant code TP01.

Copyrighted© Material

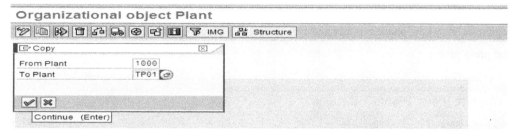

Figure 2-4 (Continue for Plant configuration)

For change of new plant name, address and other parameters go back and chose define plant and continue

Display IMG

| | | | Existing BC Sets | BC Sets for Activity | Activated BC Sets for Activity | Release Note |

☞ Choose Activity   ☒

Activities	
Perf	Name of Activity
✓	Define Plant

Figure 2-5 (For Changes in Plant Address)

Select the line of plant TP01 you just created and click on detail button mention below on screen

Change View "Plants": Overview

| | New Entries | | | | | | | |

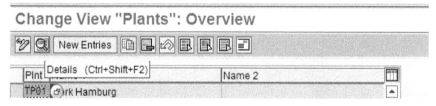

Plnt	Details (Ctrl+Shift+F2)	Name 2	
TP01	rk Hamburg		

Figure 2-6 (For Changes in Plant Address)

Copyrighted© Material

Click on address button. Here you can maintain plant address, language key, postal code, city, region, country key, phone number and factory calendar etc. relevant to your desire configuration and press save.

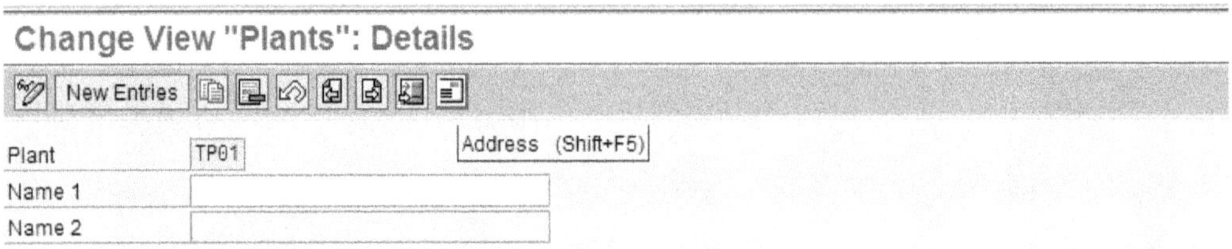

Change View "Plants": Details

| | New Entries | | | | | | | |

Plant	TP01	Address (Shift+F5)
Name 1		
Name 2		

Figure 2-7 (For Changes in Plant Address)

Copyrighted© Material

2.1.4. Storage Location

Storage location is an organizational unit where material takes place within plant. A plant has a multiple storage locations where physically your stock available for these locations. Stock falls in storage location, available for plant level. In SAP system storage location define as four digit alphanumeric keys e.g. 0001, 0002 and 0003 etc. With storage location, you can also manage your inventory in storage bin locations level. If you want to implement SAP Warehouse management module, some of warehouse management functionalities ties with materials management e.g. you assignment of warehouse with one or more storage locations.

For maintain storage location you can go to customizing IMG-SPRO > Enterprise structure > Definition >Materials Management >Maintain storage locations or directly go to transaction code OX09

Enter plant TP01 (already just created)

Click on new entries

Note: If you see already storage locations exist here, you can use the same name but changes address accordingly. When Plant TP01 copy from Plant 1000 then these storage locations was exist in 1000 Plant and was adopted from 1000 plant. If you delete previously adopted storage locations then first save after deletion and then create new storage locations

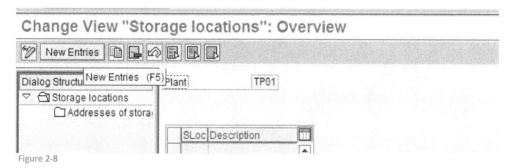

Figure 2-8

Here you maintain your necessary storage locations relevant to your configuration and addresses of that storage location as show on below mention screen and press save. For maintain of storage location addresses, you can select storage location line and double click on addresses of storage locations located in left side dialog structure.

Copyrighted© Material

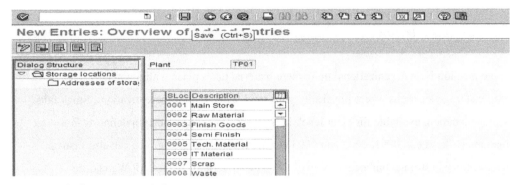

Figure 2-9 (Define Storage Location)

Note: In SAP system you have option to create storage location automatically at the time of goods inward movements. It is depending in system upon configuration of plant and movement type to allow creates storage location automatically. SAP system only allows this facility only on normal stock and special stock not is takes into account in it. It will be active on each plant which you want to create storage location automatically. It will reduce the data entry efforts, time saving and minimize error. For automatic storage location configuration you go to transaction code OMB3 or Menu path under customizing IMG-SPRO > Materials Management > Inventory Management and Physical Inventory > Goods Receipts > Create Storage Location Automatically

Copyrighted© Material

2.1.5. Purchasing organization

Purchasing organization is legally responsible for procurement of goods and services for company with specific terms and conditions negotiation, communication and co-ordination with vendor. Purchasing organization may be centralized or decentralize. Centralize purchase organization is responsible for all purchase for specific plants or company codes that are assign in enterprise structure. If all plants/ companies having their own separate purchase/ separate purchase organizations, called decentralize purchase or purchase organization. In this case you need to maintain multiple purchasing organizations and their assignments accordingly.

So you can say that purchasing organization may be enterprise level in which it is responsible to procure material and services for all company codes. For doing this you need to assign purchasing organization to all concern company codes. Purchasing organization may be at company level. For example a client have companies in different countries and it is not possible to procure material on centralize bases. So you need to configure enterprise structure accordingly. For purchasing organization at company level, you need to assign purchasing organization only to specific company code. Purchasing organization may be at plant level in which you need to assign purchasing organization with one company code and plants assign to that company code.

In SAP system purchasing organization define as four digit alphanumeric keys e.g. 1000, TPP0 and TP11 etc. So you can maintain purchasing organization by following Menu path under customizing IMG-SPRO> IMG> Enterprise Structure> Definition> Materials Management> Maintain Purchasing Organization or by transaction code OX01

Click on new entries button. Insert purchasing organization name with 4 digits alphanumeric code and put purchasing organization description.

Copyrighted© Material

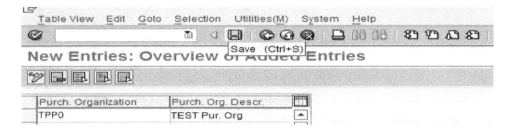

Figure 2-10 (Define Purchasing Organization)

In SAP system you can create a reference purchase organization. Some companies having strategic buying department, which work for strategic analysis and negotiating terms and conditions and best prices of material and services with global suppliers. These best rates, terms and conditions are valid for all organization level for purchasing. So in SAP system it is not assign to any company code and it is work for whole enterprise. All the best rates, terms and conditions are maintained on this purchasing organization level. You need to assign purchasing organization with reference purchasing organization for access of information.

You can assign purchasing organization to reference purchasing organization by following Menu path under customizing IMG-SPRO > Enterprise Structure > Definition > Materials Management > Assign Purchasing Organization to Reference Purchasing Organization

POrg	Ref.pur.org.	Purch. Org. Descr.	Reference purch. org.	
1000	C100	IDES Deutschland	Zentraleinkauf	▲
2000	C100	IDES UK	Zentraleinkauf	▼
2100	C100	IDES Portugal	Zentraleinkauf	
2200	C100	IDES France	Zentraleinkauf	
2300	C100	IDES Spanien	Zentraleinkauf	

Figure 2-11 (Assign Purchasing Organization to Reference Purchasing Organization)

Copyrighted© Material

2.1.6. Enterprise Structure Assignments

2.1.6.1. *Assign Plant to Company Code*

SPRO> IMG> Enterprise Structure> Assignment> Logistics General>Assignment>Assign Plant to Company Code

Click on new entries and Insert Company code 1000 and TP01 as plant you just created and press save button

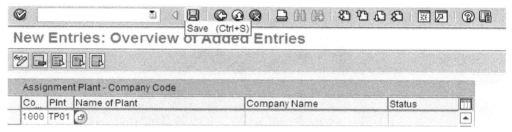

Figure 2-12 (Assign Plant to Company Code)

2.1.6.2. *Assign Purchasing Organization to Company Code*

SPRO> IMG> Enterprise Structure> Assignment> Materials Management> Assign Purchasing Organization to Company Code

Insert company code in line of TPP0 Test Pur. Org you just created and click on save button

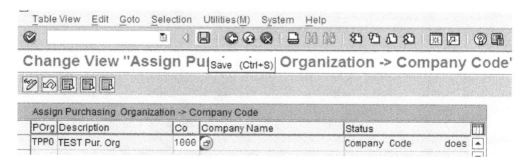

Figure 2-13 (Assign Purchasing Organization to Company Code)

Copyrighted© Material

SPRO> IMG> Enterprise Structure> Assignment> Materials Management> Assign Purchasing organization to Plant

Here enter plant TP01 for purchasing organization TPPO and click on save button

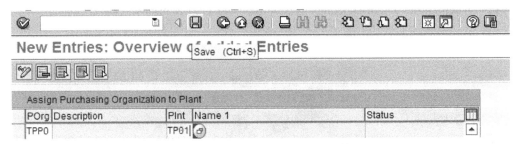

Figure 2-14 (Assign Purchasing Organization to Plant)

Note: You can assign purchasing organization to company code. If you cannot assign purchasing organization to company code then it is responsible for centralize purchasing for all company codes. A plant is must be assign to one purchasing organization or multiple purchasing organizations.

Facts:

Purchase org. must be assigning to one or more than one plant and can only assign to one company code. It can also exist without assigning to company code. Each plant must be assign to a company code. One plant may be one or more than one purchasing organizations.

Furthermore, we have already discuss three scenarios

Plant Specific Purchase (Assign Plant and company code of the plant to purchase organization)

Company specific purchase (Assign a company and company specific plants to purchasing organization)

Corporate group specific purchase (Company code not assign to purchase organization. Assign plants under different company code to purchasing organization)

2.1.7. Purchase Group

Purchase group is a group of people that are responsible for daily buying of goods and external services activities. Purchase group define as 3 digit alphanumeric key in SAP system. Purchasing groups are responsible for buying activities e.g. purchase requisition processing/ creation and monitor of purchase orders, vendor negotiations, communication and coordination's. In SAP system purchase groups are configure independently and cannot be assign with another object. For configuration of purchase groups you can go to customizing with following Menu path

IMG-SPRO > Materials Management> Purchasing> Create Purchase Groups

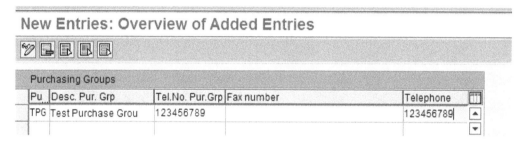

Figure 2-15 (Create Purchase Group)

Here you can maintain new purchase group, purchasing group description, telephone number of purchasing group and fax number etc.

Copyrighted© Material

Copyrighted© Material

Copyrighted© Material

Chapter 3:

Basic Concepts of Material Master Data and Configuration

Copyrighted© Material

3. Chapter: Basic Concepts of Material Master and Configuration

In this lesson you will learn

3.1.	Master Data in SAP Materials Management and Purchasing	
3.2.	Material Master Data and Configuration	
3.3.	Configuration aspects of Material types	
3.1.2.	Material types	
3.1.3.	Attributes of material types	
3.1.4.	Assign number ranges	
3.1.5.	Maintain field selection for data screen	
3.1.6.	Define industry sector	
3.1.7.	Lock Relevant Field in Material Master	
3.2.	Mass maintenance of material master	
3.3.	Bills of Material (BOM)	
3.4.	Material Master Record	
3.4.1.	Basic Data Screen	
3.4.2.	Classification *Data*	
3.4.3.	Sales and Distribution Data	
3.4.4.	Purchasing Data Screen	
3.4.5.	Forecasting Data	
3.4.6.	General Plant Data	
3.4.7.	Warehouse Management Data	
3.4.8.	Quality Management Data	
3.4.9.	Material Requirement Planning (MRP) Data	
3.4.10.	Accounting Data	
3.4.11.	Costing Data	
3.5. External Services		

Copyrighted© Material

3.1. Master Data in SAP Materials Management and Purchasing

There are three types of data in SAP. Data types include configuration data, master data and transactional data. Configuration data are created once and cannot be changed e.g. company code, plant, purchasing organization and storage locations etc. Master data changes accrue in very rare cases in system e.g. material master, vendor master, service master and purchasing info records etc. In transactional data, changes accrue on daily basis or you can maintain it on daily basis e.g. creation of purchase orders, sale orders and invoices etc. These are following types of master data in SAP materials management and purchasing

- Material master
- Vendor master
- Service master
- Purchasing info records
- Quota arrangement
- Source list

Now we will discuss briefly master data, let's talk about

3.2. Material Master Data and Configuration

Material master data consist of all material record / info regarding material, which includes material description, material unit of measure (UOM), material net and gross weight, material group (internal/ External), profit center, tax information, conversion UOM, valuation class etc. Main aim of master data includes reducing the data entry effort, accuracy in transactions' data, reduce errors, reduce time and eliminate cost.

Material master is centralized data base where every department extracts relevant information of material. Information in material master may be consisting of different department like Sales and distribution, Production planning, costing, accounting, warehouse/ store, quality management, forecasting and purchasing etc. In material master, there are different views according to above departments, where each department maintains its relevant data.

Copyrighted© Material

Material master data almost used in many modules like materials management, production planning, quality management, warehouse management and sales and distribution. It can touch all the transactions in materials management like purchase requisition, purchase orders, outline agreements, goods receipts and logistics invoice verifications.

For SAP material master transactions go to SAP easy access

Logistics > Materials management > Master data > Material > create general > immediately MM01/ change MM02/ Display MM03

3.3. Configuration aspects of Material types

3.3.1. Material types

Materials with the same basic characteristics are group together and assign to a material type. Material type is identification of particular material at client level. One material is creating under the umbrella of material type or material type must be assign to material master at the time of creation of material master record. Each material type can have its own number range, own views and own data according to client requirement. Examples of material types are raw materials, semi-finished goods, finished goods, technical spare parts, and IT materials etc.

3.3.2. Attributes of material types

When you create a material, you must specify new material belongs to which material type. So it is mandatory attributes of material type configuration. In attributes of material types you specify material type and description of material type, material master views, price control, account category reference, price and quantity update, field reference and X plant material status etc. For configuration of material type attributes, you can go to customizing under

IMG-SPRO > Logistics General >Material Master > Basic Settings > Material Types > Define Attributes of Material Types

Copyrighted© Material

As already discuss, you must adopt or copy as option for creating new object, but must chose relative and similar object. Let's suppose you create new material type Raw material (ROH), you must choose ROH and if necessary creating new Raw material type ZROH according to client requirement. So choose Raw material (ROH) material type and click on copy as button. ROH is standard ROH material type name.

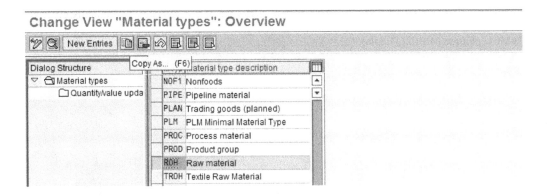

Figure 3-1 (Attribute of Material Type Configuration)

Here you change the name ROH to ZROH for new material type. You can change the description, select user departments, and external purchase order as 2 and external 0 (for raw materials and as per required material type), price control as moving average price and select price control mandatory indicator and quantity and value update indicator. Check quantity structure and external number assignment without check.

Internal/ external purchase order selection parameters select according to in-house production as well as external procurement. Quantity and value update indicator set according to requirement as well for according to material type. Quantity and value indicator shows weather movement of quantity will be update as per quantity and value or not and these are set accordingly by client and material type requirement. Field status, screen reference material types and account category references will be discuss latterly upcoming topics.

Copyrighted© Material

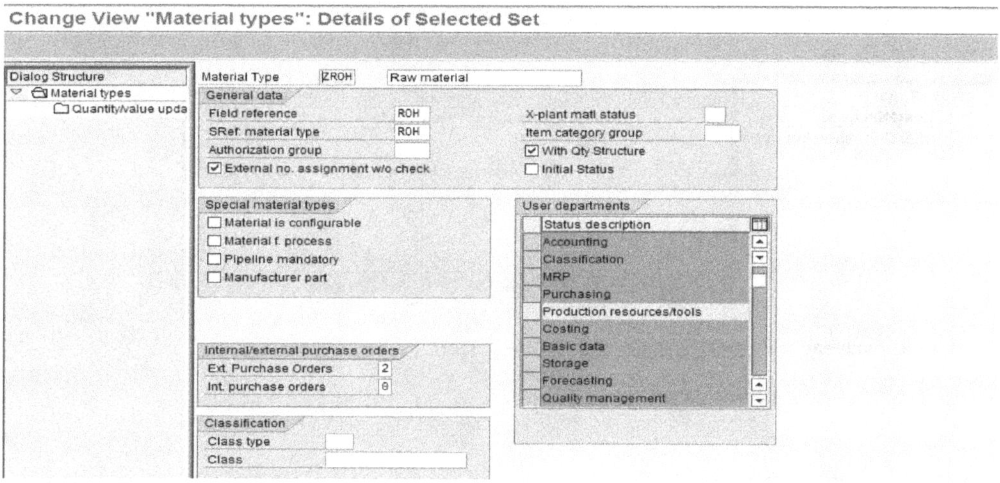

Figure 3-2 (Attribute of Material Type Configuration, selection of views and other parameters)

Quantity structure indicator control whether the material is part of costing or using costing with/ without quantity structure. If you costing with quantity structure then tick the indicator otherwise do not select indicator. Field references represent which fields will be mandatory, option or display in material master creation for this material type. Account category reference is the combination of material type and valuation class, it is the bridge where Financial (G/L account) integration of material. Field status and account category, both define another transaction screens and here you only assign field reference and account category reference number. Price control indicator determine whether it is defined for material type appear as default value or fixed value whenever material master create or change.

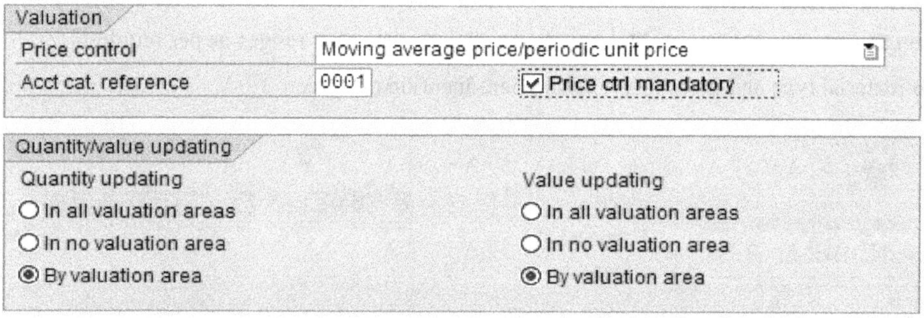

Figure 3-3 (Attribute of Material Type Configuration, Quantity and Valuation Updating)

Copyrighted© Material

Change View "Quantity/value updating": Overview

Val. ar	Matl	Qty updating	Value Upda	Pipe.mand.	PipeAllow
0001	ZROH	☑	☑	☐	☐
0005	ZROH	☑	☑	☐	☐
0006	ZROH	☑	☑	☐	☐
0007	ZROH	☑	☑	☐	☐
0008	ZROH	☑	☑	☐	☐
0099	ZROH	☑	☑	☐	☐
1000	OH	☑	☑	☐	☐
1100	ZROH	☑	☑	☐	☐

Dialog Structure — Material types — Quantity/value upda

Figure 3-4 (Quantity and Value Updating config. against Material Type)

3.3.3. Assign number ranges

After crating of material types and configuration of attributes, next step to assign number ranges for each material type in customizing. For doing this you can go to transaction MMNR or follow the Manu path under customizing IMG-SPRO > Logistics General > Material Master > Basic Settings > Material Types > Define Number Ranges for Each Material Type

Go to group and click on maintain

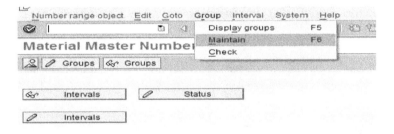

Figure 3-5 (Maintain Group for Number Range)

Go to group and press insert group. Maintain text and define number ranges as per requirement, relevant to material type and press insert button here mention on screen

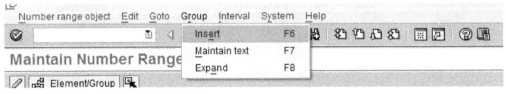

Figure 3-6 (Insert Group for Number Ranges)

Copyrighted© Material

Maintain Number Range Groups

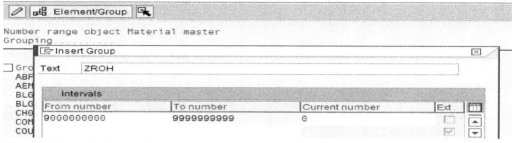

Figure 3-7 (Maintain Number Range Group)

When you insert group, you can see newly created group appear on screen mention below

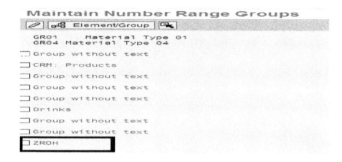

Figure 3-8 (Maintain Number Range Group)

Now click on ZROH group, select ZROH material type raw material and click on button select

element

Figure 3-9 (Select Element and Assign to Group)

Copyrighted© Material

Now click on element group button, here you can see number ranger assign to material type.

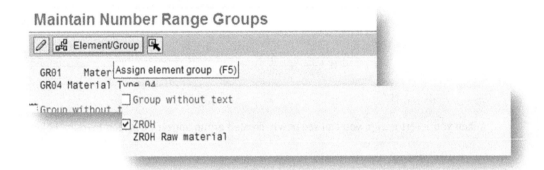

Figure 3-10 (Select Element and Assign to Group)

Note: Similarly you can create other material types (e.g. Finish goods, semi-finish, scrap, IT material types and spare parts etc.) as per client requirement, create number rangers accordingly and assign to the material type.

3.3.4. Maintain field selection for data screen

In this step of configuration we are adopt or copy as ROH field reference and create new field reference as well as selection of field as mandatory, option, hide or display. Field reference determines which field of material master will be hide, display, required or optional for entry.

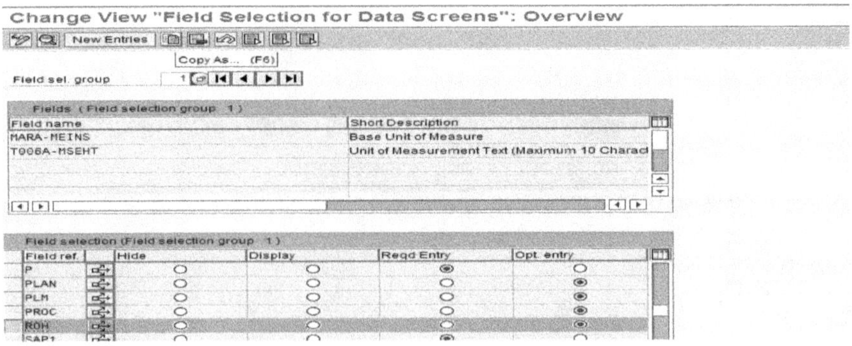

Figure 3-11 (Field Selection for Data Screen of Material Master)

Copyrighted© Material

Change field reference name and press copy and save

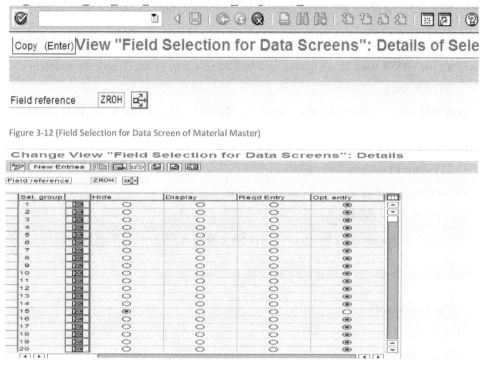

Figure 3-12 (Field Selection for Data Screen of Material Master)

Figure 3-13 (Maintain Hide, Display, Required and Optional Entry in Material Master)

If necessary, go transaction code OMS9 change the field status as hide, display, required or optional. Select the field reference line ZROH (just created) and click on detail button. Here you can select field status as per requirement. In SAP standard system there are 240 fields.

Figure 3-14 (Assign Field Reference in Material Type Attributes)

Copyrighted© Material

Now go to attribute of material type and assign field reference to material type. This field reference is valid for material type which you assign. For assignment again go to attributes of material type screen and insert ZROH as field reference for material type Raw material ZROH and press save button.

Transaction code OMSR used for assigning field to field selection group. Where we maintain whether an entry of material master is required, hide, optional or display. In SAP standard system each field selection group having number 1 to 240. These values of field selection group has been pre assign as follows

- 1 –110 material masters for industry
- 111 -120 reserved for customer (except value already used)
- 121 -150 material masters for industry
- 151 -210 material masters for retail reserve for customer

In material master, we can set field selection on the following basis

- Transaction specific
- Plant specific
- Industry specific
- Material type specific
- Customer specific
- Procurement specific (in house vs. external procurement)

We can only select only one attributes for field, (Display *, change. , hide -, required entry +.) property must determine for above mention criteria of field selection groups

Priority	Function	Character
1	Hide	-
2	Display	*
3	Mandatory	+
4	Optional	.

Table 3-1 (Field Selection Characters)

3.3.5. Define industry sector

Industry sector represent your industry in which you operate. E.g. it may be chemical industry, mechanical industry, FMCG and retail etc. some industry sectors are already configured in sap standard system. If necessary you can create new industry sector in system for your requirement. In standard system

- A represent Construction and Engineering industry sector
- M for Mechanical industry sector
- P for Pharmaceutical
- C for Chemical industry sector

3.3.6. Lock Relevant Field in Material Master

You can lock relevant field in material master as per requirement, for doing this go to

SPRO> IMG> Logistics General> Material Master> Field Selection> Define Lock-Relevant Fields

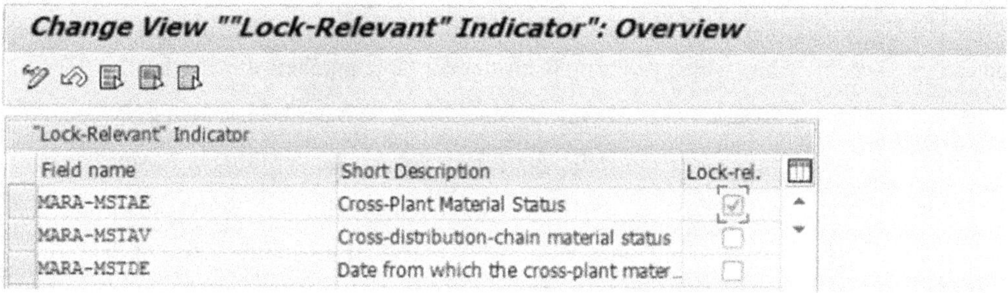

Figure 3-15 (Lock Relevant Indicator)

In material Master Basic data1 view you can see lock relevant field

Note: In standard system there are no fields are flag as lock relevant.

Copyrighted© Material

3.4. Mass maintenance of material master

Sometime client required change in master data of many materials. It may be change of one field or many fields. In target field may be enter new data or may be change an existing data. For doing this, use the transaction code MM17 for mass maintenance of material master data. Here following are showing maintenance screen, which represent the field description and technical name of field.

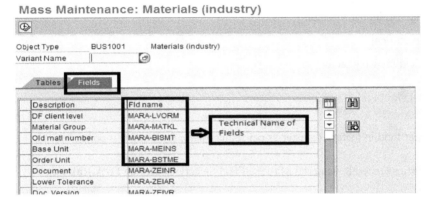

Figure 3-16 (Mass Maintenance of Material)

You can select the field line which you want to change for large numbers of materials collectively by name description or by technical name. By name it has been showing on description and for technical name confirmation of field, you can go to MM02 or MM03 transaction. Let's suppose requirement is to change x-plant material status. Select desire field you want to change and press F1 and press button of technical information [icon] of field. Here you can see technical name of field

Figure 3-17 (Mass Maintenance of Material)

Copyrighted© Material

Now find the technical name of field MSTAE (X-Plant material status) in MM17 transaction code and select field then press execute button

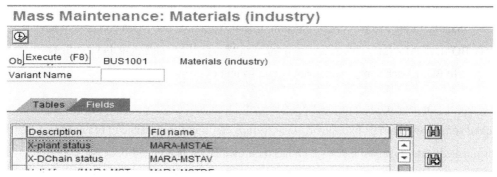

Figure 3-18 (Mass Maintenance of Material)

Now select the materials you want to change. You can select the range as well selective materials for mass maintenance as

Mass Maintenance: Materials (industry)

Figure 3-19 (Mass Maintenance of Material)

Enter the desire value in line new value, press carry out mass change button and press save

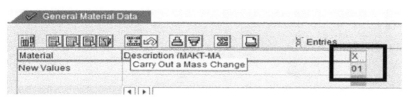

Figure 3-20 (Carry Out a Mass Changes)

Copyrighted© Material

3.5. Bills of Material (BOM)

List of materials or components required for creating or building new product. It is used for discrete manufacturing and parts of production. It is also possible one BOM component having its own BOM. BOM master data is essential for both Materials Management and Production Planning. In BOM, each component quantity and its unit of measure mention.

For example you have a finish product XYZ biscuit. For manufacturing of XYZ biscuit you required some raw materials like flavor, sugar, syrups etc. It is also possible to require some semi-finished material mixed batch which has their own BOM like mixed flour and corn. In XYZ Biscuit BOM, three raw materials and one semi-finished material according to above scenario are required. Semi-finished material can have its own BOM which can include two or more than two raw materials.

In BOM structure, it is possible many BOM exist for required of finish good. It is essential before creating a product you must create a BOM master data in SAP.

A BOM contain header data and item data. Header data include plant, material name and description, BOM usage, BOM group, base quantity and validity period etc. Item data includes item category, quantity of component, base unit of measure etc.

For creation of BOM in SAP system, go to SAP easy access under Logistics > Production > Master Data > Bills of Material > Bills of Material > Material BOM > Create/ Change/ Display or directly use transaction codes CS01, CS02 and CSO3 respectively.

BOM can be creating for different usage, e.g.

- BOM for production planning
- BOM for engineering
- BOM for costing
- BOM for plant maintenance

Copyrighted© Material

3.6. Material Master Record

As previously discuss, material master data maintain by different departments or functional areas. For example purchasing data maintain by procurement/ sourcing department, quality control data maintain by quality management department, sales and distribution data maintain by sales and marketing department. There are different views in material master data according to different functional areas. These different views are consist of basic data, purchasing, material classification, quality management, material requirement planning views, accounting and costing views etc. So let's talk about on these views with important fields

Note : You can create material master data by transaction MM01, change material master by transaction MM02 and display it by transaction MM03.

Copyrighted© Material

3.6.1. Basic Data Screen

In basic data screen views consist of basic information of material regarding material description, material number, base unit of measure, material groups, and gross and net weight etc. As already discuss, obligatory fields in material master can be done in configuration as per client requirement. Basic data is relevant for non-organizational level.

Note: You can maintain basic data views without assignment of plant and storage location in material master record.

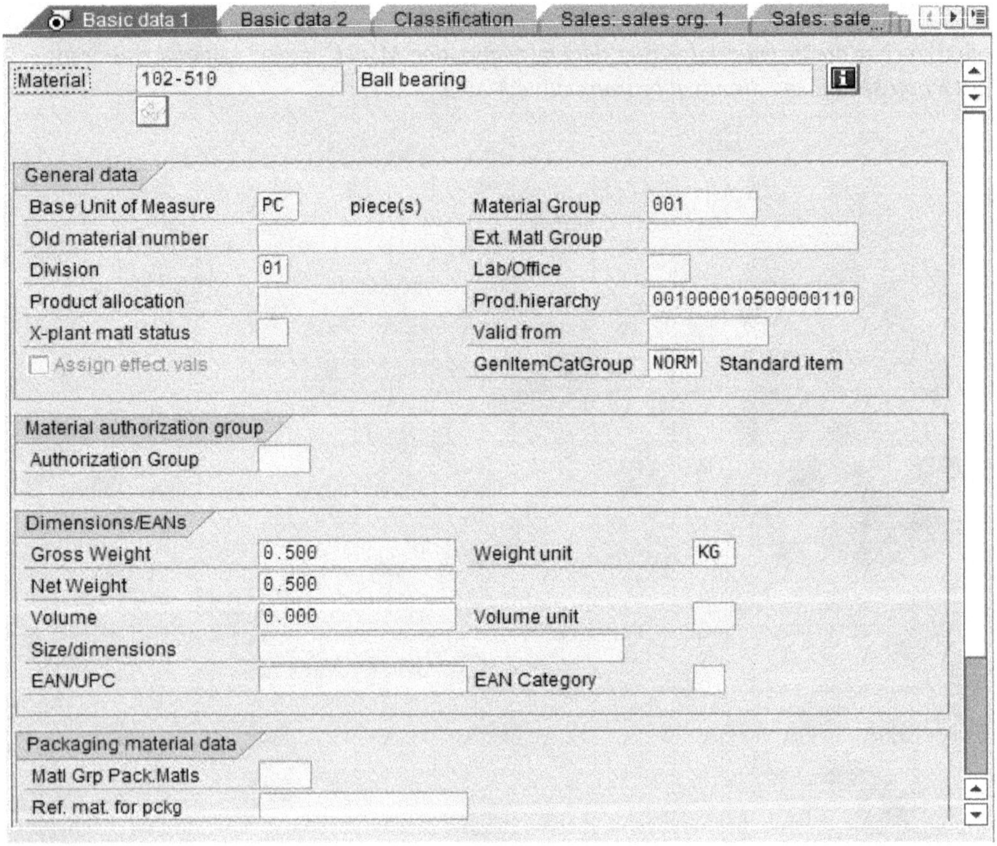

Figure 3-21 (Basic Data)

Copyrighted© Material

3.6.1.1. *Material Description*

It is the first basic and mandatory field in material master record. In system we have option to maintain description in different languages as per settings. We can add only 40 character description in material master. In standard behavior of system, you can change it whenever required.

3.6.1.2. *Unit of Measure*

Unit of measure describe a physical size of material in which material stock can manage. For example some materials are manage in pallets, some are manage in bottles, packets, feet's, square feet's, bags and meters etc. In Material master data you have to option to maintain conversions unit of measure e.g. selling unit of measure, issuance unit of measure. Base unit of measure cannot be change once any transaction (e.g. PR, PO or RFQ) accrue in record.

3.6.1.3. *Materials group*

In material group we are grouping together that material which having same characteristics and assign them a material group. Let suppose materials of Ball Bearing with descriptions as Ball Bearing 12235 or Ball Bearing 223354. These two materials consist of under material group Bearing. Similarly office supply is material group and under this material group relevant materials may be pencils, rubber and stapler etc. Material group is mandatory element of material master record. Its assignment in material master is mandatory for each material master record. In material master there are two material groups, internal material group and external material group. Configuration of both groups is

For internal material groups go to IMG-SPRO > IMG > Logistics General > Material Master > Setting for key fields > Define material groups and

for external material groups go to IMG-SPRO > IMG > Logistics General > Material Master > Setting for key fields > Define external material groups

Copyrighted© Material

3.6.1.4.   Old Material Number

Old material number field required you for material number that is used in legacy system of your company. This field consists of 18 characters in length.

3.6.1.5.   Division

You can assign one division to one material master record. It can use for differentiate different areas of distribution channels. You can configure division under customizing IMG-SPRO > Sales and Distribution > Master Data > Define Common Divisions

3.6.1.6.   Cross plant material status

This field describes whether the material may be used in purchasing, inventory management, production planning, plant maintenance, costing or for quality purpose. In basic data screen, any changes in cross plant material status field can be relevant for all plants belong to concern material master record.

Copyrighted© Material

3.6.2. Classification Data

The classification data is used primarily when searching for material. The characteristics values enter into the classification for each material can be find and the material which that set of characteristics can be found. This view is very useful when a customer has allocated significant efforts into identifying and creating characteristics and classes as well entering the characteristics values for material and other objects, such as in case of batches.

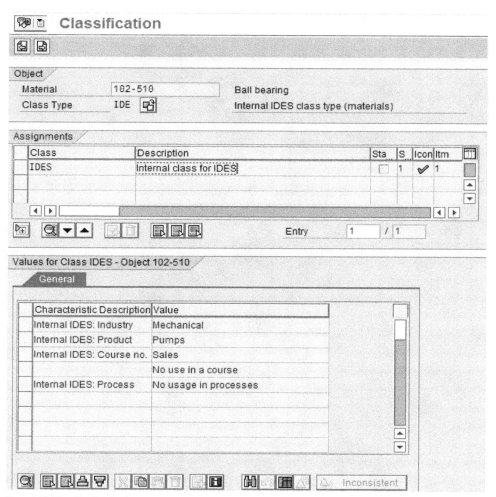

Figure 3-22 (Classification data)

Copyrighted© Material

3.6.3. Sales and Distribution Data

Sales and distribution data screen includes, sale organization data screen 1, sales organization data screen 2 and sales general plant data. These screens allow users to enter data relevant to sales organization. These materials may be sold on various sales organizations but data may be differing from one sale organization to another sale organization. Sales relevant fields includes, sales unit, division, delivering plant of material, sale tax fields includes tax country, tax category and tax classification, sales material groups, general item category group, product hierarchy, material pricing group, account assignment group, transportation group and loading group etc.

Figure 3-23 (Sale Data Screens)

Copyrighted© Material

3.6.4. Purchasing Data Screen

Every material which is relevant for purchasing is obligatory to maintain purchasing view in master data. Material number, material short description, base unit of measure and purchase group field by default comes from basic data screen. Some other purchasing data fields consist of following

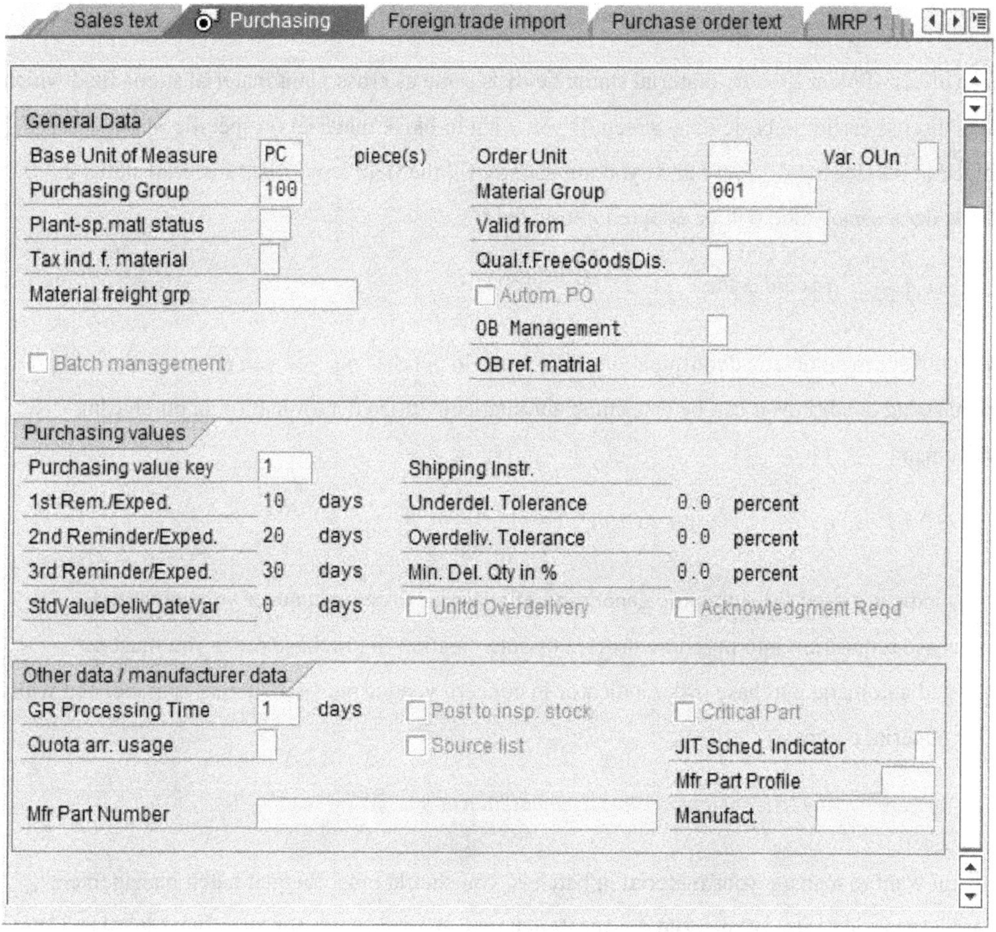

Figure 3-24 (Purchasing Data)

Copyrighted© Material

3.6.4.1.   Order unit

Order unit is a unit which is used in purchasing (purchase order) of material. If a material having base unit of measure is each (EA) may be it can procure in Feet (FT) or packet (PAC). Base unit of measure is treated as ordering unit for purchasing, if system not found any value in the order unit field.

3.6.4.2.   Plant-specific material status

The effect of plant specific material status fields is same as cross plant material status field which was discuss earlier in basic data screen. If you want to block material on specific plant, you can block in purchasing data screen. If you are already fill the field cross plant material status in basic data, same value will be adopted in this field.

3.6.4.3.   Tax indicator

If you want to automatic determination of tax code in purchasing, you can check it. By using purchasing conditions it can be determine automatically price determination in purchasing document.

3.6.4.4.   Automatic Purchase Order indicator

This indicator used for automatic generation of purchase order, whenever you converted purchase requisition into purchase order. For auto creation of purchase order you must set flagged automatic purchase order indicator in concern vendor master data that is associated with this material purchase.

3.6.4.5.   Batch Management Requirement indicator

If you want to manage your material in batches, you should must flagged batch management requirement indicator of material master. Batch management indicator also found in other views of material master record e.g. quality management view.

Copyrighted© Material

3.6.4.6. Purchasing value key

Configuration of purchasing value key allow the entry of purchasing values of tolerance limits (under and over delivery tolerances), reminder days, standard value for delivery date variances and minimum deliver quantity in percentage. You can configure purchasing value keys under customizing IMG-SPRO > Materials Management > Purchasing > Material Master > Define Purchasing Value Keys.

3.6.4.7. Unlimited over delivery indicator

If you flagged unlimited over delivery indicator in material master, you can receive and accept any over delivery from supplier. This indicator also located in vendor master record. So both are must be active for this function.

3.6.4.8. Goods Receipt Processing Time

Goods receipt processing time is number of work days that are required after receiving the material for quality inspection or for placement and movement into storage location.

3.6.4.9. Critical Part

Critical part indicator use and specify for sampling of inventory in SAP system.

3.6.4.10. Post to inspection stock indicator

This indicator allows you to whether a material is subject to quality inspection without inspection lot processing and material needed for post inspection stock. Whenever you create purchase order or perform goods receipts, indicator adopted from material master automatically.

3.6.4.11. Source List Indicator

This indicator is very important for sourcing/procurement department. This indicator must be flag if you want to maintain source list in procurement. Source list is the kind of master data in purchasing for plant specific. This master data use for automatic source determination in purchase requisition. Source list will be discussed later with brief details.

Copyrighted© Material

3.6.4.12.   *Quota Arrangement Usage*

In SAP system you have functionality to arrange quota of purchasing materials. You can distribute your procure quantity from different suppliers on percentage basis or on quantity basis. You can configure quota arrangement under customizing IMG-SPRO > Materials Management > Purchasing > Quota Arrangement > Define Quota Arrangement Usage.

Here you can configure and active quota for mention functions

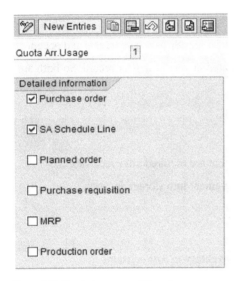

Figure 3-25 (Quota Arrangement Usage)

Copyrighted© Material

You can configure this key for following procurement functions

- Purchase requisition
- Purchase order
- Scheduling agreement
- Planned order
- Material requirement planning
- Production order

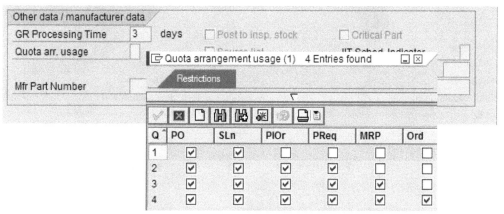

Figure 3-26 (Quota Arrangement Usage)

3.6.4.13.   Just In Time (JIT) Delivery Schedule

This indicator allow the system whether it is created schedule lines with Just in time based or forecast based for scheduling agreement schedule lines. If you use this function in material master, system automatically adopt information from material master in additional data for the item of scheduling agreement.

Copyrighted© Material

3.6.5. Forecasting Data

Forecasting data is used for calculated forecast as well consumption values for material requirement planning.

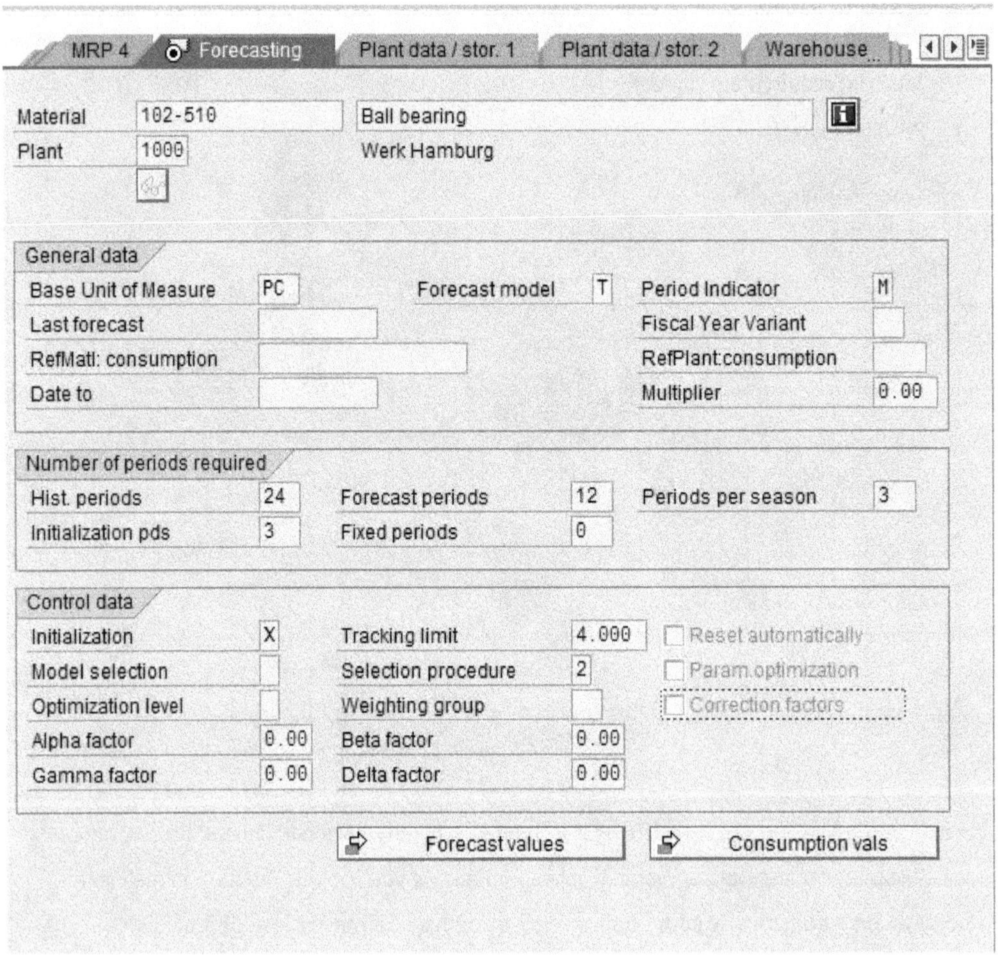

| MRP 4 | ☉ Forecasting | Plant data / stor. 1 | Plant data / stor. 2 | Warehouse | ◀ ▶ ▤ |

Material	102-510	Ball bearing	ℹ
Plant	1000	Werk Hamburg	

General data

Base Unit of Measure	PC	Forecast model	T	Period Indicator	M
Last forecast				Fiscal Year Variant	
RefMatl: consumption				RefPlant:consumption	
Date to				Multiplier	0.00

Number of periods required

Hist. periods	24	Forecast periods	12	Periods per season	3
Initialization pds	3	Fixed periods	0		

Control data

Initialization	X	Tracking limit	4.000	☐ Reset automatically
Model selection		Selection procedure	2	☐ Param.optimization
Optimization level		Weighting group		☐ Correction factors
Alpha factor	0.00	Beta factor	0.00	
Gamma factor	0.00	Delta factor	0.00	

⇨ Forecast values   ⇨ Consumption vals

Figure 3-27 (Forecasting data)

Copyrighted© Material

3.6.5.1.   Forecast models

Forecast models are used to calculate the material requirement. Before you run forecast, you must select model for calculate forecasting values. Forecasting models can be select automatically by system or you can select manually in system. Forecasting models with examples are shown below image

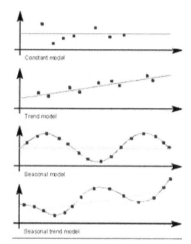

Figure 3-28 (Forecast models)

3.6.5.2.   Period Indicator

Period indicator field determine the time frame for which the consumption or historical values are held for forecasting.

3.6.5.3.   Physical year variant

Field describes the variant of the physical year and it is relevant for accounting.

3.6.5.4.   Reference Material for Consumption

If the material you are entering has no historical record or data from which to create forecast, you can define a material that may be related characteristics to be used as reference material.

Copyrighted© Material

3.6.5.5.   Reference Plant

You mention reference plant in material master for the purpose of drive consumption values.

3.6.5.6.   Date to

This date determine from which date figures/values taken of reference material.

3.6.5.7.   Multiplier

The multiplier field is figure between D and 1 where the values are relating to percentage to the reference material consumption values. These values should be used in new material.

3.6.5.8.   Historical periods

Forecast values calculate on the basis of historical periods enter in historical period field. No period will be used if this field remains blank.

Forecast Period

The number enters in this field, system will calculate the forecast period accordingly.

3.6.5.9.   Number of period initialization

This field determines historical values of consumption that you want to be used for the initialization of forecast. No value will be used in initialize forecast if this field value remains blank.

3.6.5.10.   Fixed Periods

For avoidance of fluctuation in calculation of forecast, fixed period value has used by system. The value you enter in this field, forecast will be fixed accordingly that value.

3.6.5.11.   Initialization Indicator

This field determines the system to initialize forecast manually.

Copyrighted© Material

3.6.5.12. Tracking Limit

The tracking limit field value determines the amount by which the forecast value may deviate from the actual value.

3.6.5.13. Reset Forecast Model Automatically

With this indicator, the forecast is reset if the tracking limit (describe above) is exceeded.

3.6.5.14. Model Selection

If you not entering any value into the forecast model, then this field will active. It is used when user want system automatically select a forecast model. Model will be selected by system one of the following three indicators

- ➤ T: Examine a trend
- ➤ S: Examine for seasonal fluctuations
- ➤ A: Examine for a trend and seasonal fluctuations

3.6.5.15. Selection Procedure

Selection procedure determines system select automatically forecast model. In standard SAP system there are two there are two procedures

- ➤ To find a best forecast seasonal model or trend pattern, perform significant test
- ➤ Carries out forecast for all the model and select the model which having lowest mean absolute deviation (MAD)

Note: *SAP system can automatically select a forecast model on the basis of past consumption values. For doing this, system carried out statistical tests and check whether seasonal requirement pattern or trend pattern applies. In seasonal test system clear the historical values of any possible trends and carries out auto correlation test. In trend test system subjects the historical values to regression analysis. System also checks whether trend patterns are exist in system or not. In automatically model selection, system also select model with the help of using combination of Alpha, Beta and Gamma. The smoothing factor is also varied between 0.2 to 0.8 and it will be interval of 0.2 and System will be chose lowest mean absolute deviation model*

Copyrighted© Material

3.6.5.16. *Alpha*

The default value of alpha factor is 0.2 if the field remains blank by user. For the basic value alpha is a smoothing factor.

3.6.5.17. *Beta*

It is smoothing factor for trend values. The default beta factor is 0.1 in case of absence of any value in beta factor field.

3.6.5.18. *Gamma*

This smoothing factor is used for seasonal index. The default gamma factor is 0.3 in case of absence of any value in gamma factor field.

3.6.5.19. *Delta Factor*

This smoothing factor is used for means absolute deviation (MAD). The default delta factor is 0.3 in case of absence of any value in delta factor field.

Copyrighted© Material

3.6.6. General Plant Data

This plant data is directly relevant for inventory management. Inventory staff may be relevant for entering information about storage location, shelf life of materials relevant data, storage bins and storage condition etc. some of important fields of general plant data are

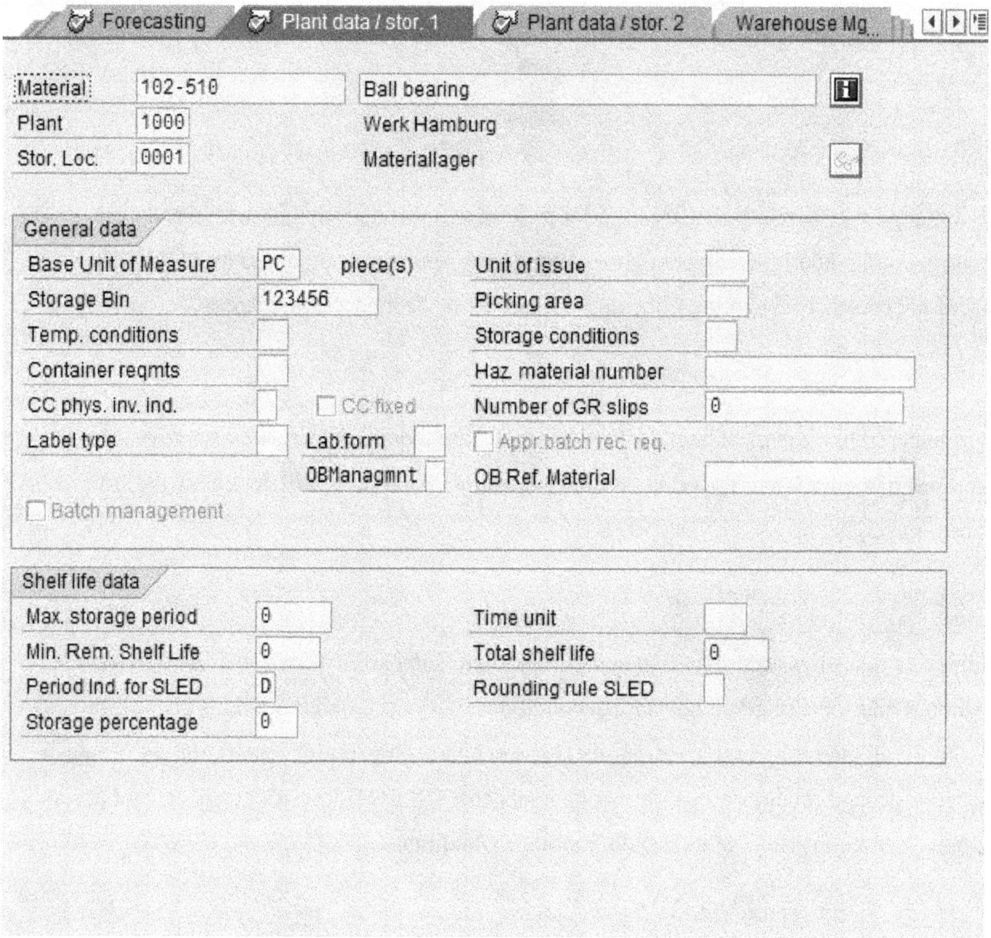

Figure 3-29 (General Plant Data)

Copyrighted© Material

3.6.6.1. *Storage Bin*

Storage bin is a 10 character field. Storage bin is a place with in storage location where materials actually take place. This field can use without warehouse management module. It is used for reference field and not configure in customizing. In materials management standard, you can define only one storage bin against one storage location. You can enter storage bin at the time of creation of material master data or with the change view of material master or by the transaction code MMSC.

3.6.6.2. *Picking Area*

It is a group of storage bins that are used for picking and it is directly link with warehouse management module. You can configure picking area in customizing under the IMG-SPRO > Logistics Execution > Shipping > Picking > Lean WM > Define Picking Areas

3.6.6.3. *Temperature Conditions*

Some material like chemical, metals, food items etc. are required a particular temperature for avoidance of expiration of material. So this temperature conditions will determine the storage of concern materials.

3.6.6.4. *Storage Conditions*

In different industries according to nature of materials, some of materials required refrigerated conditions and some required hot storage conditions. Storage condition field is client level and it is valid for all plants. Storage condition field is same like temperature condition field. You can configure storage conditions in customizing under IMG-SPRO > Logistics General > Material Master > Setting for Key Fields > Define Storage Conditions.

3.6.6.5. *Hazardous Material Number*

Hazardous material number field is also based on client level and valid for all plants. Hazard material number is linked with material. Hazard materials are dangerous and harmful. You can define hazardous material in front end by transaction code VM01 or by Menu path SAP easy access under Logistics > Logistics Execution > Master Data > Material > Hazardous Material > Create

Copyrighted© Material

3.6.6.6. *Cycle Counting Physical Inventory Indicator*

For cycle counted of inventory, indicator must be set in material master data. The indicator specify how the count is taken and how often. It is identify by four characters that are followings mention below

- Physical inventory number per fiscal year performed
- Maximum interval days between counts
- Time of float allowed for the date of planned count after the required date
- Consumption percentage allocated to each of the indicator (A, B, C, D etc.)

You can configure cycle counting indicator by transaction OMCO or in customizing under IMGP-SPRO > Materials Management > Inventory Management and Physical Inventory > Physical Inventory > Cycle Counting

3.6.6.7. *Cycle Counting Indicator is fixed*

If cycle counting indicator is flag than the cycle counting physical inventory indicator define mention above and cannot be changed by the ABC functionality that can be run periodically. If it is not set then the indicator will be changed if ABC functionality specifies that the material have in change status. If it is set and no changes can carried out via ABC functionality, then the indicator can still be set by changing in the master data.

3.6.6.8. *Number of Goods Receipt slips*

The field of number of goods receipts slips allow the receiving store / receiving room to mention figure that specifies number of goods receipts documents that will be printed after goods receipts posting.

3.6.6.9. *Maximum Storage Period*

Maximum storage period field describes maximum storage period for a material before it expire. Mostly it is used by reporting purpose.

Copyrighted© Material

3.6.6.10. Time Unit

It is a measuring unit of maximum storage period of material. It may be in days, weeks, and month or year.

3.6.6.11. Minimum Remaining Shelf Life

Minimum remaining shelf life field work for client level and it is valid for all plants. During goods receipts (e.g. today) the system check the shelf life expiry date of the batch of the material being transected and compare it with the date of today. If there is any difference accrue in days between today and shelf life expiration date, the system showing error or warning message as per your setting of configuration messages in customizing.

3.6.6.12. Total Shelf Life

Total shelf life field also at client level and valid for all plants. Total shelf life of a material is the time frame for which the material will keep in shelf from the production life to the shelf life expiration date. The shelf life is checked by system only if the shelf life expiration dates indicator flag in customizing settings. You can flag it by transaction OMJ5 or via IMG-SPRO > Logistics-General > Batch Management > Shelf Life Expiration Date (SLED) > Set Expiration Date Check

Plnt	Name 1	BBD/ProdD	
0008	New York	☑	▲
1000	Werk Hamburg	☑	▼
1100	Berlin	☑	
1200	Dresden	☐	

Figure 3-30 (Set Expiration Date Check)

3.6.6.13. Period Indicator for Shelf Life Expiration Date

This field is defined for the SLED fields used in this material master screen. The period can be defined as days, months or years etc. you can configure period indicator by transaction code O02K or by customizing IMG-SPRO > Logistics-General > Batch Management > Shelf Life Expiration Date (SLED) > Maintain Period Indicator

Copyrighted© Material

3.6.7. Warehouse Management Data

The warehouse management data fields are relevant for warehouse management module. For example these fields consist of warehouse management measuring unit, warehouse issuance unit of measure, storage strategies includes stock removal and stock placement and storage section etc. mention on below screen

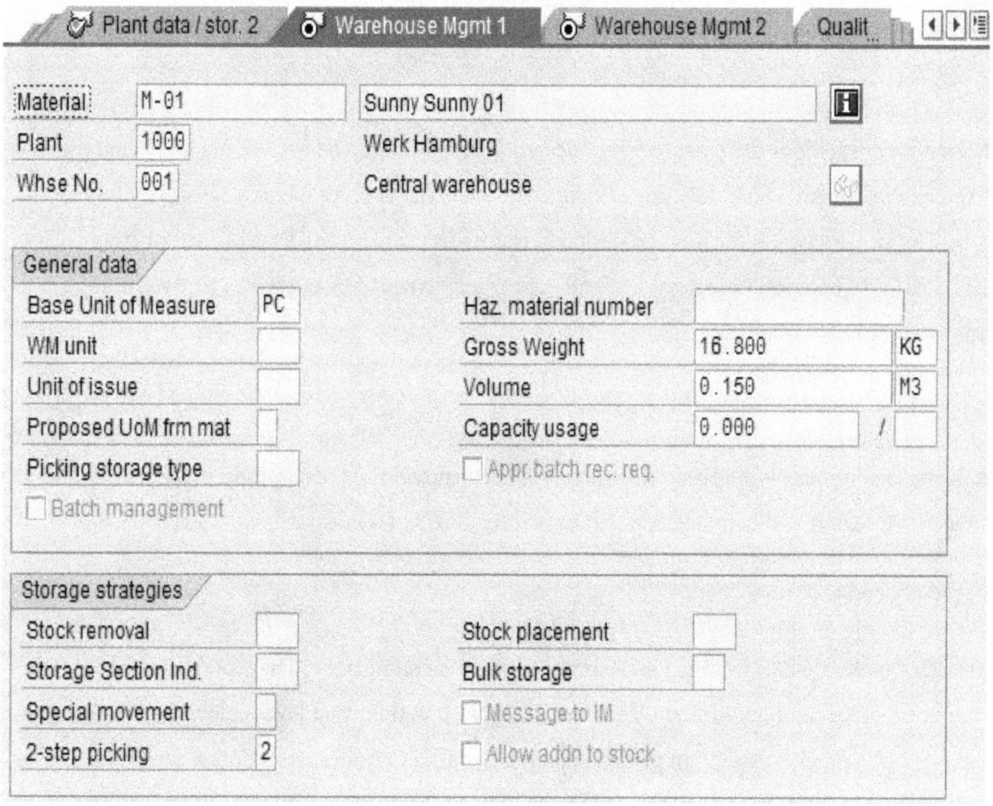

Plant data / stor. 2	Warehouse Mgmt 1	Warehouse Mgmt 2	Qualit

Material	M-01	Sunny Sunny 01
Plant	1000	Werk Hamburg
Whse No.	001	Central warehouse

General data

Base Unit of Measure	PC	Haz. material number	
WM unit		Gross Weight	16.800	KG
Unit of issue		Volume	0.150	M3
Proposed UoM frm mat		Capacity usage	0.000	/
Picking storage type		☐ Appr. batch rec. req.
☐ Batch management		

Storage strategies

Stock removal		Stock placement	
Storage Section Ind.		Bulk storage	
Special movement		☐ Message to IM
2-step picking	2	☐ Allow addn to stock

Figure 3-31 (Warehouse Management Data)

Copyrighted© Material

Some important fields in warehouse management data screen are

3.6.7.1.   WM Unit

It specifies unit of measure in which material will manage in warehouse management module.

3.6.7.2.   Picking Storage Type

Picking storage type field is used in rough-cut planning and detailed planning in system.

3.6.7.3.   Storage Type Indicator for Stock Removal

This indicator specifies the storage type selected by the system when removing stock and the preference in system which they are accessed. Storage type is predefined in system by hieratical order. The storage type indicator can define in transaction code OMLY or by customizing IMG-SPRO > Logistics Execution > Warehouse Management > Strategies > Active Storage Type Search

3.6.7.4.   Stock Placement

Stock placement field is similarly working as stock removal field, except the strategy is define in storage type search will be placement strategy instead of removal strategy.

3.6.7.5.   Storage Section

For each warehouse and storage type, storage section is compulsory. The storage section search is a more specific strategy for the placement of stock. It defines one level below the storage type search for placement of stock. In placement strategy up to ten storage section sequence can be define in system. You can configure storage section by transaction code OMLZ or under customizing IMG-SPRO > Warehouse Management > Strategies > Activate Storage Section Search.

3.6.7.6.   Bulk Storage

In the strategies of placement of stock, you can define how bulk material stock should be place. This indicator is used in bulk storage placement strategies for warehouse management module. It also indicates the width and height of respective storage type. It can be define by transaction

Copyrighted© Material

code OMM4 or in customizing under IMDG-SPRO > Logistics Execution > Warehouse Management > Strategies > Putaway Strategies > define strategy for bulk storage

3.6.7.7.   Two Step Picking

In warehouse management you have option for picking a material with one step or with two steps. One step picking is good option for large and bulky materials. One step picking not a good option for small or numerous material stock. For minimize your work load, you can use two step picking process. The interim storage process in which item is picked and transfer to the interim storage type from there the final pick takes place. You can configure it under customizing IMG-SPRO > Logistics Execution > Warehouse Management > Interfaces > Shipping > Define Two Step Picking

Copyrighted© Material

3.6.8. Quality Management Data

Quality management data is relevant to quality management department. Quality department specifies quality requirement of material against plant specific. This data screen field includes material authorization group for activities in QM which use to restrict users to access material related data in quality management. Inspection setup indicator specifies existence of inspection setup for concern material and for relevant plant. Post to inspection stock indicator which specifies stock posted forcedly for inspection. Inspection setup button where you enter inspection plans and make activations that plans. Inspection interval days specify the interval between different quality inspections. QM control key that determine which conditions are valid for material in quality management for procurement process. QM proc. active check determines QM in procurement for all plants relevant to a client and certificate type specifies the contents of quality certificate.

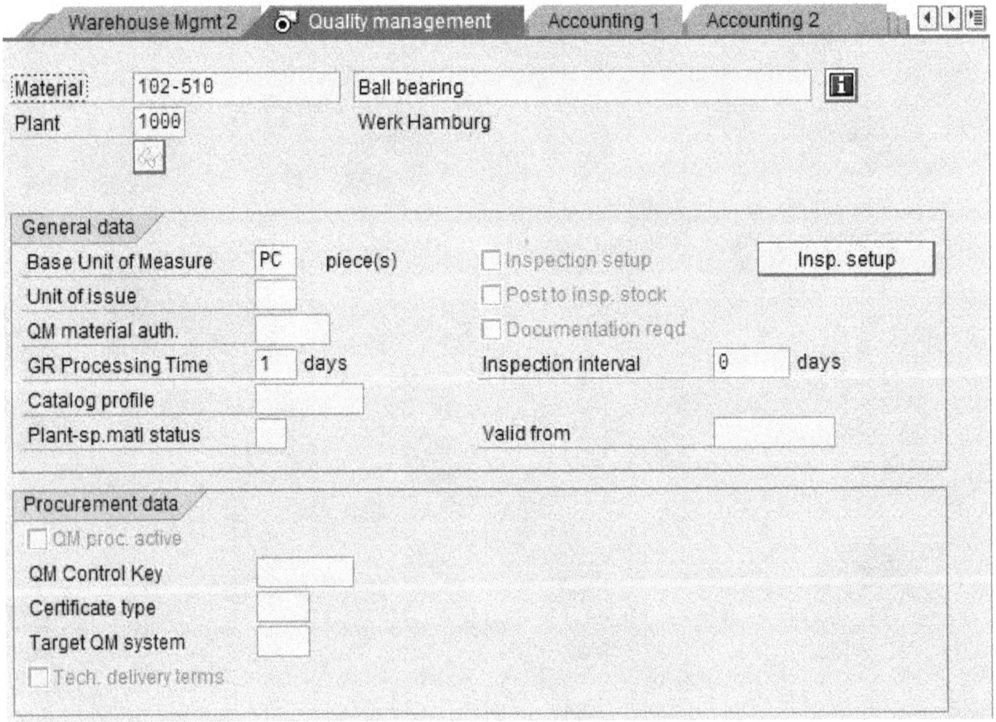

Figure 3-32 (Quality Management Data)

Copyrighted© Material

3.6.9. Material Requirement Planning (MRP) Data

The main aim of Material requirement planning (MRP) is raw materials are available for production and finished goods are available for sale. MRP master data consist of multiple screens which includes MRP1, MRP2, MRP3 and MRP4. . It contains information regarding how your material plan and how to produce. Fields includes in MRP screens are

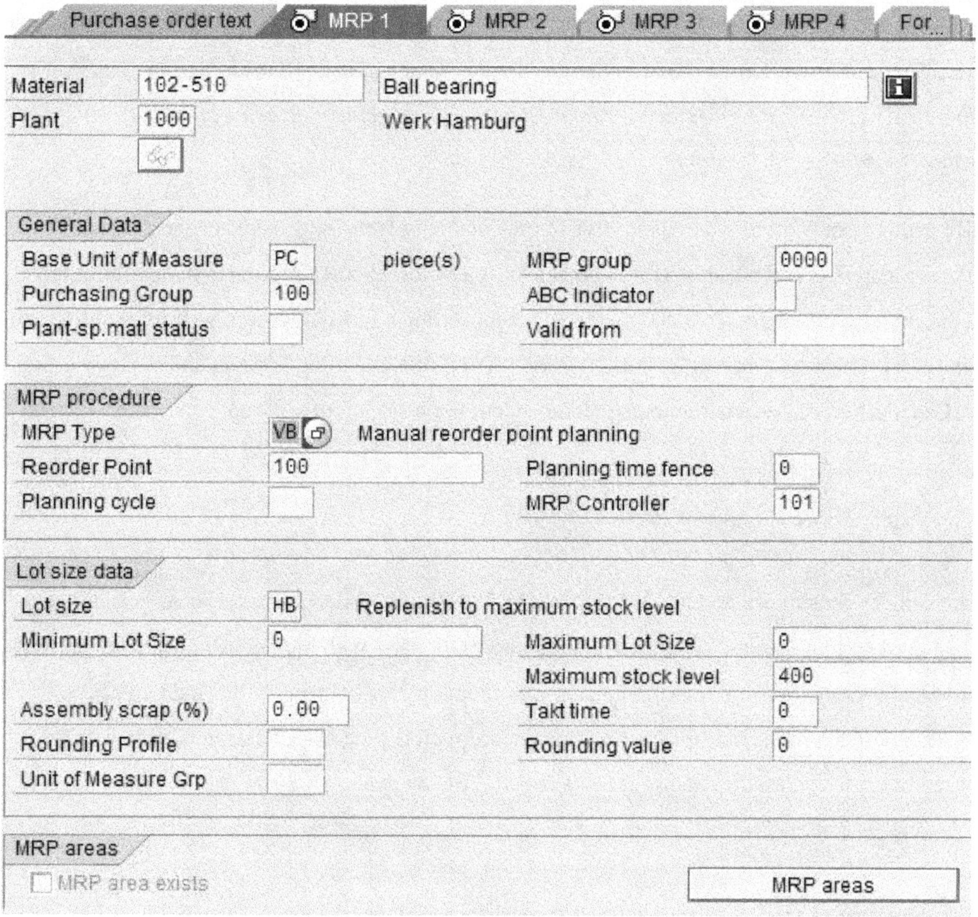

| Purchase order text | MRP 1 | MRP 2 | MRP 3 | MRP 4 | For... |

| Material | 102-510 | Ball bearing |
| Plant | 1000 | Werk Hamburg |

General Data

Base Unit of Measure	PC	piece(s)	MRP group	0000
Purchasing Group	100		ABC Indicator	
Plant-sp.matl status			Valid from	

MRP procedure

MRP Type	VB	Manual reorder point planning
Reorder Point	100		Planning time fence	0
Planning cycle			MRP Controller	101

Lot size data

Lot size	HB	Replenish to maximum stock level
Minimum Lot Size	0		Maximum Lot Size	0
			Maximum stock level	400
Assembly scrap (%)	0.00		Takt time	0
Rounding Profile			Rounding value	0
Unit of Measure Grp				

MRP areas

☐ MRP area exists | MRP areas |

Figure 3-33 (MRP1, MRP2, MRP3 and MRP4 DATA Screens)

Copyrighted© Material

3.6.9.1. MRP Group

The responsibility of MRP group is to planning separately of your material. We create planning group by transaction OPPR or OPPZ codes or by customizing IMG-SPRO > Materials Management > Consumption-Based Planning > MRP Groups > Carry out Overall Maintenance of MRP Groups.

Note: *After configuration, you assign these groups to material types. For doing this, go to customizing IMG-SPRO > Materials Management > Consumption-Based Planning > MRP Groups > Define MRP Group for Each Material Type*

MRP groups can be used when plant division for planning is not sufficient for the division of the different materials MRP necessities. You can assign different MRP groups to material master according to requirement for MRP run by different settings. In MRP group, you define MRP run parameters. These parameters includes consumption mode, planning horizon and strategy group etc. Calculations of these parameters are dependent upon setting of your concern material master data.

3.6.9.2. ABC Indicator

According to consumption value of material, ABC indicator classifies material A, B and C. e.g. in standard system, A classification specifies important parts with high consumption value, B classification specifies less important parts with medium consumption value and C type classification determine unimportant parts compare with B type classification with low vale of consumption. The classification process is called ABC analysis.

3.6.9.3. MRP Type

For controlling of MRP procedures MRP type is used in system and it is specifies how and whether your material will plan. MRP types includes, manual reorder point planning, automatic reorder point planning, time phase planning and forecast based planning etc. it also determine other parameters in material master record maintenance.

Copyrighted© Material

3.6.9.4.   Reorder Point

Reorder point field use for reorder point planning. When your stock reaches or drops below the quantity mention in this field, system creates procurement proposals during MRP run. It is only use for reorder point planning that will discuss latterly in material requirement planning section.

3.6.9.5.   Planning Cycle

Planning cycle field specifies the number of days in which material will be planned as well as order or when material will create or when it will be order. Planning cycle is a planning calendar that you define in customizing for MRP. You can configure it in customizing IMG-SPRO > Production > Material Requirement Planning > Master Data > Maintain Planning Calendar

3.6.9.6.   MRP Controller

MRP controller is a person or a group of people that are responsible for planning run of material. You can configure MRP controller in customizing IMG-SPRO > Production > Material Requirement Planning > Master Data > Define MRP Controller

3.6.9.7.   Lot Size

This field specifies lot size procedures. These procedures calculate quantity in material requirement planning. Latterly in MRP section, it will discuss briefly. You can configure lot size in configuration IMG-SPRO > Materials Management > Consumption Based Planning > Planning > Lot Size Calculations > Check Lot Sizing Procedures

3.6.9.8.   Minimum Lot Size

This field specifies minimum lot size for procurement.

3.6.9.9.   Maximum Lot Size

This field specifies maximum lot size for procurement.

Copyrighted© Material

3.6.9.10. Maximum Stock Level

This field is only on used for lot size procedure as replenishment to maximum (HB) and determine the maximum stock level for respective material at plant level.

3.6.9.11. Procurement Type

Procurement type field specifies whether the material procure from externally or internal in-house. The following procurement types can be possible for it

- Material will be produce in-house
- Material will be produce externally
- Material will be produce both in house and externally

3.6.9.12. Batch Entry

Batch entry field is used to identify where the batches has have to be entered in the process of production. There are following options for the field of batch entry are

1. Batch in goods issue; no confirmation required
2. Manual batch determination required upon release of order
3. Batch not required in production/ process order; confirmation required
4. Automatic batch determination upon release of order

3.6.9.13. Special Procurement Type

The special procurement type field describes a procurement scenario more accurately. It can be specify procurement type, procurement from another plant and BOM characteristics. You can configure it in customizing IMG-SPRO > Consumption Based Planning > Master Data > Define Special Procurement Type

3.6.9.14. Production Storage Location

If your material produce in-house then the production storage location enter in this field will be used in planned order, production order and run schedule quantity.

Copyrighted© Material

3.6.9.15. *Quota Arrangement Usage*

In SAP system you have functionality to arrange quota of purchasing materials. You can distribute your procure quantity from different suppliers on percentage basis or on quantity basis. You can configure quota arrangement under customizing IMG-SPRO > Materials Management > Purchasing > Quota Arrangement > Define Quota Arrangement Usage.

3.6.9.16. *Backflush*

With backflush option system automatically issues/consumed goods (against movement type 261) at the time of confirmation of operations. Consumption is automatically posted when withdrawal of material. It may be useful for fixed relationship materials.

3.6.9.17. *Storage Location for EP (External Procurement)*

Storage location for external procurement specifies whenever you run MRP, system automatically suggest this storage location in planned order or subsequent storage location for purchase requisition.

3.6.9.18. *Safety Stock*

The safety stock is designate for any unexpected rise of demand. The purpose of safety stock is to ensure to production that there is no shortage of material in case of increase of demand.

3.6.9.19. *Minimum Safety Stock*

Minimum safety stock is the lower limit of safety stock range. Your mention safety stock must be exceeded by minimum safety stock during maintenance of master record.

Copyrighted© Material

3.6.10. Accounting Data

In material master, accounting data is relevant to account department. Account department is responsible for maintaining the valuation and pricing data relevant for inventory transactions'. Fields in accounting data includes

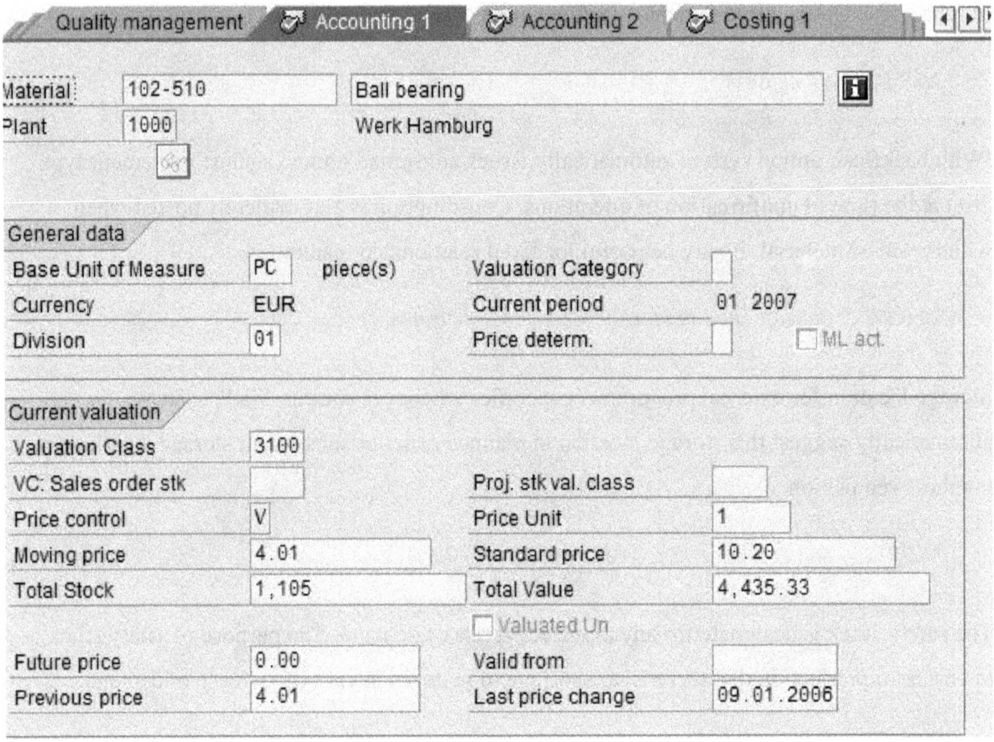

Quality management	Accounting 1	Accounting 2	Costing 1	◀ ▶

Material	102-510	Ball bearing	ℹ️
Plant	1000	Werk Hamburg	

General data

Base Unit of Measure	PC	piece(s)	Valuation Category	
Currency	EUR		Current period	01 2007
Division	01		Price determ.	☐ ML act.

Current valuation

Valuation Class	3100		
VC: Sales order stk		Proj. stk val. class	
Price control	V	Price Unit	1
Moving price	4.01	Standard price	10.20
Total Stock	1,105	Total Value	4,435.33
		☐ Valuated Un	
Future price	0.00	Valid from	
Previous price	4.01	Last price change	09.01.2006

Figure 3-34 (Accounting Data)

Copyrighted© Material

3.6.10.1. Valuation category

Valuation category is criteria in which material is subject to split valuated. It specifies whether your material valuated separately or together. For configuration of valuation category you first required to set valuation area in system. In standard SAP system contain several by default valuation categories e.g.

- H for origin
- B for procurement type
- C for quality

3.6.10.2. Material Ledger Active Check

Material ledger active check field determine whether material is relevant for material ledger valuation or not.

3.6.10.3. Valuation Class

For determination of stock account of material, valuation class use and plays an important role. It is a mechanism (discuss briefly in automatic account determination chapter) where your material is link with GL account. Every accounting relevant movement GL account will be updating according to mention valuation class. Valuation class linked with materials type via account category reference in configuration. You can configure valuation class by transaction OMSK or in customizing IMG-SPRO > Materials Management > Valuation and Account Assignment > Account Determination > Account Determination without Wizard > Define Valuation Class

3.6.10.4. Valuation Class for Sale Order Stock

If account department want, you can enter a different valuation class for sale order stock.

3.6.10.5. Price Control

For valuation of stock, price control is used. There are two price control indicator i.e.(V) moving average price and (S) standard price.

Copyrighted© Material

3.6.10.6.   Price Unit

The value enter in price unit field specifies the number of units that standard price or moving average price relates to. Suppose that the material (ABC) having moving average price is EUR 3.25 and price unit value is 100, then the actual cost of per unit will be 0.0324.

3.6.10.7.   Moving Average Price

Moving average price is used for those materials which having dynamic fluctuating rates. Moving average price also called as weighted average price of material with "V" indicator. Most likely companies used moving average price for Raw materials (ROH), Packaging materials (VERP), Spare parts (ERSA), IT materials and trading goods (HAWA) etc. In moving average price, price of material will be impact after every goods receipts entry. These materials purchase order price fluctuating may be take place on daily basis, or continuously basis. The benefit of moving average price is raw materials or other related material which having moving average price, always represent current market price.

3.6.10.8.   Standard Price

Standard price is used for those materials, which having low fluctuating prices or no fluctuating frequently. Most likely companies use standard prices for Semi Finished (HALB) and finished goods (FERT) that are producing internally in production premises. Price is remain constant at specified period of time and don't change whenever goods receipts perform in with in that period. In simple word, it is planned value of particular material for some specific period (may be 15 days or may be 30 days) of time with actual costing/ material ledger. Standard price maintain in two ways in material master

- With manual insert/ enter
- Automatically suggest by SAP system (e.g. Cost run)

In material master for standard price it is mandatory

- Price control "S" should be maintained in material master account one view screen.
- Attributes of material type configure accordingly

Copyrighted© Material

Standard price of material can be changed through an entry in the future price field. According to date mention in valid from field, future price is enter in the field will be valid till that that.

Copyrighted© Material

3.6.11. Costing Data

This data contain information regarding costing of material. Some fields includes in costing data are

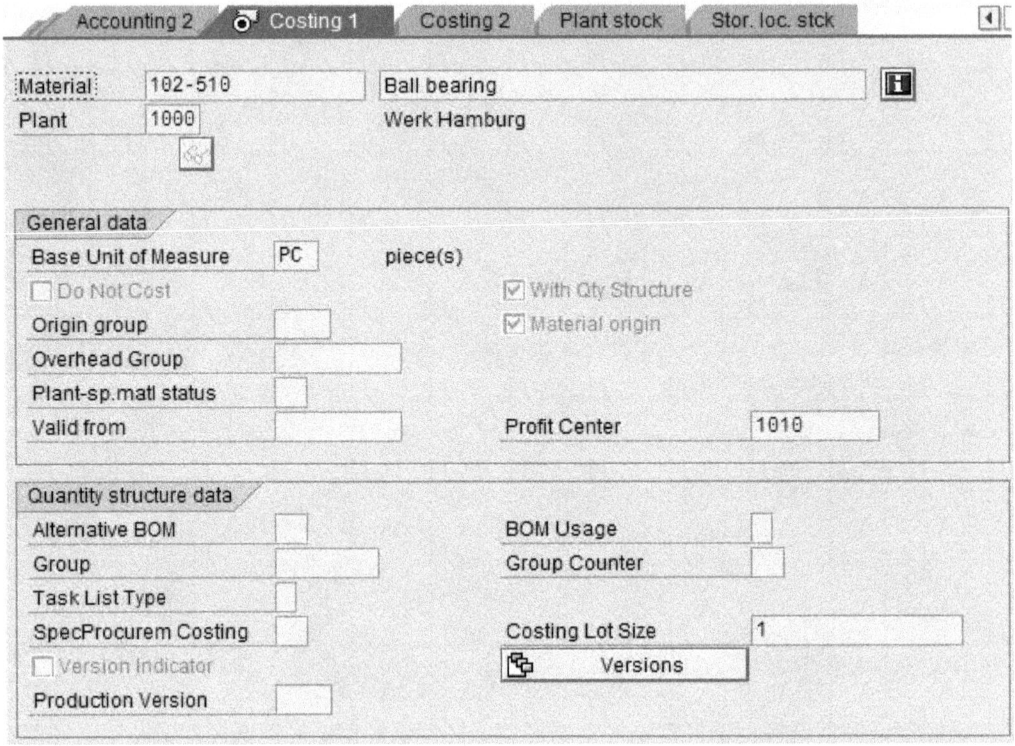

| Accounting 2 | Costing 1 | Costing 2 | Plant stock | Stor. loc. stck |

Material 102-510   Ball bearing
Plant   1000   Werk Hamburg

General data

Base Unit of Measure	PC	piece(s)	
Do Not Cost		☑ With Qty Structure	
Origin group		☑ Material origin	
Overhead Group			
Plant-sp.matl status			
Valid from		Profit Center	1010

Quantity structure data

Alternative BOM		BOM Usage	
Group		Group Counter	
Task List Type			
SpecProcurem Costing		Costing Lot Size	1
Version Indicator		Versions	
Production Version			

Figure 3-35 (Costing Data)

Copyrighted© Material

3.6.11.1. Origin group

These groups are used to further more subdivide the cost of material. Materials assign to same cost element by automatic account determination can be separate into origin groups. Material assign to the origin group and overhead cost are assign to different origin groups at different rates with percentage or at a flat cost.

3.6.11.2. Material Origin Indicator

If the indicator is flag, the number of material will be written to the cost element itemization in the controlling area.

3.6.11.3. With Quantity Structure Indicator

This indicator specifies whether your material costing with or without a quantity structure.

3.6.11.4. Costing Overhead Group

It applies cost of overheads from the costing sheet of production order to materials in the group.

3.6.11.5. Task List Group

With task list you can combine the processes related to production that are similar and are for similar materials.

3.6.11.6. Group Counter

It is used to combine the task group list so it indicates a unique list for task the material.

3.6.11.7. Task List Type

It specifies the type of task list according to its functionality. You can configure it by transaction OP8B or under customizing IMG-SPRO > Production > Basic Data > Routing > Control Data > Maintain Task List Types

Copyrighted© Material

3.6.11.8. Costing Lot Size

The field of costing lot size allow product costing department to specify a lot size of material in material master that would use in cost estimate of product.

Copyrighted© Material

3.5. External Services

Similarly material purchase, there is also option in SAP for procurement of external services. You can manage services same like as material. So in SAP there is a difference between procurement of materials and procurement of external services.

External services management incorporates functionality that is relevant to the procurement and execution of services at a company. Similarly material master records, SAP system having functionality for maintain and build service master record. Service master data consist of all information regarding service which includes service description, service UOM, service category, valuation class and conditions etc.

For creation of service master go to SAP easy access under Manu path

Logistics > Materials Management > Service Master > Service > Create AC03

For maintain of conditions

Logistics > Materials Management > Service Master > Service > Service conditions > for vendor with plant/ for vendor without plant

You can procure services with normal purchase order creation transaction ME21N, but the difference accrues in item category in purchase order. In services purchase order item category D (Services) is used. Buyer can add a necessary service master number in purchase order. In purchase order, service master number is entering with quantity and price. Once all necessary information is entered, save and sent services purchase order to supplier.

When a supplier has performed services fully or partially, the relevant information will be enter in SAP system. The entry of this date is recorded in service entry sheet. The information mention in service entry sheet can be planned and unplanned service. The service entry sheet can be entering with reference to service purchase order. You can maintain service entry sheet by transaction code ML81N or by Menu path under Logistics > Material Management > Service Entry Sheet > Maintain

Copyrighted© Material

Copyrighted© Material

Copyrighted© Material

Chapter 4:
Basic Concepts of Vendor Master Data and Configuration

Copyrighted© Material

4. Chapter 4: Basic Concepts of vendor Master Data and Configuration

In this lesson you will learn

4.1.   Vendor Master

4.2.   Vendor Master Configuration

   4.2.1.   Account groups for vendor and field selection

   4.2.2.   Vendor Number Ranges

4.3.   Vendor Master Record

   4.3.1.   General Data Screen

   4.3.2.   Accounting Information Data

   4.3.3.   Purchasing Data

   4.3.4.   Partner role for vendor master record

4.4.   Mass Maintenance of Vendor Master

Copyrighted© Material

4.1. Vendor Master

Vendor master data consist of all vendor record including vendor name/ company name, vendor address, contact information, sales person, partner role, reconciliation account, terms of payments, payment currency and tax information etc. Vendor master is maintain by both purchase and account department. It can be created centralize or by purchase organization.

For Vendor Master (Purchasing) creation goes to sap easy access

Logistics > Materials Management > Purchasing > Master data > Vendor > Purchasing > Create MK01/ Change MK02/ Display MK03

For centrally creation of Vendor Master goes to SAP easy access under

Logistics > Materials Management > Purchasing > Master Data > Vendor > Central > Create XK01/ Change XK02/ Display XK03

XK04 Vendor changes centrally, XK05 Block vendor centrally, XK06 Mark vendor for deletion, XK07 Change vendor account group, XK11 Create condition, XK99 Mass maintenance

4.2. Vendor Master Configuration

- Account Groups for vendor
- Field Selection for vendor master
- Number ranges assignment

4.2.1. Account groups for vendor and field selection

Whenever you create vendor master it is mandatory to mention account group of vendor. It determine whether

- Vendor is one time?
- Number range of vendor master?
- Screen sequence?
- What Partner role?

Copyrighted© Material

- What Field sections?

- What Partner determination schema use?

- Reconciliation account?

Common examples of vendor account groups are goods supplier, alternative payee, Plant, forwarding agent, invoicing party and one time vendor etc.

Let suppose we create one time vendor account group. If necessary you can maintain vendor account group in customizing, under

SPRO> IMG> Logistics General> Business Partner> Vendor> Control> Define Account Group and Field Selection (Vendor) or Transaction code OMSG

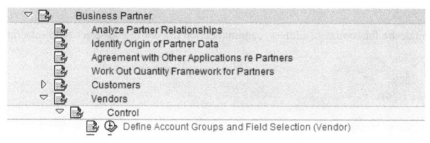

Figure 4-1 (Account Group and Field Selection Configuration)

Select new entries,

Figure 4-2 (Account Group and Field Selection Configuration)

Now enter here account group name, account group description. If vendor is one time, tick one time vendor indicator. For field selection for one time vendor account group, double click on (Field Status section) General data, company code data and purchasing data etc. as mention below

Copyrighted© Material

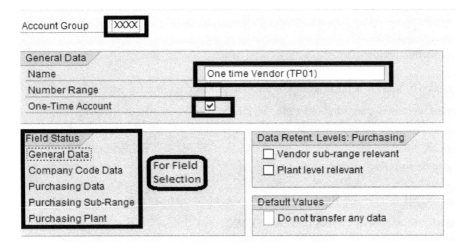

Figure 4-3 (Account Group and Field Selection Configuration)

Double click on desire function e.g., address, communication or control and select field selection

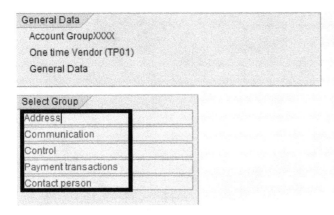

Figure 4-4 (Account Group and Field Selection)

Select your desire entry, double click then field selection (Required entry, optional, display or hide an entry) according to requirement

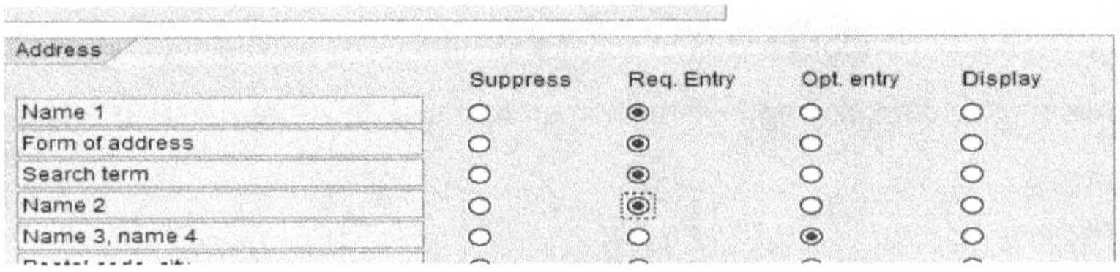

Address	Suppress	Req. Entry	Opt. entry	Display
Name 1	○	◉	○	○
Form of address	○	◉	○	○
Search term	○	◉	○	○
Name 2	○	◉	○	○
Name 3, name 4	○	○	◉	○

Figure 4-5 (Account Group and Field Selection)

Copyrighted© Material

4.2.2. Vendor Number Ranges

For number ranges assignment again go to Logistics General > Business partner> Vendor > Control >Define Number Ranges for Vendor Master Record

Here you maintain interval number range by clicking intervals and this interval number range assign to account group by clicking on number range

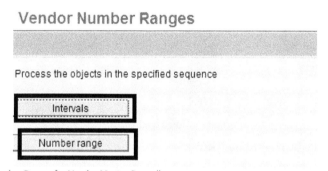

Figure 4-6 (Number Ranges for Vendor Master Record)

Copyrighted© Material

4.3. Vendor Master Record

Account department and purchasing department is responsible to maintain vendor master data. Vendor relationship having two folds with your company, first one is to negotiating price, conditions and deliver materials through purchasing. Second fold is to receive payment against invoicing through accounts payable. Vendor master data contain the information of relationship with your company.

You can create, change and display vendor master data by transaction XK01, XK02 and XK03 respectively or follow the Menu path SAP Essay Access under Logistics > Materials Management > Master Data > Vendor > Central > Create / Change / Display or

> ➤ Create via purchasing by transaction MK01
> ➤ Create via financial accounting by transaction FK01
> ➤ Create via centrally by transaction XK01

Vendor master (Central) data initial screen mention below. You must mention here relevant company code, purchasing organization and account group.

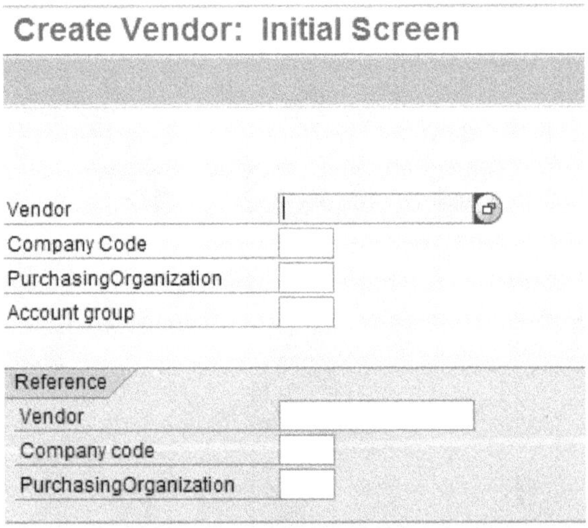

Figure 4-7 Vendor master (central) data creation initial screen

Copyrighted© Material

4.3.1. General Data Screen

4.3.1.1. Title

It specifies the title of the vendor e.g. Company, Individual, Mr., Ms. and Dr. etc. You can also define title of vendor in customizing under IMG-SPRO > Flexible Real Estate Management > Address Management > Maintain Texts for Form of Address

4.3.1.2. Name

Name field contain the information regarding name of your vendor. Before creation of vendor master record, make sure there is no duplication of vendor master record.

4.3.1.3. Search Term

Search term field use to find a vendor. You can define search criteria to find a vendor that will help for your users for easily search.

4.3.1.4. Street Address

The street address is the address of vendor. For calculation of tax jurisdiction code, you can use vendor country, vendor region and postal code.

4.3.1.5. PO Box Address

Some of companies are using post office boxes address. So it contains information relevant to post of box.

4.3.1.6. Communication

Communication fields include vendor communication language, vendor telephone number, extensions, E-Mail addresses and fax numbers.

Copyrighted© Material

4.3.2. Accounting Information Data

Accounting data is relevant to account department. It is enter by account department and important fields in this data includes

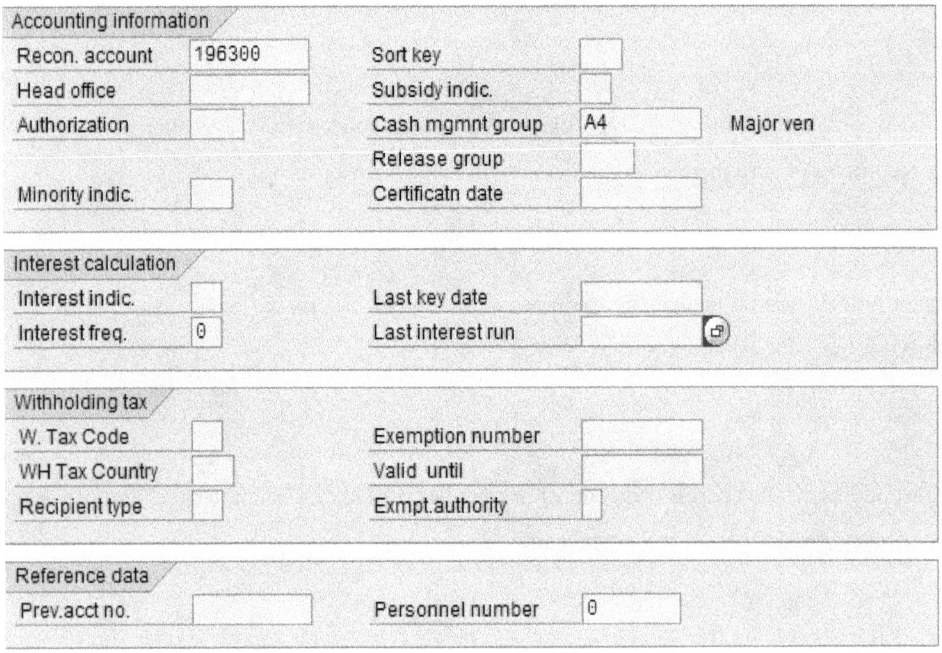

Figure 4-8 (Accounting data)

4.3.2.1.   Reconciliation account

The reconciliation accounts are individual general ledger accounts. It is recorded in the line item detail in the sub ledger and sum up in general ledger. In depth information enter into the reconciliation account is all line item data from the vendor account.

In addition with vendor, the reconciliation accounts are also maintained for customer accounts and asset accounts. You can create reconciliation account by transaction FS01 and make sure

Copyrighted© Material

account should be a balance sheet account, account group is mandatory to select as reconciliation account and you must assign reconciliation account to vendor master.

4.3.2.2. *Sort Key*

It specifies the rule of lay outs for the allocation field in line item of document. System sorts the document line item according to the key enters in allocation field.

4.3.2.3. *Head Office*

Head office field specifies head office or master account of concern vendor. You specify this account only for branch accounts. Any item posting relevant to branch accounts will be auto posting to head office accounts.

4.3.2.4. *Authorization Group*

It is a course of maximize or extend authorization protection security on certain objects. You can define authorization object independently. You can make assignment of authorization object by using object F_LFA1_BEK

4.3.2.5. *Cash Management Group*

With this functionality it is possible to allocate vendor to a planning group. The planning group directly relevant to cash management department for clear cut information about to plan or to produce company's cash forecast.

4.3.2.6. *Release Group*

It is allow only those in the group to be able to release for payments. These release approval groups freely assign. You can also use these groups to classify customers and vendors. You can configure release groups in customizing SPRO-IMG > Financial Accounting > Account Receivables and Account Payables > Business Transaction > Release for Payment > Define Release Approval Groups for Release for Payment

Copyrighted© Material

4.3.2.7. Minority Indicator

It is relevant to implementation in U.S. configuration is required to enter the relevant information. Many companies in U.S. ask their local or federal officials to report on the level of minority vendor supplying material to them.

4.3.2.8. Certification Date for Minority Vendor

It is also relevant to U.S. implementation and it indicated that expiration date of minority vendor. The expiry consists of two years. After two year must be renewal required.

4.3.2.9. Interest calculation indicator

If the account is suitable for interest, it use to automatic calculation of interest. You can define these indicators in customizing under IMG-SPRO > Financial Accounting > Account Receivable and Accounts Payable > Business Transactions > Interest Calculation > Interest Calculation Global Setting > Define Interest Calculation Types

4.3.2.10. Interest Calculation Frequency

The indicator use when interest calculation made for concern vendor. Period can be range through month to year.

4.3.2.11. Withholding Tax Code

Withholding tax relevant for foreign vendor from another country or applies vendors who are not belongs to resident in country. But drive income from interest, profit, royalties, rentals, and other income source of resident country. There are also numbers of different exceptions as well as rules that are defined by tax experts.

4.3.2.12. Withholding tax country key

The tax calculation can be relevant to payee's country specific

Copyrighted© Material

4.3.2.13.   Vendor Recipient Type

Vendor recipient type is used for I.R.P.F (Impuesto sobre la renta de las personas fisicas, Spanish income tax) reporting in Spain and used for 1042 (annual taxable return used by withholding agents to report tax withheld on US source income paid to certain non-resident corporations or individuals) reporting in United States of America.

4.3.2.14.   Exemption Number

If a vendor having exemption certificate and exempt from withholding tax, then exemption number will be used in master data of vendor.

4.3.2.15.   Validity Date of Exemption

It specifies the expiry date of exemption certificate.

4.3.2.16.   Authority for Exemption

Authority for exemption from withholding tax is used for 1042 reporting in the United States.

4.3.2.17.   Previous Account Number

It specifies the legacy system account number which was used in previous system.

4.3.2.18.   Personnel Number

Personnel number is used if your vendor is also your employee.

Copyrighted© Material

4.3.3. Purchasing Data

Vendor purchasing data can be entering via transaction MK01 or XK01. Purchasing department is custodian to enter this purchasing data.

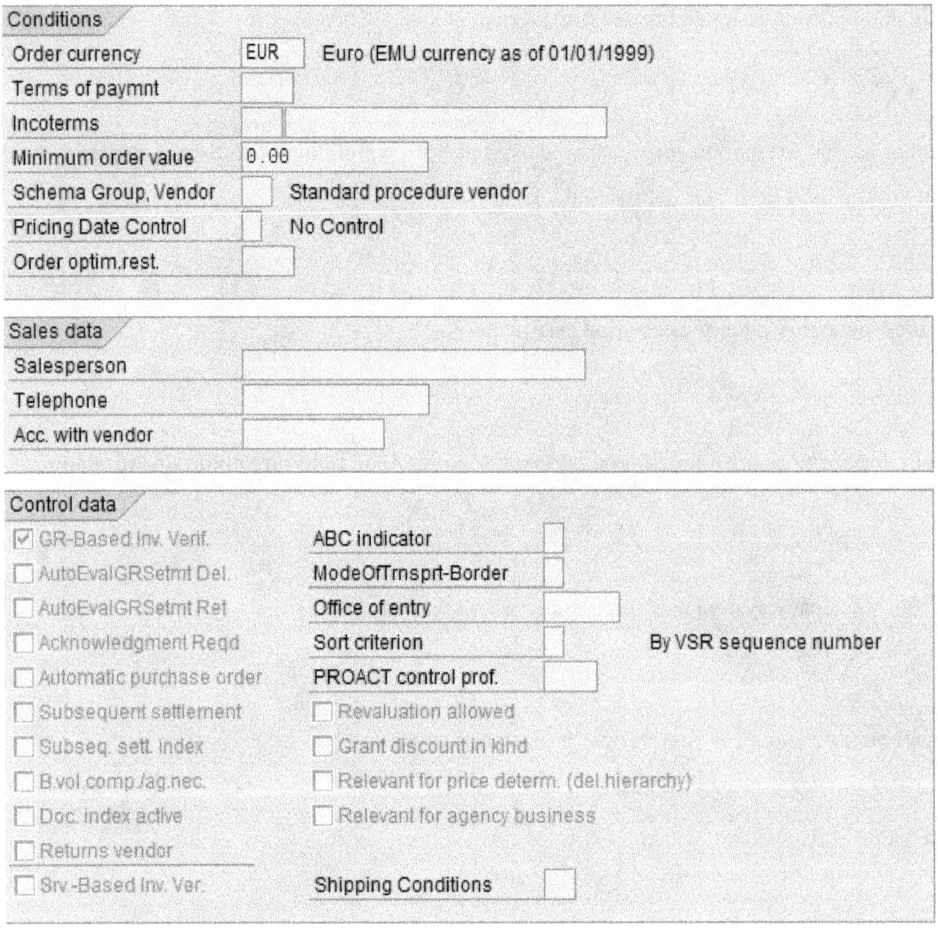

Conditions		
Order currency	EUR	Euro (EMU currency as of 01/01/1999)
Terms of paymnt		
Incoterms		
Minimum order value	0.00	
Schema Group, Vendor		Standard procedure vendor
Pricing Date Control		No Control
Order optim.rest.		

Sales data	
Salesperson	
Telephone	
Acc. with vendor	

Control data

☑ GR-Based Inv. Verif.	ABC indicator
☐ AutoEvalGRSetmt Del.	ModeOfTrnsprt-Border
☐ AutoEvalGRSetmt Ret	Office of entry
☐ Acknowledgment Reqd	Sort criterion By VSR sequence number
☐ Automatic purchase order	PROACT control prof.
☐ Subsequent settlement	☐ Revaluation allowed
☐ Subseq. sett. index	☐ Grant discount in kind
☐ B.vol.comp./ag.nec.	☐ Relevant for price determ. (del.hierarchy)
☐ Doc. index active	☐ Relevant for agency business
☐ Returns vendor	
☐ Srv.-Based Inv. Ver.	Shipping Conditions

Figure 4-9 (Purchasing Data)

Copyrighted© Material

4.3.3.1. Order Currency

It is a currency in which order will be placed to your vendor. For example, currency use in purchase orders will be mention here. It may be a vendor country specific currency.

4.3.3.2. Incoterms

It is use in international trade and makes your procurement easier. It also facilitates both vendors and customers in procurement process. These are international standard trade definitions used in international contracts between buyers and sellers. These are created by international chamber of commerce (France, located in Paris). There are thirteen incoterms which consist of four groups mention below

Group	Incoterm	Long name	Location
E – Departure	EXW	EX Works	Named Place
D – Arrival	DAF	Delivered at Frontier	Named Place
D – Arrival	DES	Delivered Ex Ship	Port of destination
D – Arrival	DEQ	Delivered Ex Quay	Port of destination
D – Arrival	DDU	Delivered Duty Unpaid	Destination
D – Arrival	DDP	Delivered Duty Paid	Destination
C – Paid	CFR	Cost and Freight	Port of destination
C – Paid	CIF	Cost, Insurance, Freight	Port of destination
C – Paid	CPT	Carriage Paid To	Destination
C – Paid	CIP	Carriage, Insurance Paid	Destination
F – Unpaid	FCA	Free Carrier	Named Place
F – Unpaid	FAS	Free Alongside Ship	Port of Shipment
F – Unpaid	FOB	Free On Board	Port of Shipment

Figure 4-10 (incoterms)

Copyrighted© Material

4.3.3.3.   Vendor Schema Group

Vendor calculation schema group is used to determine the effective pricing procedure for supplier in purchasing document. You can configure schema group under customizing IMG-SPRO > Materials Management > Purchasing > Conditions > > Define price determination Process > Define Schema Group

4.3.3.4.   Pricing Date Category

Pricing date category field is used to specify the date on which the effective price determination will take place.

4.3.3.5.   Good Receipt-Based Invoice Verification

If this indicator is flagged, system will perform invoice verification based on goods receipts.

4.3.3.6.   Automatic Evaluated Receipt settlement

Automatic evaluated receipt settlement agreement is created between purchasing department and vendor. In this agreement purchasing department make payment to vendor for the goods received at the time those materials are posted into the inventory stock and latterly vendor not submit an invoice to purchasing department. System automatically posts an invoice with reference to purchase order and respective goods receipt.

Following goods movements can be relevant to evaluated receipt settlement

- Goods Receipts
- Return Delivery
- Reversals
- Returns

4.3.3.7.   Automatic Evaluated Receipt settlement - Return

If this indicator is flagged, system will auto reverse the same entry (evaluated receipt agreement) mention above.

Copyrighted© Material

4.3.3.8.   Order Acknowledgement Requirement

This indicator specifies the procurement documents (e.g. purchase order, outline agreement) whether to be required acknowledge by the vendor or not.

4.3.3.9.   Automatic Purchase Order

If after creation of purchase requisition assignment made to respective vendor in which automatic purchase order indicator is flagged, system create automatic purchase order respectively

4.3.3.10.   Subsequent Settlement

If you procure some additional or more material, vendor offer you some incentive regarding. For example it is due to promotional offers or incentive may be form of subsequent settlement. So it can be an agreement between vendor and purchase department depending upon how much material is procured. At the end of the period rebate will be given.

4.3.3.11.   Business Volume Comparison/Agreement Necessary

Before any subsequent is posted, evaluate and comparison of data must be between vendor and purchase department before any subsequent is posted. It is relevant if this indicator is flagged.

4.3.3.12.   Document Index Active

This indicator allows auto adjusting of purchasing documents if any condition changes.

4.3.3.13.   Return Vendor

If this indicator is flagged Vendor return is carried out using shipment processing.

4.3.3.14.   Service-based Invoice Verification

If this indicator is flagged, system will post invoice based on release and acceptance of service entry sheet.

Copyrighted© Material

4.3.3.15. *ABC Indicator*

You can use this indicator for different purposes e.g. it classifies your vendor according to significance for company. For example A is highly significant, B is moderate and C is less significant. It is enter manually in vendor master data.

4.3.3.16. *Mode of Transport for Foreign Trade*

This field specifies whether your respective vendor engage in foreign trade or not. It is identifying from which transportation source (Rail, Air Plane, Truck etc) goods are cross from border during import and export. You can define these transportation modes in customizing under IMG-SPRO > Materials Management > Purchasing > Foreign Trade/Customs > Transportation Data > Define Mode of Transport

4.3.3.17. *Office of Entry*

Office entry field specify custom office code in which goods are leave or enter the country. This field is used only in import and export case. You can configure it in customizing under IMG-SPRO > Materials Management > Purchasing > Foreign Trade/Customs > Transportation Data > Define Customs Offices

4.3.3.18. *Vendor Sort Criterion*

Vendor sort criterion field specifies in which criteria is used for sort the delivery item from this vendor in specific manner.

4.3.3.19. *Shipping Conditions*

It is a strategy for general shipping for the delivery of materials from vendor to specific customers.

Copyrighted© Material

4.3.4. Partner role for vendor master record

Vendor or business partner perform different roles for your company. A business partner may be ordering address of company, may be a good supplier, invoicing party or payee. We mention these roles in vendor master record. These partner role values appear as default values in concern documents. E.g. when we create purchase order, partner data is automatically pick from vendor master record. At the time of posting logistics invoice verification, these partner roles define the rights duties and task of each partner in business transaction. Furthermore in purchasing, if one partner is supply goods for your company, another partner give you service for custom clearance and one partner is payee for all. You have option to maintain these roles in vendor master. At the time of logistics invoice verification system automatically split amount according to your setting of vendor master. In Vendor master having separate screen for partner function master data e.g. you can see under vendor master mention in below screen. There are three different partner roles, first one is ordering address, second and third partner roles are vendor and invoicing party respectively.

Figure 4-11 (Partner Function)

For configuration aspects

- Define partner role
- Define permissible partner role as per account group
- Define partner schema
- Assign partner schema to account groups

Copyrighted© Material

Define partner Role

SPRO> IMG> Materials Management> Purchasing> Partner Determination> Define Partner Role

Insert function code CR (must be two digits randomly and can be alpha numeric), description of role and LI vendor as type of partner

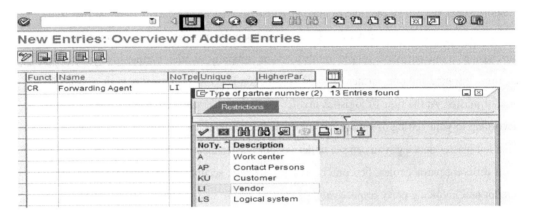

Figure 4-12 (Partner Function)

Define Partner Schema

SPRO> IMG> Materials Management> Purchasing> Partner Determination>Partner Setting in Vendor Master> Define Partner Schema

Click on new entries

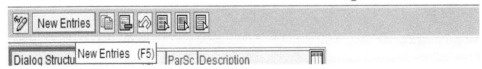

Figure 4-13 Define Partner Schema

L1 as partner schema and Vendor as description

Copyrighted© Material

View "Partner Schemas Vendor Master" Change: Overview

Dialog Structure	ParSc	Description	
▽ 🗁 Partner determination ｐ	L1	VENDOR	▲
🗀 Partner Functions iɾ			▼

Figure 4-14 Define Partner Schema

Now select line of L1 schema (Just schema is created) and double click on partner function in procedure, here you maintain parameter according to requirement. E.g. for L1 (Vendor) and press save button. No change indicator shows after an entry vendor will not be changed. Mandatory indicator determines partner function mandatory in particular object.

PartnDet.Proc.   L1

Funct	Name	No Chnge	Mand.
AD	Additionals	☐	☐
PE	Sales Employee	☐	☐
CP	Contact person	☐	☐
AZ	A.payment recipient	☐	☐
OA	Ordering address	☐	☑
VN	Vendor	☑	☑
PI	Invoicing Party	☐	☑
CA	Contract address	☐	☐

Figure 4-15 Define Partner Schema

Assign partner schema to account group

Here you assign L1 Partner schema (Just created) to account group

Figure 4-16 (Assign partner schema to account group)

Copyrighted© Material

Figure 4-17 (Assign partner schema to account group)

Press save button.

Define Permissible partner role as per account group

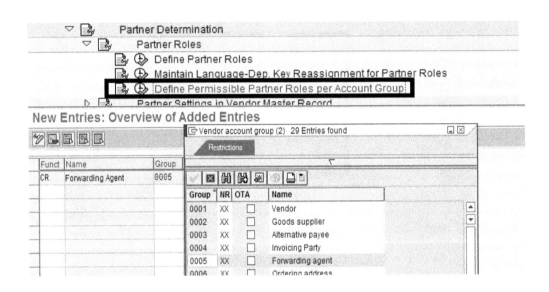

Figure 4-18 (Define Permissible partner role as per account group)

Select function forwarding agent and account group and save configuration.

Copyrighted© Material

4.4.   Mass Maintenance of Vendor Master

Sometime client required to mass change in vendor master record. It may be change of one field or many fields. In target field may be enter new data or may be change an existing data. For doing this use the transaction code XK99 for maintenance of vendor master record. Vendor master change similarly as material master record discuss earlier, Here following are showing maintenance screen, which represent the field description and technical name of field.

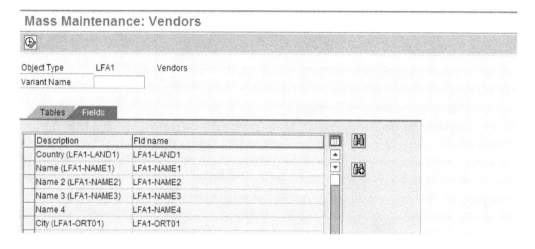

4-19 (Mass Maintenance of Vendor Master Record)

Note: Follow the same steps for mass changes in vendor master that use in material master earlier.

Copyrighted© Material

Copyrighted© Material

Copyrighted© Material

Chapter 5:

Master Data in Purchasing

Copyrighted© Material

5. Chapter: Master data in Purchasing

In this lesson you will learn

5.1.   Master data in Purchasing

    5.1.1.   Purchase info Record

    5.1.2.   Source list

    5.1.3.   Conditions

    5.1.4.   Quota arrangement

Copyrighted© Material

5.1. Master data in Purchasing

There are three types of data in SAP. Data types include configuration data, master data and transactional data. Configuration data are created once and cannot be changed e.g. company code, plant, purchasing organization and storage locations etc. Master data changes accrue in very rare cases in system e.g. material master, vendor master, service master and purchasing info records etc. In transactional data, changes accrue on daily basis or you can maintain it on daily basis e.g. creation of purchase orders, sale orders and invoices etc. These are following types of master data in SAP purchasing

- Purchasing info records
- Quota arrangement
- Source list
- Conditions

5.1.1. Purchase info Record

Purchasing info record contains the information regarding a certain vendor and material. This information may be at Plant level or purchasing organization level. The info record includes purchase organization data, general data, conditions data and texts. Purchasing organization data includes terms of payment, planned delivery time, purchase group, delivery tolerances, net price, conversion and base unit of measure and tax code etc. General data include reminders, vendor sale person and telephone number etc. Condition data includes conditions related to purchasing as well as conditions validity period. Text data includes two types of text, first one is info record notes and second one is purchase order text. Purchasing info record created both automatically and manually. For manual creation, SAP Manu path is

Logistics > Materials Management > Purchasing > Master data > Info record Create ME11/ Change ME12/ Display ME13

Copyrighted© Material

For automatically creation of purchase info record, you must flag info update indicator in purchasing documents such as purchase order, quotation, contract and scheduling agreement. Example of info update indicator in Purchase order showing in item detail, material data tab.

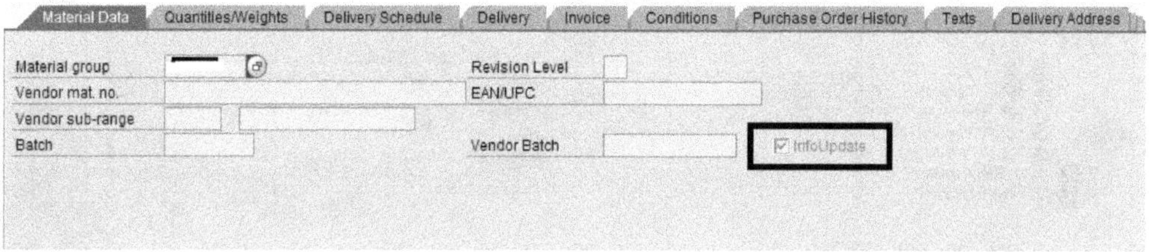

Figure 5-1 (Info Update Indicator in Purchase Order, Material Data Tab)

Info update indicators set then have one of the following values

"Blank" info record not updated

"A" if info record exists at plant level, it is updated. Otherwise an info record at purchasing organization is updated.

"B" If plant conditions are allowed for plant, an info record updated at plant level.

"C" If plant conditions are not necessary for the plant. An info record is updated at purchasing organization level.

If indicator of purchasing info record is set in purchasing document, then following cases are most likely probable

If just one info record (with or without a plant) exists, the record is updated.

If no info record exist and "Plant conditions requirement" has been specified in customizing, an info record with a plant is created. Otherwise info record without a plant is created.

If two info records exist, one record with a plant and one without a plant, the info record with the plant is updated.

For purchase info record update indicator, we can select default values on the EVO parameters under

Copyrighted© Material

SPRO > MM > Purchasing > Environment Data (OLME) > Define default values for buyer/ OMFI

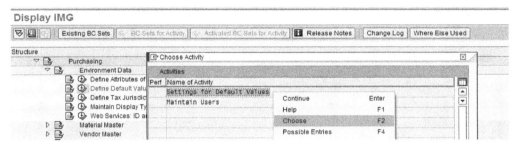

Figure 5-2 (Default Values for Buyers)

Then, select line and click on detail button

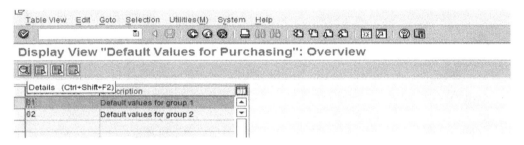

Figure 5-3 (Default Values for Purchasing)

Then these default values assign or allocate that code to the EVO parameter in the user parameters.

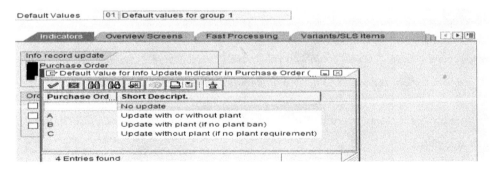

Figure 5-4 (Default Values for Info Update in Purchase Order)

Copyrighted© Material

Or

SU03 or SU01 chose tab parameters and enters parameter EVO along here with value 01 for all users.

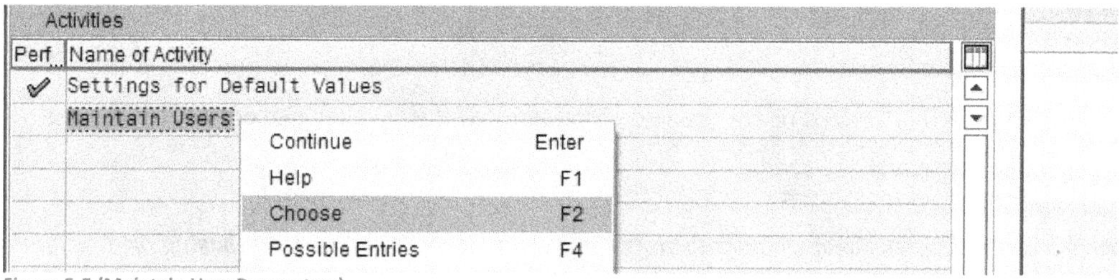

Figure 5-5 (Maintain User Parameters)

5.1.1.1. *Procurement types in info records*

- Standard
- Subcontracting
- Pipeline
- Consignment

5.1.1.2. *Role of conditions with info update indicator*

The conditions are used to determine the effective purchase order price with systematically consideration of all the relevant pricing elements. Condition are playing important role with info update indicator in purchasing documents. In customizing we can control the conditions with or without plant level. For doing this you can

SPRO > Materials Management > Purchasing > Conditions > Define condition control at plant level

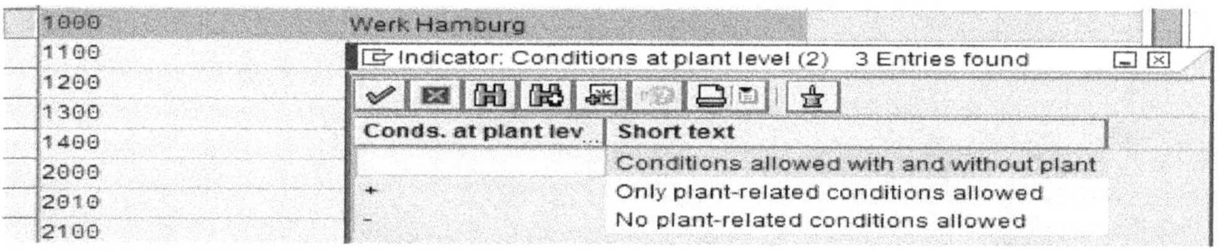

Figure 5-6 (Condition Control at Plant Level)

Copyrighted© Material

Here you can specify

- Conditions are allowed with or without plant
- Only plant related conditions are allowed
- No plant related conditions are allowed

In purchase order, info update indicator has the two characteristics that are purchasing Info record is updated or created or not updated and created. If it is updated and created, then most likely following situations accrue

An info record exists either on purchasing organization level only or on purchasing organization level and plant level only (exactly one info record (with or without plant)) and is updated.

An info record exists both with purchasing organization data and with purchasing organization/plant data and plant-specific data is updated.

If no info record exists and Plant condition requirement was determined in Customizing, the system creates an info record with a plant. Otherwise, the system creates an info record without a plant

Copyrighted© Material

5.1.2. Source list

Source list consist of possible source of supply of particular material for specific time period for specific plant. Material was purchase with different sides with different numbers of vendors. Source list helps you a suitable source determination in procurement. Source list contain you a fixed source of supply with mention validity period in source list. E.g. you can tick the indicator of fixed source of supply. When you create a purchase order/ purchase requisition for specific material then always fix vendor will be part of procurement as mention in source list with in mention validity period. You can also block a vendor/ supplying plant with check block vendor with specific period of time. Purchase order cannot be out putted to block vendor with in specific validity period. Source list also integrate with material requirement planning. When Purchase requisition generated from material requirement planning are automatically consider source of supplies mention in source list. It can also consider block and fixed vendor mention in list.

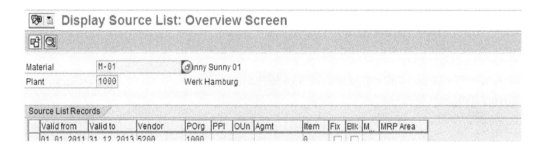

Figure 5-7 (Source List Overview)

You can

- Maintain source list ME01
- Display source list ME03
- Display changes ME04
- Analyze source list ME06
- Generate source list ME05
- Display source list for materials ME0M

Copyrighted© Material

You can create source list manual or automatically. For manual creation of source list, use transaction code ME01 and for automatically creation, first go to change material master (MM02) screen and tick the indicator source list in purchasing view.

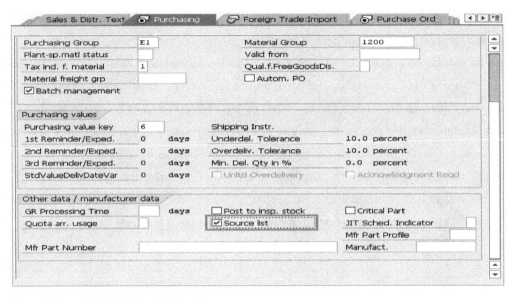

Figure 5-8 (Source List Check in Material Master)

Then go to ME05 for automatically generation of source list or by transaction code ME01. Mention your material and Plant

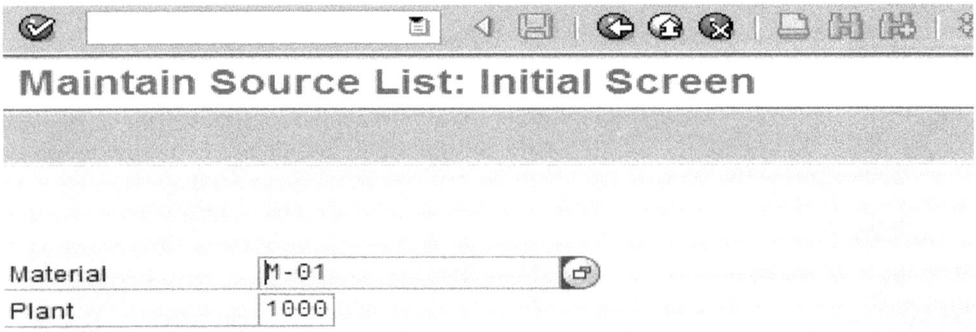

Maintain Source List: Initial Screen

Material   M-01

Plant   1000

Figure 5-9 (Maintain Source List Initial Screen)

Copyrighted© Material

Press Generate button

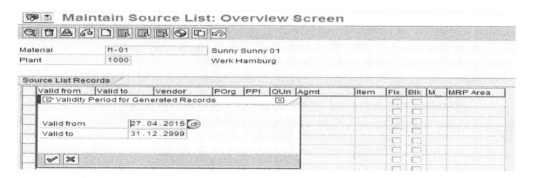

Figure 5-10 (Generate Records via Source List)

Maintain validity period and press continue

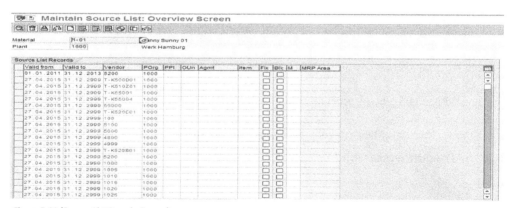

You can see all possible sources of supply and then press save button for updating your record.

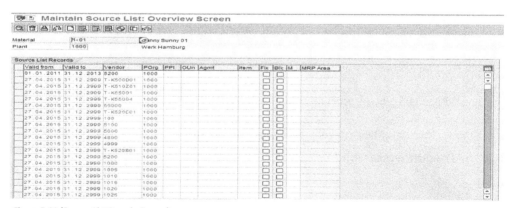

Figure 5-11 (Source List Sample Screen)

Copyrighted© Material

5.1.3. Conditions

Procurement Conditions are used for pricing terms and conditions negotiating with vendor. These are may be gross price, net price, freight, delivery charges and insurance etc. Conditions are used in outline agreements, purchase order, quotations and purchasing info records. Conditions are time dependent and time independent. Time dependent conditions are valid for specific period of time. Time dependent conditions are on contracts info records and quotations. In time independent conditions, there is no validity period. Purchase order conditions are always time independent conditions. Conditions are may be at header level or an item level. Header level condition is applied on all purchase documents. Item level conditions are only applied on respective line item of concern purchase document.

5.1.4. Quota arrangement

In quota arrangement, material procures from various sources of supply with allocating the quantity of certain material with specific validity span of time. Source of supply may be in-house plant or may be by external source. In quota arrangement split the total quantity of material over a period among desire sources of supply by assign quota. Source of supply can be

- An individual vendor or outline agreement
- May be your another plant

In quota arrangement, there is some configuration required. If necessary

Define number ranges (already discuss how to create number interval and assign to document)

For doing this, go to SAP easy access

SPRO-IMG > Materials Management > Purchasing > Quota arrangement > Define number ranges or (Transaction code OMEP)

Copyrighted© Material

SPRO-IMG > Materials Management > Purchasing > Quota arrangement >Define Quota
Arrangement Usage

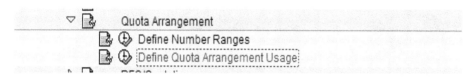

Figure 5-12 (Define Quota Arrangement Usage)

Click on new entries

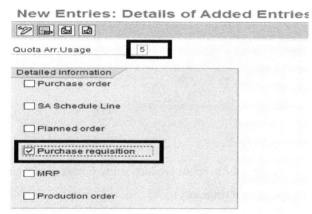

Figure 5-13 (Define Quota Arrangement Usage)

Insert new number and set parameters according to requirement e.g. quota split in purchase
requisition and press save.

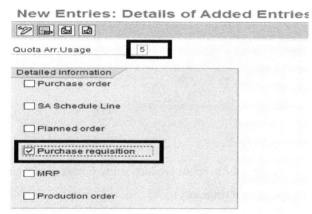

Figure 5-14 (Details of Edit Entries)

Then go to MM02 and change the material master, purchasing view

Copyrighted© Material

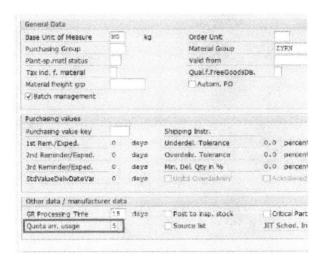

Figure 5-15 (Quota Arrangement Usage indicator in Material Master)

For creation of quota arrangement, go to SAP easy access

Logistics > Materials Management > Purchasing > Master Data > Quota arrangement > Maintain
or MEQ1

Enter validity period and click on item overview button

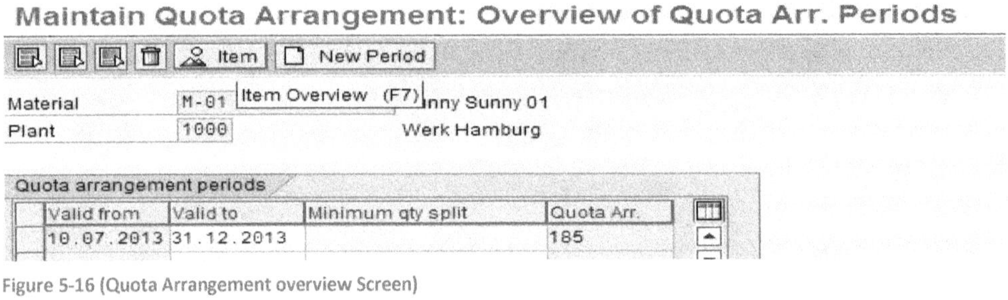

Maintain Quota Arrangement: Overview of Quota Arr. Periods

| 🗐 🗐 🗐 🗑 | 👤 Item | 🗋 New Period |

Material   M-01 | Item Overview (F7) | nny Sunny 01
Plant   1000   Werk Hamburg

Quota arrangement periods

	Valid from	Valid to	Minimum qty split	Quota Arr.	
	10.07.2013	31.12.2013		185	

Figure 5-16 (Quota Arrangement overview Screen)

Procurement type F use for external procurement (for in house production use E instead of F and
mention plant on PPL (Procurement plant) Colum if necessary)

Copyrighted© Material

QAI	P	S	Vendor	PPI	PVer	Qu...	in %	Allocated Qty	Maximum Quantity	
1	F		4999			1	25.0	0.000		
2	F		5200			2	50.0	0.000		
3	F	U	10000	1200		1	25.0	0.000		

Figure 5-17 (Quota Allocation among Plants and Vendors)

We have a lot quota on 1:2:3 among three vendors. In above case when you create purchase requisitions, then system create PR maximum 100 quantities of vendor 4999 (line item 1). From 101 to 150 quantity PR automatically split to vendor 5200 (line item 2) and 151 to 200 respectively vendor 10000 (line item 3) that is your plant.

Copyrighted© Material

Copyrighted© Material

Copyrighted© Material

Chapter 6:

Components of Purchasing

Copyrighted© Material

6. Chapter: Components of Purchasing

6.1.   External Procurement

   6.1.1.   External Procurement Activities

6.2.   Components of Purchasing

   6.2.1.   Request for quotation

   6.2.2.   Purchase Requisition

   6.2.3.   Purchase Order

   6.2.4.   Account assignment categories and Item Categories

   6.2.5.   Outline Agreements

   6.2.6.   Framework Order

Copyrighted© Material

6.1. External Procurement

External procurement process is the process of procurement of material and external services from external supplier for your company. Every organization need external procurement to run and complete business needs. This procurement requires correct quantity, right quality, with a proper value and minimum time. External procurement life cycle includes

- ➢ Requirement and gathering procurement information
- ➢ Contact with supplier
- ➢ Background review (product/service quality, after sale services and warranties etc.)
- ➢ Negotiation and communication with supplier about prices and conditions
- ➢ Order fulfillment
- ➢ Payment process

6.1.1. External Procurement Activities

External procurement activities includes

6.1.1.1.   Determination of requirement

The user department sent necessary and needful demand and requirement of material to purchase department. This requirement can be sent manually or electronically via purchase requisition. If you have planned item in MRP, purchase requirement generates through material requirement planning run.

6.1.1.2.   Determination of Source of Supply

Purchase department is responsible and support pillar during determination of possible and suitable sources of supply. Purchase department can user determination of the source of supply to create request for quotation (RFQs) and then enter a quotations as well as comparison statement. For selected and suitable source of supply, purchase department refer to purchase order, contract, scheduling agreement and conditions that already exist in the system.

Copyrighted© Material

6.1.1.3. Vendor Selection

By comparative statement of different suppliers, system simplifies the vendor selection procedure. For rejected suppliers, system automatically sends rejection letters.

6.1.1.4. Purchase order Processing and Monitoring

For suitable and selected supplier, purchase department create a purchase order in system with reference to purchase requisition or via request for quotation for reduction data entry efforts and for reference. After creation of purchase order, responsible purchaser sends purchase order to supplier. Then Purchaser monitors the processing status of purchase order via SAP system. Purchaser determines whether the goods receipts or invoice against concern purchase order has been entered. If necessary, purchaser can remind the supplier for full or partial outstanding deliveries.

6.1.1.5. Goods Receipts

When store supervisor enter inward deliveries in SAP system, he/she refer relevant purchase order for that particular purchase. With this purchase order reference, data entry time, efforts and error will minimize, and store supervisor can easily match goods receipts quantity with reference purchase order.

6.1.1.6. Logistics Invoice Verification

Logistics invoice verification is the last portion of procurement process. In logistics invoice verification, incoming invoices are comparing with purchase order, goods receipts as well as service entry sheet contents like price and quantity etc. and post them. When posting these invoices, notification sent to account and financial department for further payment process.

6.1.1.7. Payment Processing

The payment program authorizes the payment to the creditor liabilities and in financial accounting regularly executes this program regular basis.

Copyrighted© Material

6.2. Components of Purchasing

6.2.1. Request for quotation

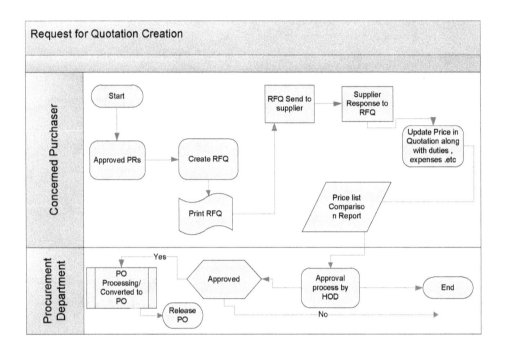

Figure 6-1 (Request for Quotation Process)

Request for quotation (RFQ) is a request to vendor by purchase department to submit bid or quotation for the supply of material or performance of specific services. Request for quotation can be created with reference to purchase requisition and other request for quotation or can be created independently without any reference of any document. You can create purchase order and contract as proceeding documents with reference to quotation.

Copyrighted© Material

You can create RFQ by transaction ME41, change by ME42 and for display by ME43. Maintain quotation by transaction ME47 and make price comparison list by transaction ME49. You can find these transaction under SAP Easy transaction under Logistics > Material Management > Purchasing > RFQ/Quotation

An RFQ involves of the RFQ header and item.

RFQ Header:

It consist of general information regarding RFQ type, Company code, Purchasing organization, vendor address, language, collective number, quotation deadline and validity date start and date etc.

RFQ Items:

It consists of Item category, RFQ quantity, delivery date, and plant and storage location.

In Procurement process, RFQ and Quotation are separate screens form a single document. Rates of quantities and Conditions send by vendor are entering in quotation. You can send RFQ to vendor via electronic data interchange, by E-mail or fax. If you send RFQ to more than one vendor, you can have the system determine the most favorable quotation submitted and automatically generate rejection letter to unsuitable vendors.

 If your procurement process starts from purchase requisition, after creation and release of PR (if release strategy exist), SAP system can easily convert purchase requisition into request for quotation and it sent to different suppliers. When each vendor sends respective rates, terms and condition, purchaser put these values into quotation maintain screen. After maintain quotation in SAP system, you can easily generate price comparison list with the help of collective number and then it will suggest you suitable source of supply. Purchase can easily convert suitable / approved quotation convert into purchase order.

If Info update indicator in request for quotation is mark, all the conditions of RFQ copy in purchasing info record. Whenever you create purchase order, these conditions copy from info record and system suggest you to use these conditions in respective purchase.

Copyrighted© Material

Collective number is a random number which is use to make comparison statements of rates, conditions etc. of different suppliers. In case of RFQ creating with reference to purchase requisition, system copy purchase requisition number as collective number.

For creating RFQ, Go to transaction ME41 Insert Plant, purchasing organization and purchase group then enter. Create RFQ screen will be appearing. Here you put RFQ date and quotation deadline date and press enter,

Enter Collective RFQ number, it's up to your choice which number is insert that latterly help you for comparison of suppliers or If RFQ of particular procurement process have been assign to a collective number, it is then possible to list and process to all individual RFQs are grouped under this number.

Create RFQ

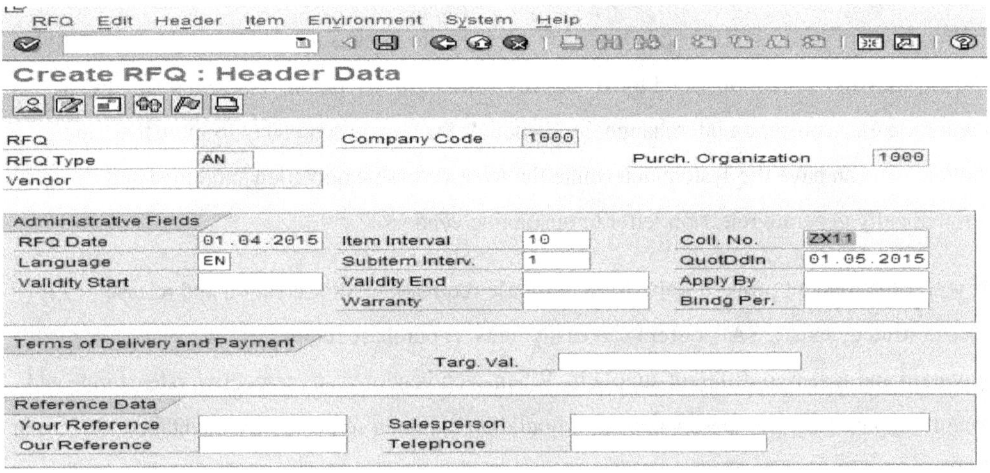

Figure 6-2 (RFQ Header Data Screen)

Note: Collective number is any random number, ZX11 is not compulsory. It may be your purchase requisition number.

Copyrighted© Material

After insert collective number click enter. Insert following information and press vendor address button that is mention below

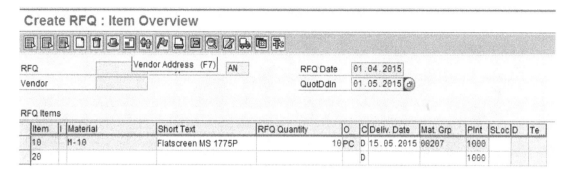

Figure 6-3 (RFQ Item Overview Screen)

After press the vendor address button new window will be open. You put respective vendor name here which you want to use for RFQ, e.g. enter vendor 1000 and press enter and click on save button.

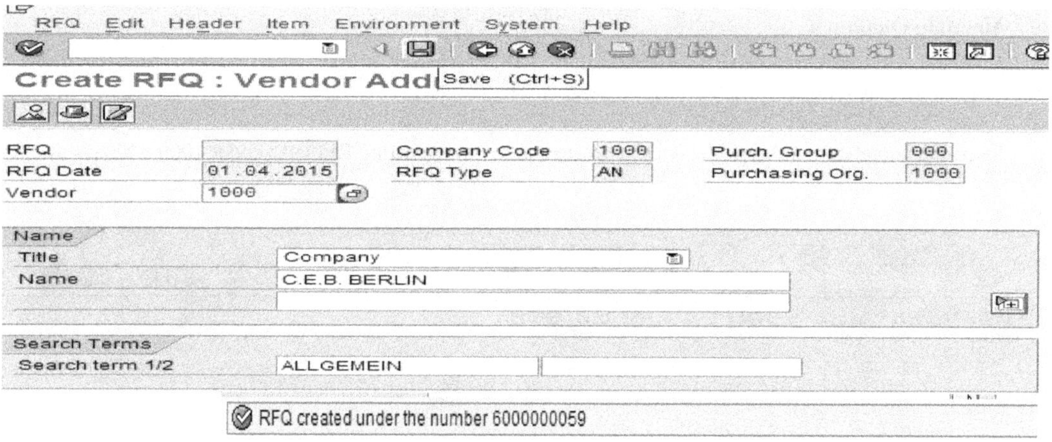

Figure 6-4 (Vendor Address Screen)

Note the quotation number after saving.

Similarly you will same process RFQ of another vendor; here it is for processing for new vendor

Insert vendor 2000 and press enter,

Copyrighted© Material

After processing Request for quotation then next step is to maintain quotation of vendor 1000 and 2000 (Concern vendors relevant to your respective RFQ).

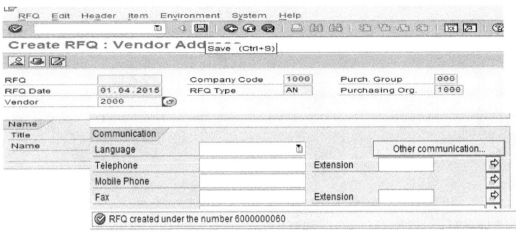

Figure 6-5 (Vendor Address Screen)

Click on save button and note down another document number

Maintain Quotation

For maintain quotation, go to Transaction Code ME47 and press enter

Insert the quotation number which was generated at the time creating RFQ of vendor 1000 which is as follows,

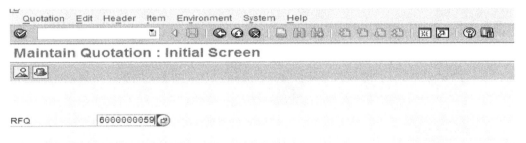

Figure 6-6 (Maintain Quotation Initial Screen)

Copyrighted© Material

Here you put the price of vendor 1000 which is given after conversation of vendor.

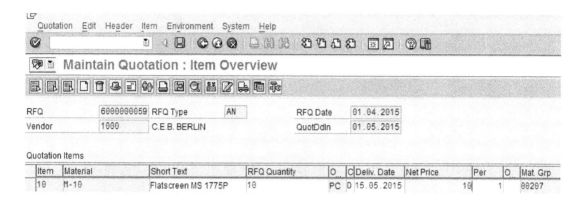

Figure 6-7 (Quotation Item Overview Screen)

You may also maintain conditions of that vendor (1000). For maintaining of conditions you can press condition button as mention.

Press item condition button, if necessary you may maintain condition here.

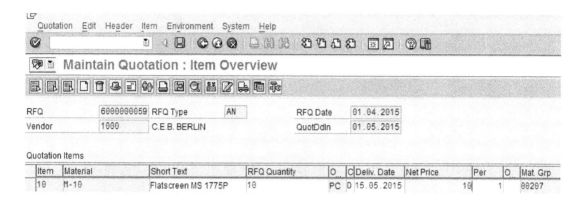

Figure 6-8 (Condition in Quotation)

Click on back button and press save.

Similarly follow the same procedure for vendor 2000, go to again transaction code ME47 and follow same procedure for quotation # 6000000060. Maintain price and maintain conditions and press save button.

Copyrighted© Material

Price Comparison Statement

Now for price comparison you go to transaction code ME49

Press enter and insert Collective RFQ number and execute

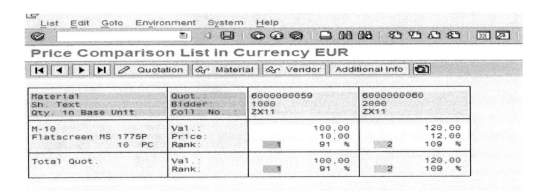

Figure 6-9 (Price Comparison List Selection Screen)

Here the new screen shows that represent price comparison for both vendors. System prefer vendor 1000 for best source due to rank one. Here in price comparison you can decide which vendor is suitable for procurement and then use of quotation number of suitable vendor, you convert respective quotation number into PO.

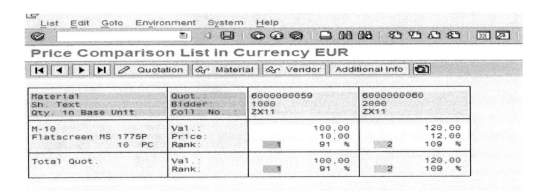

Figure 6-10 (Price Comparison List)

Copyrighted© Material

6.2.2. Purchase Requisition

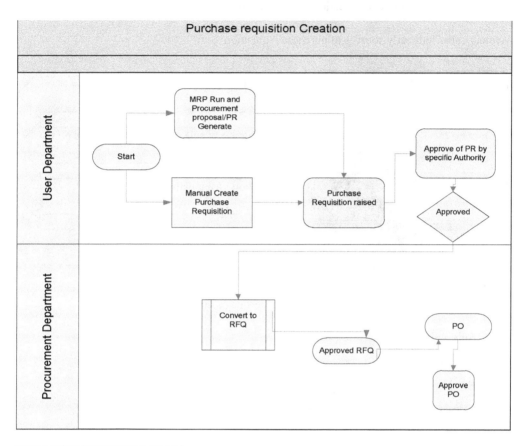

Figure 6-11 (Purchase Requisition Process)

Purchase requisition is a formally request from user department to purchase department to procure a required quantity of material or services within certain date. User department can use these materials for production, Plant maintenance or sales and distribution department etc. Purchase requisition can be created with reference to another purchase requisition, request for quotation, contract or scheduling agreement and can be creating without reference. With purchase requisition document, you can create purchase order, request for quotation, contract and scheduling agreement as processing documents.

You can also create purchase requisition automatically. Automatically generate PR means purchase requisition is initiated with another component or by other module. It may be from

Copyrighted© Material

Plant maintenance, production planning, and project system or by Sales and distribution. Manual purchase requisition is directly creating by user department.

Automatically/ indirectly sources of purchase requisition

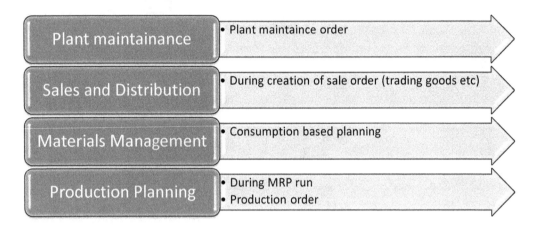

Purchase Requisition can be created with following mention procurement types

- Subcontracting
- External services
- Stock transfer
- Consignment
- Standard

Path to create Purchase requisition:

Go to SAP easy access

Logistics => Materials Management => Purchasing => Purchase Requisition =>Create /Change/Display

Directly go to transaction code ME51N

For Change transaction code ME52N

For Display transaction code ME53N

For necessary configuration of purchase requisition, you need to configure document type, purchase requisition releases procedures (release strategy) as well as number ranges. Release strategy will be discussed latterly with details.

Number ranges configuration

For configuration of number ranges of purchase requisition go to transaction code: OMH7 or using Manu path under customizing IMG-SPRO > Materials Management > Purchasing > Purchase Requisition > Define Number Ranges

Here you can see display interval button which show current configure intervals of number ranges and current number status. Change status button use for checking status of current number ranges and changes of current numbers. By clicking on change interval button you can insert new interval for number ranges. Ext check box determine whether number range internal or external. If it is not checked in configuration, system automatically assign number to purchase requisition. If it is checked in configuration, you need to enter a number for external number issue. The number you enter manually, must be between concern number ranges. For creation of new number range, click on change interval button. After that new window will appear here you click on insert interval button which is mention on below

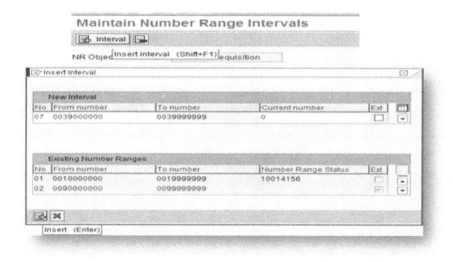

Figure 6-12 (Maintain Number Ranges Interval)

Copyrighted© Material

Now put new number range in "from number" to "to number" Colum and press insert and then press save button. No range number

Document type configuration

Use T-code: S_ALR_87002168 or Manu path, go to SAP Easy Access

IMG-SPRO > Materials Management > Purchase Requisition > Define Document Types

For most of configuration in SAP system where you have option for adopt or copy as, here you can use it. It will save your time and reduction of error and data entry, for PR document type configuration you can select the line of respective document type and press adopt or Copy as button. Than "copy all" if necessary

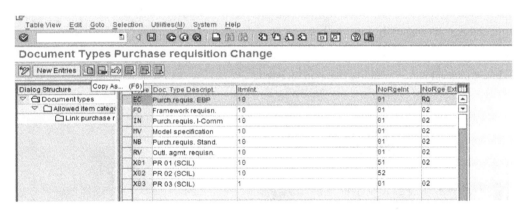

Figure 6-13 (Purchase Requisition Doc. Type Configuration)

Changes the type and Doc. type description, press copy/enter button and other parameters if necessary and press save button.

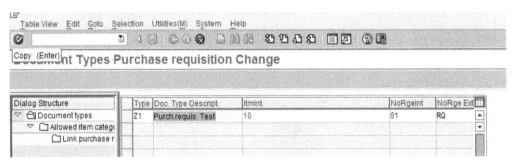

Figure 6-14 (Purchase Requisition Doc. Type Configuration)

Copyrighted© Material

"Type" column represent the technical name of document type. These technical names are consisting of maximum four digits alphanumeric and differentiating with each other. "Doc. Type Descript." Column represent the description of document type e.g. service PR, General PR, Raw materials PR, Production PR etc. "Itmint" column represent the size of the steps between the default item numbers. In standard SAP system configuration, it shows "10" number. You can change it as per your requirement. "NoRgeInt" column shows number range of PR document. Here you can assign respective number range with document type. "FieldSel." column shows the relevant field selection key. Here you can assign relevant field attributes. Field attributes in PR, represent which fields are compulsory, which are hide or which one is only for display in document.

Now you can assign the number range to document type. For doing this

Go to SPRO > Materials Management > Purchase > Purchase Requisition >Define Document type

Go to number range Coolum and press f4, select the number range 07 (0039000000) which you created earlier and assign the document type and press save button.

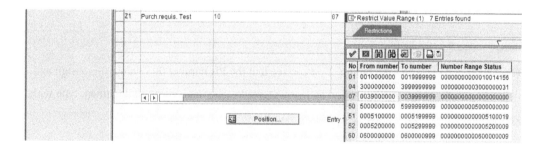

Figure 6-15 (Assign Number Range to Purchase Requisition Document Type)

Newly created document type appears in Front end transaction ME51N. Whenever you create PR with this document type number range will be automatically assign by SAP system from your created number range 07 (39000000 to 39999999).

Copyrighted© Material

Note: *In SAP Materials Management, Purchase order, Request for quotation and Contracts having same procedure for creating document types, number ranges and their assignments with each other.*

Directly go to ME51N

Select Document type you just configure

Insert material, quantity, date etc

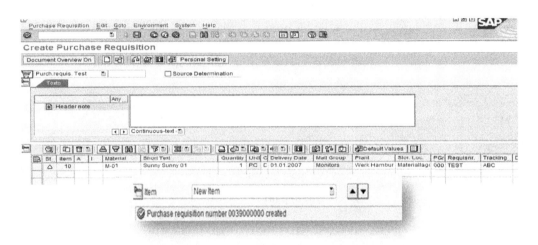

Figure 6-16 (Purchase Requisition)

Press enter and click on save button. You can see that the PR number 0039000000 is assign and note that number range 0039000000 which you created earlier and assign to document type with variant 07.

Copyrighted© Material

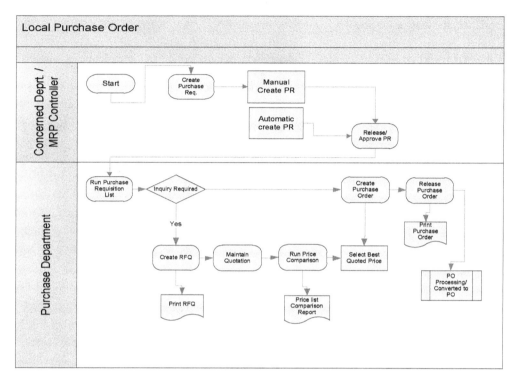

Figure 6-17 (Purchase Order Process)

In SAP standard system there are following types of purchase orders and document types

- Stock Transfer Purchase order
- Standard Purchase order
- Subcontracting Purchase order
- Consignment Purchase order
- External Services Purchase order
- Framework order
- Foreign purchase order etc.

Note: *Purchase order Document types and number ranges similarly configure as purchase requisition configuration that discuss earlier.*

Purchase order is a formal request from Purchase organization to vendor for the purpose of providing goods or services at specific conditions, specific quantity, a specific time and negotiated rates etc.

Purchase order consists of document header section, item section and item detail section. Header section consist of conditions, purchase organization, purchase group, Company code exchange rates, incoterms, status of purchase order, header text, address of supplier, payment terms and release strategy etc. Item section include account assignment, item category, material number and material short text, purchaser order per unit price, quantity, plant and storage location etc. Item detail section includes conditions, tax codes, purchase order history, item text and delivery address etc.

Note: Header level conditions apply on all items in purchase order and item level conditions apply only on selected item.

Account assignment category consists of project, Asset, Cost center and so on. It defines which account to be charge at the time of goods receipts as well as logistics invoice verification. It can also use for Material that directly consume with purchase order.

Purchasing organization is an organization unit that is responsible for purchase a material or services for centralized or decentralized. Purchase organization is legally responsible for procuring a material or service for company. Centralize purchase organization is responsible for all purchase for assign plants or company codes. Decentralized purchase organization is responsible for specific plant.

Purchase group is a group of people that are responsible for daily buying of goods and external services activities.

Item category consists of standard, consignment, subcontracting, services and limits etc. in adding, it is used for distinguish the different types of purchase processes.

Copyrighted© Material

In SAP system for purchase order

Create Transaction code: ME21N

Change Transaction code: ME22N

Display Transaction code: ME23N

For Manu path in SAP easy access go to Logistics > Materials Management > Purchasing > Purchase order > Create > vendor supplying plant known /Change /Display

We can directly create purchase order or can be create with reference to RFQ, PR, Contract and another PO. For doing this, we can use selection variant button in purchase order screen. In SAP system there is an option for converting multiple purchase requisition into purchase order automatically by transaction ME59.

When you create purchase order, most of the data comes from master data of material and vendor. It reduces your data entry efforts, time saving and minimizes error rates. Vendor master data includes vendor description, ordering address, payment currency and terms of payments etc. some data comes from material master, which include material description, base unit of measure and material group etc. if you create purchase order with reference to purchase requisition, most of the data similarly adopted from it.

If your info record already created with the combination of material and vendor than gross price, conditions, delivery tolerances and confirmation controls etc. will be suggest by system automatically.

Purchase order can be printed and fax to the vendor. It can also send via electronic data interchange technology or can be sent directly to vendor via E-mail or can be uploaded in sales system of vendor.

Copyrighted© Material

6.2.4. Account assignment categories and Item Categories

6.2.4.1. Account Assignment Category

Account assignment category consists of project, asset, cost center, network and so on. Account assignment category defines which account to be charge at the time of goods receipts as well as logistics invoice verification. Various settings consist of account assignment category e.g. goods receipts indicator shows whether a goods receipts necessary or not, valuated goods receipts indicators shows whether a non-valuated goods receipts. Similarly invoice receipts indicator defines whether an invoice receipts or not on this assignment. It can also use for material that directly consume with purchase order. In SAP standard system, account assignment category shows in screen

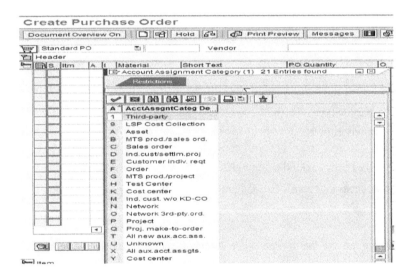

Figure 6-18 (Account Assignments)

Account assignment categories determine which account to be charge during goods receipts and logistics invoice verification, nature of assignment of accounts and which account assignment data must be provide. You can also set field selection attributes against account assignment categories e.g. which fields of purchase orders are mandatory, which are hidden, which one only for display and which one is optional.

Copyrighted© Material

In standard SAP system whenever you create PO or PR without material, system demand relevant account assignment as per selective account assignment category. You can enter account assignment manually. In account determination system attempts to suggest a particular or needed G/L account for a given preliminary account assignment. We can enter G/L account both manually and automatically.

Note:

If you want Automatic account determination in case of account assignment, it is compulsory to configure G/L against material group. For automatic account determination without material master following steps chart

- *Create material Group (OMSF)*
- *Create valuation class (OMSK)*
- *Assign valuation class to Material group in*
  - *SPRO-IMG-Materials management-Purchasing-Material Master-Entry aids for items without Material master*
- *Assign General Modification to account group*

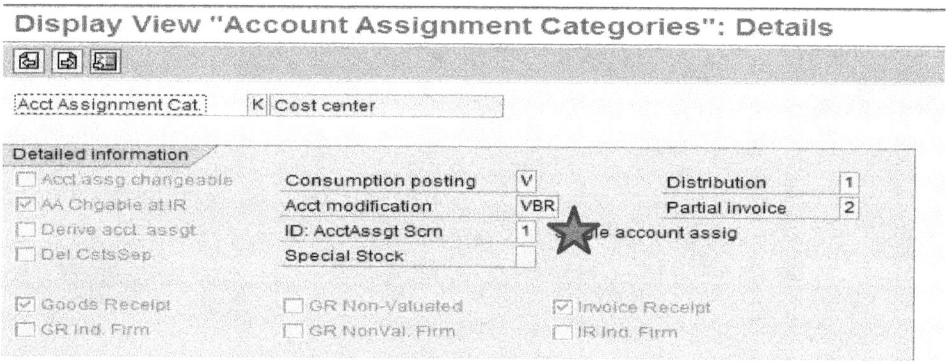

Figure 6-19 (Configure Account Assignment Category)

- *Maintain G/L account against valuation class*

  Note: Under the SPRO >Materials Management >Account determination> Account determination without wizard> Configure automatic posting (OBYC)

Copyrighted© Material

Maintain G/L account under the transaction event key GBB (Use for consumption debit entry, along with general modification VBR) and transaction event key WRX (offsetting entry for inventory posting)

Note: Behind valuation class there is G/L account assignment, account category reference and material types configure. These are all link together for automatic account determination in SAP Materials Management. It will discuss briefly in Automatic account determination chapter latterly.

You can specify single account assignment or use multiple account assignment categories. For multiple account assignments cost is splitting to multiple orders, assets or cost centers etc. You can split cost both in Purchase order as well as logistics invoice verification. In framework order, mostly use multiple account assignment. Framework order discuss laterally with explanation.

Account assignment category can configure through following menu path

IMG-SPRO> Materials Management>Purchasing> A/C assignment> Maintain account assignment category

And then

Define Combination of item category/ account assignment category

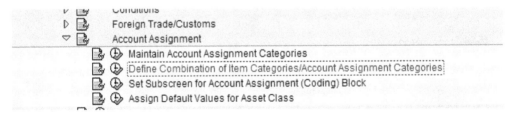

Figure 6-20 (Combination of item category/ account assignment category)

Note: There is no need to configure new item category because standard account assignment categories almost fulfill all requirement of necessary business and client requirements. If any new requirement exists, you can configure it accordingly.

Copyrighted© Material

6.2.4.2.   Item category

Item category consists of standard, consignment, subcontracting, services and limits etc. In addition, it is used for distinguish the different types of purchase processes. In SAP standard system there are following item categories mention on below screen

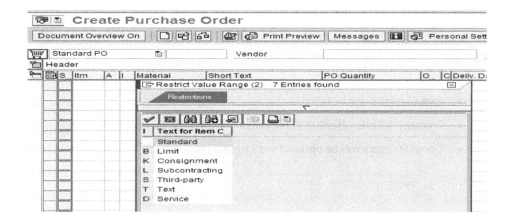

Figure 6-21 (item categories)

Item category has many control functions. It determines order item has

- Goods Receipts are mandatory or not?
- Logistics invoice verification mandatory?
- Which procurement process will be used?
- Material number is entering in Order or not?
- Account assignment of material is required or not?
- Material will be a part of stock or not?

6.2.4.2.1.   Standard item category

- Item category blank as shown in screen shoot
- Goods receipts and logistics invoice verification entry mandatory

Copyrighted© Material

6.2.4.2.2.   Consignment item Category

- Material Procure on consignment basis
- Material Master (Material number) mandatory
- Goods Receipts will be mandatory
- Consignment stock non valuated until with drawl
- Logistics invoice not mandatory
- Item category use K for consignment

6.2.4.2.3.   Limits Item Category

- Item Category will be use B
- Framework Order/ Blanket PO document type will be mandatory
- Goods Receipts will be optional and Logistics invoice verification will be mandatory

6.2.4.2.4.   Subcontracting Item Category

- Material number is compulsory
- Goods Receipts entry can be perform
- Logistics invoice verification is mandatory
- Item Category L is used

6.2.4.2.5.   Services Item Category

- Material number not required but material short text is required
- Service master optional
- Services entry sheet perform
- Invoice is mandatory
- Item Category D will be use

6.2.4.2.6.   Third Party item category

- Goods Recipient is customer

Copyrighted© Material

- Account assignment is mandatory
- Item category S will be used

Copyrighted© Material

Outline agreements are longer term agreements between buyer and vendors regarding the procurement of material or services that can be specific quantity, specific value, specific period of time with negotiated terms and conditions. These conditions are valid only for some specific time span and with mention quantity and value in contract. In outline agreements, delivery dates are not specified. Outline agreements include both contracts as well as scheduling agreements.

6.2.5.1. *Contracts*

Contracts are outline agreements with supplier for supply of materials and services. Delivery dates are not take into account in contracts and these are imposed on vendor via contract release order. Contracts agreements are created for longer term in SAP system e.g. may be for 1 year or two years. With reference to contracts, POs are created. All the conditions mention on contracts will be carrying forward to PO's. The validity period is mention on contract header. Contracts can be created manually without reference or with reference to

- Another Contract
- Request for quotation/ quotation
- Purchase requisition

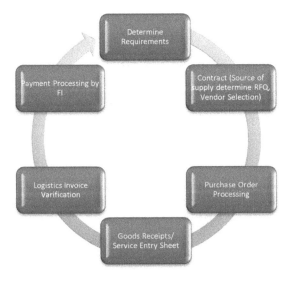

Figure 6-22 (Contract Process Flow)

Copyrighted© Material

Above mention is process flow of contract. You can create contract by transaction code ME31K and for change and display respectively ME32K and ME33K transaction codes are used. List display of contract with transaction code ME3L

Manu path for creating contract is SAP Easy Access, Logistics > Materials Management > Purchasing > Outline Agreement > Contract

In outline agreements, contracts include distributed contracts and centrally agreed contracts.

6.2.5.1.1.   Distributed Contracts

Distributed contracts create in SAP system and then these contracts are available on another SAP system. Contract data is linkage between two systems via ALE (Application link enabling) or transmitted to other SAP systems in the form of an intermediate document (IDOC) via ALE import. In order to be able to distributed contracts you must have matching or identical Purchase groups, Material, Vendor number and purchasing organizations in central as well local system. In standard SAP system, distributed contract document is used VK (Distributed contract).

Copyrighted© Material

6.2.5.1.2. Centrally agreed contracts

A central purchase organization procures materials or external services to all plants that are falls under the umbrella of that purchase organization. E.g. a purchase organization ABCD having four plants 3100, 3200, 3300 and 3400. A contract is created with purchase organization ABCD is valid for all assign plants.

6.2.5.2. Contract Types

There are two types of contract

- Quantity Contracts
- Value contracts

6.2.5.2.1. Quantity Contracts

Quantity contracts consist of particular quantity of material. When total quantity of respective duration of contract is known then quantity contracts are use. MK agreement type is used in quantity contracts.

6.2.5.2.2. Value Contracts

Value contracts consist of particular value of the material. When total value of concern duration of contract is known then value contracts are use. WK agreement type is used in value contracts.

6.2.5.2.3. Item categories in Contracts

M - Material is unknown

W – Value and quantity of material is unknown

D – Procurement of external services

K – Consignment material

L – Subcontracting

Copyrighted© Material

6.2.5.2.3.1.   Item categories M and W

Item categories M and W both are used for material group contracts and both categories are not permitted for contract release orders.

6.2.5.2.3.2.   Item category M

- Similar material with same price but different material numbers
- Not specify the material number
- Material group contract
- All material include in contract that have concern material group hit in contract.
- In contract, use short text, quantity, unit of measure and prices

6.2.5.2.3.3.   Item category W

- Material belonging to same material group but different prices
- Value and quantity are unknown
- W allow you enter material group without entering value and material quantity
- During creation of contract, enter short text, unit of measure and material group, not enter price and condition of item.

Note: Item category M is used for both value (WK) and Quantity contract (MK). But in value contracts (WK) only item category W is used

6.2.5.3.   Contract release orders

Purchase order is consider as contract release order. In SAP standard system it is created with reference to contract.

We can create PO with reference to contract or automatically in ME32K by

Go to SAP Easy Access

Logistics > Materials Management > Purchasing > Outline agreements > Contract > Change (ME32K)

Copyrighted© Material

Put number of contract and execute

Go to Contract and click on contract release order.

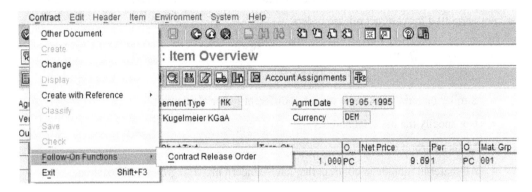

Figure 6-23 (Contract Release Order)

Copyrighted© Material

6.2.6. Scheduling Agreements

Scheduling agreements are longer term agreement between buyer and vendor to procure a particular quantity of material or services with predefine dates, terms and conditions. In scheduling agreements, you make sure release creation profile copy from vendor master data. SAP having functionality to create forecast based and just in time based delivery schedule. These schedules are based on material master settings.

Scheduling agreements can be created manually or can be created with reference to purchase requisition, quotation and centrally agreed contracts. You can also create scheduling agreements for subcontracting, stock transfer and for consignment. So following procurement types exist in scheduling agreements

- Standard
- Consignment
- Subcontracting
- Stock transfer

In SAP system, you can create scheduling agreements by transaction ME31L, for change ME32L and for display ME33L. You can maintain delivery schedule via transaction ME38 or can use menu path SAP easy access under Logistics > Materials Management > Purchasing > Outline Agreement > Scheduling agreement

Copyrighted© Material

Figure 6-23 (Scheduling Agreement Process Flow)

6.2.6.1.   Scheduling Agreement types

Scheduling agreements has two types. Release without documentation and release with documentation.

6.2.6.1.1.1.   Release with documentation

In Scheduling agreements with release documentation delivery schedules maintain with MRP. Schedule agreements release documentation is created on the basis of these schedule lines. Then these are issued to concern vendor.

Inventory / warehouse supervisor check schedule line in system then create manually just in time (JIT) or forecast (FRC) delivery schedules

In SAP Standard system, during material requirement planning run system automatically create schedule lines with JIT or FRC based.

We have option to maintain JIT schedule lines or FRC based schedule lines on the basis of requirement and concern material master setting according to chosen schedule.

Copyrighted© Material

In scheduling agreements, Release without documentation once the schedule lines are created and save in system based on settings the details are transmitted to supplier.

Copyrighted© Material

Framework order is used to bulk purchase of consumable materials having low value and low cost. It is also called blanket purchase order. It can use for large procurement of external services. Framework purchase order is created with longer validity period may be one, two or more than two years with concern item value specific limit. In framework order you can skip many steps of procurement process as per requirement. Skipping E.g. Purchase requisition, Request for quotation, Contract, Goods receipts and service entry sheet. Logistics invoice verification will be performing with the reference to framework order.

In SAP standard system there is separate document type for framework order name as Framework Order. Item category B (limit) represents the framework order in PO screen. Goods receipts and service entry sheets are optional and you must insert limits validity period as well as limits in header data of framework order. Account assignment category U is allowed and service or material group is mandatory for blanket/ framework order. In standard system when you create order for specific amount limit, after completed that limit there is no more logistics invoice will be post.

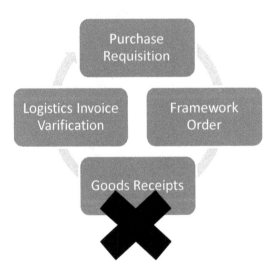

Figure 6-24 (Framework Order Process Flow)

Copyrighted© Material

Copyrighted© Material

Chapter 7:

Inventory Management with SAP Material Management

Copyrighted© Material

7. Chapter: Inventory Management with SAP Material Management

7.1.   Inventory Management in SAP

7.2.   Types of stock in Materials Management

   7.2.1.   Unrestricted stock:

   7.2.2.   Restricted stock:

7.3.   Movement types in SAP

7.4.   Stock transfer and transfer posting

   7.4.1.   Transfer Posting

   7.4.2.   Stock Transfer

7.5.   Stock Materials and Consumable Materials

   7.5.1.   Difference between stock material and consumable material

   7.5.2.   Financial Accounting impact in Stock and consumable materials

7.6.   Standard Price and Moving Average Price of Material

   7.6.1.   Standard Price

   7.6.2.   Moving Average Price

7.7.   Variances in GR IR account

   7.7.1.   Price Variance

   7.7.2.   Quantity Variance

   7.7.3.   Price Quantity Variance

7.8.   Reservations and Goods issue

   7.8.1.   Reservations

   7.8.2.   Goods Issues

7.9.   Automatic Create Purchase Order at the Time of Goods Receipt

7.10.   Consignment Stock

   7.10.1.   Consignment Purchase Order

   7.10.2.   Process Flow with Reservation

7.11.   Subcontracting

   7.11.1.   SAP Process in Subcontracting

7.12.   Tolerances in Goods receipts

   7.12.1.   Tolerance key B1 (Error Message

   7.12.2.   Tolerance key B2 (Warning message

   7.12.3.   Configuration aspects of tolerances

7.13.   Physical Inventory in SAP Materials Management

   7.13.1.   Inventory Stock Management Unit

   7.13.2.   Reasons of Accurate Physical Inventory

   7.13.3.   Physical Inventory Procedures

   7.13.4.   Physical inventory audit Process in SAP

Copyrighted© Material

7.1. Inventory Management in SAP

Inventory management is one of an important part of materials management and linked with whole logistics execution system. It directly linked with material requirement planning and provides information of inventory of physical stock as well as also planned goods movement like issues and receipts. After goods procure from vendor, goods receipts take place in inventory management as reference with concern purchase order. If a material is produce internally by means of production, inventory management provides provisions of components/ materials. Goods receipts of finished goods also take place in inventory management.

In warehouse management you can view full stock available at plant as well storage location level. It also show you where is and which material quantity located in restricted stock (block stock and stock in quality inspection) and which stock quantity located on unrestricted stock. Inventory management allows you to manage stock on quantity bases, value bases or both quantity and value bases in warehouse management.

It also determine you to display your entire warehouse stock in the system with full detail include storage locations as well storage bin levels. It also shows you which time which movement of material takes place. It is not only showing total quantity of respective material but also show you where is located.

Inventory management also caters information about internal goods movement as well as also external goods movement. External goods movement includes goods receipts from vendor (reference to purchase order), Goods issue to customer (sales and distribution) and internal goods movement includes goods receipts from production, goods issue to project or internal order or cost center etc.

Copyrighted© Material

7.2. Types of stock in Materials Management

There are possible two types of stock in materials Management

- Unrestricted stock
- Restricted stock

7.2.1. Unrestricted stock:

It physical type of stocks that easily and freely move in sap system and available at plant and storage location level.

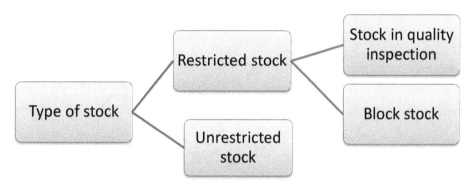

Figure 7-1 (Types of Stock in MM)

7.2.2. Restricted stock:

Restricted stock includes stock in quality inspection and block stock. Stock in quality inspection means stock is located in quality control department for checking of quality. You can block stock in several reasons e.g. due to checking for quality queue, defective reasons, rejected for quality inspection, for return to vendor or may be reservation for sales etc. You cannot consume block stock and quality inspection stocks until it move to unrestricted stock.

Copyrighted© Material

There are also some special stocks available in sap system that already discuss. These special stocks includes,

- Pipeline
- Subcontracting stock
- Consignment stock
- Sale order stock
- Project stock
- Third party processing
- Stock transfer using stock transport order
- Returnable transport packaging

Copyrighted© Material

7.3. Movement types in SAP

When you want to goods movement in SAP system, the movement types indicate where goods are move. Movement type is 3 digits key. Here following are the examples

Goods Movement	Movement type
Goods receipts for purchase order	101
Goods issues against order	261
Goods issues against project	241
Goods issues against cost center	201
Stock transfer between storage locations	311
Goods receipts into block stock	103
Goods receipts from block stock	105
Return to vendor	122
Initial stock entry	561

Table 7-1 (Different Goods Movements and Movement Types)

Movement type plays an important role in

- Field selection
- Quantity update
- Value update
- Quantity and value update
- Which accounts are update
- Indicate goods movement
- Accounting transaction generate or note
- Determine the screen structure

There are possibilities in system that maximum two documents will generate during goods movement

- Accounting document
- Material document

Copyrighted© Material

These documents generates according to stock movement type configuration. For creating/ changing or display movement type go to

SPRO> IMG> Materials Management>Inventory Management and Physical Inventory> Movement Types> Copy, Change Movement Types

Check indicator movement type

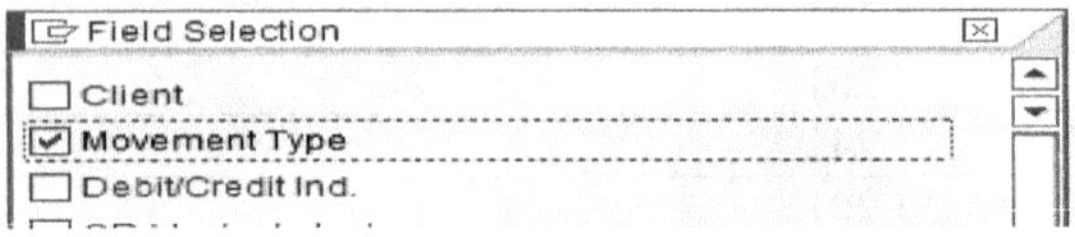

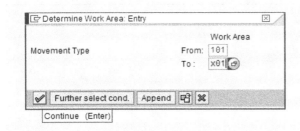

Figure 7-2 (Copy, Change Movement Types)

Enter movement type 101 (from) and X01 new MVT name insert in field to and press continue,

Figure7-3 (Movement Type Configuration)

Select relevent movement type and click on copy as button

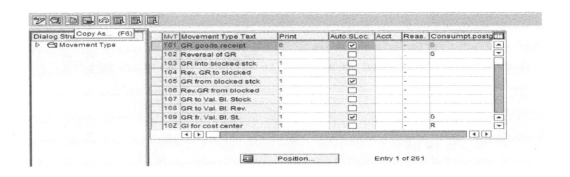

Figure 7-4 (Copy as Movement Type)

Copyrighted© Material

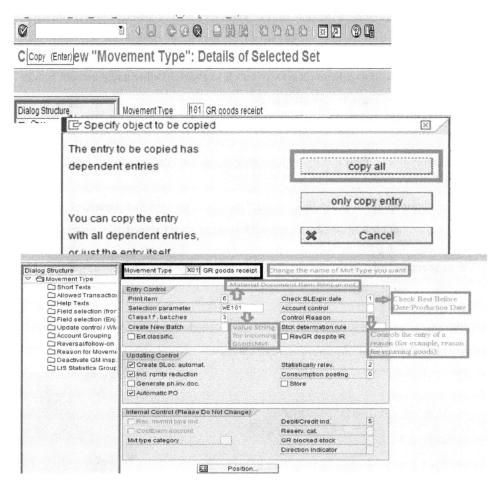

Figure 7-5 (Movement Type Configuration)

Change the name of new movement type (use alpha numeric or numeric key) must be 3 digits. In entry control section print item shows which document is printed during with certain movement type? Check SL Expire. date indicate stock check best before date/ production date. Selection parameters determine the selection parameters in purchase list (e.g. for searching of goods receipts purchase order)? Control reason indicates control the entry of a reason e.g. reason for returning of goods. Classif. batches field determine system branches to batch classification upon goods movement or when you create or change a batch (not in material master).

Copyrighted© Material

At updating control section, create storage location indicator specify automatically creation of storage location data at the time of first goods receipts is allowed or not. If you have goods movement to special stock (e.g. Project stock), the data is not created.

Requirement reduction indicator shows system is to check whether a requirement is to be partially offset or reduce to zero for the material document item in question at time of goods receipts is entered.

"Statistically relev." field specify with concern movement type update the statistics and whether this update is carried out online or in batch mode.

Control consumption field determine control posting of planned and unplanned consumption. Consumption is updated whether stock is withdrawal planned or unplanned.

Create purchase order indicator specify, PO created at this Mvt automatically at the time of goods receipts or not.

Debit credit field specify during goods movement which side (debit or credit)is updated or indicate whether movement of goods inward or outward.

Change View "Short Texts": Overview

Dialog Structure	L.	MVT	Spec.Stock	Mvt ind.	Receipt	Consumpt.	Movement Type Text	
▽ ☐ Movement Type	ZH	01		B			GR 收货	▲
☐ Short Texts	ZH	X01		B		A	有关资产的收货	▼
☐ Allowed Transaction								

Figure 7-6 (Change View Short Texts)

In short text section you maintain short text of movement type. In SAP system you can also maintain movement type short text as per SAP default languages.

Copyrighted© Material

Change View "Allowed Transactions": Overview

New Entries

Dialog Structure	MvT	TCode	Transaction Text
▽ ☐ Movement Type	X01	CIP2	CC2: Update PDC messages
☐ Short Texts	X01	CIP3	CC3: Update PDC messages
☐ Allowed Transactio	X01	CIP4	CC4: Update PDC messages
☐ Help Texts			

Figure 7-7 (Change View Allowed Transaction)

In allowed transaction section you specify which transactions will be valid for this movement type.

There is also option available to allow number of selectable transaction for respective movement type (e.g. Goods issue, goods receipts and transfer posting etc.) and reference documents (material and accounting doc.) for enjoy transaction.

Change View "Field selection (Enjoy)": Overview

New Entries

Dialog Structure				
▽ ☐ Movement Type	**Field selection (Enjoy)**			
☐ Short Texts	Mv	Field Name	Required Entry	Optional Entry
☐ Allowed Transactio	101	CUSTNAME	○	◉
☐ Help Texts	101	SGTXT	○	◉
☐ Field selection (fror	101	WEMPF	○	◉
☐ Field selection (Enjoy)				
☐ Update control / Wh				
☐ Account Grouping				
☐ Reversal/follow-on				

Figure 7-8 (Change View Field Selection (Enjoy))

In account grouping section, you specify against movement type which transaction event key is valid. Under transaction event key there is G/L account is assign as transaction OBYC. It is a bridge that helps for automatic account determination against movement type. In account grouping as per below image, here movement type also specify quantity and value update or not. Updating of value is directly link with accounting document. Value string is a sequence or way

Copyrighted© Material

for account determination. WE01 is used for incoming goods receipts, WA14 used for free of charge delivery and WA01 is used for consumption.

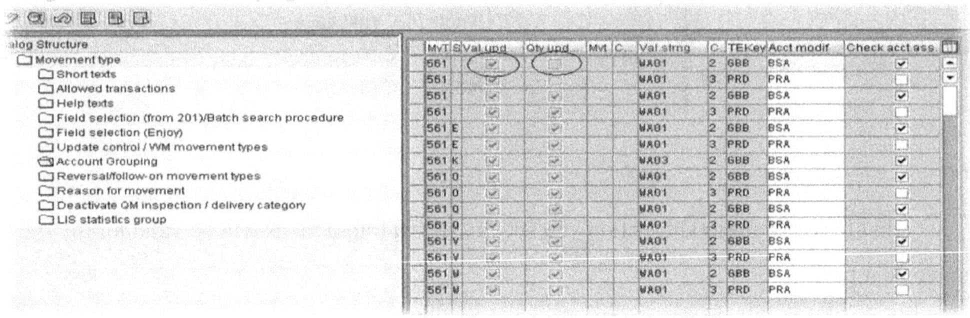

Figure 7-9 (Change View Account Configuration)

Copyrighted© Material

7.4. Stock transfer and transfer posting

Transfer Posting

- Stock to Stock
- Material to Material
- Consignment to warehouse

Stock Transfer

In SAP system stock transfer can be

- Plant to Plant
- Company to company
- Storage Location to Storage Location

7.4.1. Transfer Posting

7.4.1.1. Stock to Stock Transfer Posting

Stock to stock transfer posting includes material movement between unrestricted stocks, stock in quality inspection and block stock e.g.

- Movement of stock from block stock to unrestricted stock or unrestricted stock to block stock
- Movement between block stocks to quality inspection stock or quality inspection stock to block stock
- Movement between stock in quality inspection to unrestricted stock or unrestricted stock to stock in quality inspection

Copyrighted© Material

Here following are the detail of stock transfer from stock to stock with movement types

Figure 7-10 (Stock to Stock Transfer Posting With Movement Types)

Example:

Material procures and goods receipts against purchase order and posting to block stock. Store keeper post same stock to stock in quality inspection. After quality inspection quality control department post it unrestricted stock.

7.4.1.2. *Material to Material Transfer Posting*

Material to material transfer posting will be accrue when state of material changes over time. For example,

In chemical industry ABC chemical raw material is used for production. After some time this chemical is obsolete and new chemical DEF Raw material having same characteristics is used for production in replacement of ABC. The available quantity of ABC material is 10 Ton. We have an option to transfer ABC Material quantity transfer to DEF material but it is mandatory

Copyrighted© Material

- Both materials having same unit of measure e.g. kg
- Cannot be preplanned in reservation
- Movement type should must be 309 for material to material transfer posting
- Transfer posting will be in one step process
- It will be possible the movement should must be from unrestricted stock to unrestricted stock

7.4.2. Stock Transfer

7.4.2.1. Plant to Plant Stock Transfer

In case of stock transfer between plants, you can transfer stock plant fall in same company code or can be fall on different company codes. There are following possible procedures for transfer of stock.

7.4.2.1.1. One step procedure

In one step, goods issue and goods receipts only in one material document. You insert movement type 301 and enter respective issuing plant, issuing storage location, Receiving Plant and receiving storage location and material.

7.4.2.1.2. Two step procedure

In two step procedures, first you remove respective material from storage location with movement type 303 and then place in storage location in second step with movement type 303. At the time of removal, you mention receiving plant, issuing organizational level and concern material because mandatory for valuation. Material remove from issuing plant and receive from receiving plant will be reference to the material document. In case of same plant valuation is not mandatory.

Copyrighted© Material

7.4.2.1.3.   Stock Transport order (STO)

In stock transport order, you create stock transport order in PO screen (separate document type as Stock Transport Order), at vendor field mention issuing plant, and mention purchasing organization of receiving plant, receiving Plant Company, receiving plant and its storage location. It is mandatory material is extending at both plant. Then goods issue with reference to stock transport order with movement type 311 and then goods receipts with reference to material document (just created with 311) with movement type 315.

Note: In SAP stander system there is also option available to view stock in transit. For doing this you can go to MB5T. It shows you stock between 311 posted and 313 is yet to be posted.

Example of STO:

Let's suppose you have two plants. One plant produce biscuits and second plant produce chocolates. You have raw material sugar use in both plants. Your biscuits plant suddenly out of stock of sugar material. At the same time there is access sugar material in chocolate plant. In SAP system, you have an option to take material from chocolate plant with stock transport order.

7.4.2.2.   *Storage Location to Storage Location Stock Transfer*

There are two procedures available for storage location to storage location stock transfer.

7.4.2.2.1.   One Step Procedure

In one step procedure, there is an advantage to stock transfer in single transaction however in two steps has an advantage to monitoring of stock in transit easily in SAP system. In one step, first you remove stock from storage location and then place storage location in receiving plant. There will be no impact in financials but MM document will be generated. Accounting document will be generating only in the case of split valuation. It is mandatory the material is split valuated and valuation type will be change of that material. You can use 313 movement type for one step procedure.

Copyrighted© Material

7.4.2.2.2.   Two step procedure

In two step procedure, you only transfer materials from unrestricted stock. For doing this you issue material from issuing plant from issuing storage location and receive that material receiving plant at receiving storage location. There are two material documents will be generate in two step procedure. One at the time of goods issue from issuing storage location and second one will be at the time of goods receipts in receiving storage location. At the time of issuance 313 movement type and at the time of receiving 315 movement type will be used. There is no accounting document will be generate in this case.

Copyrighted© Material

7.5. Stock Materials and Consumable Materials

Stock materials are those materials which you store in storage location. You manage stock at storage locations of these materials. In stock materials, it is mandatory material master record must exist for procurement. Consumable materials are those materials which consume after purchase and not manage their stock in storage locations, and it can be possible

- Consumable materials procure with material master record
- Consumable materials procure without material master record

You can also procure stock material with account assignment. For doing this, account assignment is mandatory for stock materials. You mention account assignment as cost center, internal order or by charge to an Asset.

7.5.1. Difference between stock material and consumable material

Stock Materials	Consumable Materials
Master Data of Material Mandatory	May or may not, by choice
Necessary to mention material in PO	Not Mandatory
No account Assignment in PO	Account Assignment is mandatory
Goods Receipts must be in Stock materials	Optional, by choice
Stock Account update when GR	Consumption account update at the time of GR
Impact on material moving average price	No impact

Table 7-2 (Difference between stock material and consumable material)

Copyrighted© Material

7.5.2. Financial Accounting impact in Stock and consumable materials

7.5.2.1. *Financial Accounting impact of Stock material*

When goods receipts perform

Debit	Credit
Stock/ Material Account	
	GR/ IR Account

Table 7-3 (Goods Receipt Entries)

At the time of invoice receipts

Debit	Credit
GR/ IR Account	
	Vendor Account

Table 7-4 (Invoice Receipt Entries)

7.5.2.2. *Financial accounting impact of consumable materials*

When goods receipts perform

Debit	Credit
Consumption Account	
	GR/ IR Account

Table 7-5 (Goods Receipt Entries)

At the time of invoice receipts

Debit	Credit
GR/ IR Account	
	Vendor Account

Table 7-6 (Invoice Receipt Entries)

Copyrighted© Material

7.6. Standard Price and Moving Average Price of Material

7.6.1. Standard Price

Standard price is used for those materials, which having low fluctuating prices or no fluctuating frequently. Most likely companies use standard prices for Semi Finished (HALB) and finished goods (FERT) that are producing internally in production premises. Price is remain constant at specified period of time and don't change whenever goods receipts perform in with in that period. In simple words, it is planned value of particular material for some specific period (may be 15 days or may be 30 days) of time with actual costing/ material ledger. Standard price maintain in two ways in material master

- With manual insert/ enter
- Automatically suggest by SAP system (e.g. Cost run)

In material master for standard price it is mandatory

- Price control "S" should must be maintain in material master account one view screen.
- Attributes of material type configure accordingly

Note: After save such material, the price field fix and don't change in material master. For price changes in MM of concern material, you can use transaction code MR21.

7.6.1.1. Silent Features of Standard Price

- In standard price valuation of all concern materials having price control "S" at standard price.
- Variances or differences go to separate price difference account
- Price changes can be taking into account
- Variances are updated

Copyrighted© Material

Quantity $_{(new)}$ = **Quantity** $_{old}$ + **Quantity Receipts**

Value $_{(new)}$ = **Value** $_{old}$ + **Quantity Receipts** * **Price** $_{Material\ Master}$ / **Price Unit** $_{Material\ Master}$

Price $_{(new)}$ = **Price** $_{old}$ = **Price** $_{Material\ Master}$

Total Value = Standard price Material master * Total stock

Note:

   If the difference accrues in purchase order price and standard price, the variance between two prices is posted as follows

Purchase order value > Goods Receipts then expense account will be update

Purchase order value < Goods receipts then revenue account will be update

7.6.1.3.   Financial Accounting impact

Debit	Credit
Stock Account	
	GR IR Account

Table 7-7 (Goods Receipt Entries @ Standard Price without Difference)

Copyrighted© Material

If difference accrue, difference impact will be as follows when Goods receipts

Debit	Credit
Stock Account	
Price Difference Account	
	GR IR account

Table 7-8 (Goods Receipt Entries @ Standard Price with Difference)

When invoice received without difference then

Debit	Credit
GR IR Account	
	Vendor Account

Table 7-9 (Invoice Receipt Entries @ Standard Price without Difference)

When invoice received with difference, then

Debit	Credit
GR IR Account	
	Price difference Account
	Vendor Account

Table 7-10 (Invoice Receipt Entries @ Standard Price with Difference)

Copyrighted© Material

7.6.2.   Moving Average Price

Moving average price is used for those materials which having dynamic fluctuating rates. Moving average price also called as weighted average price of material. Most likely companies used moving average price is used for Raw materials (ROH), Packaging materials (VERP), Spare parts (ERSA), IT materials and trading goods (HAWA) etc. In moving average price, price of material will be impact after every goods receipts entry. These materials purchase order price fluctuating may be take place on daily basis, or continuously basis. The benefit of moving average price is raw materials or other related material which having moving average price, always represent current market price. Moving average price maintain

At the time of creation of material

Update regular basis at every goods receipts

Note: Some other transactions are also impact on moving average price. These entries discuss in next topic.

For moving average price, it is mandatory

- Price control "V" select in material master
- Attributes of material types configure accordingly

7.6.2.1.   Silent features of Moving average price

Goods receipts are book at GR value

Material master price is adjusted to delivered price

Manual price change generally unnecessary, but can be changed

Price differences/ Variances charge to material (Stock Account)

Variance automatically adjust in Material master at every goods receipts

Note: For split valuation, it is recommended to use moving average price

Copyrighted© Material

7.6.2.2. Moving average price calculation

Quantity new = Quantity old + Quantity receipt

Value new = value old + quantity receipt * Price receipts / Price Unit receipt

Price new = Price unit material master * Value new / quantity new

Total Value = MAP price Material master * Total stock

7.6.2.3. Financial accounting impact

Debit	Credit
Stock Account	
	GR IR Account

Table 7-11 (Goods Receipts Entries @ Moving Average Price without Difference)

If difference accrue, difference impact will be as follows when Goods receipts

Debit	Credit
Stock Account/ material account	
	GR IR account

Table 7-12 (Goods Receipts Entries @ Moving Average Price with Difference)

When invoice received without difference then

Debit	Credit
GR IR Account	
	Vendor Account

Table 7-13 (Invoice Received Without Difference)

When invoice received with difference, then

Debit	Credit
GR IR Account	
	Vendor Account

Table 7-14 (Invoice Received With Difference)

Copyrighted© Material

7.6.2.4.   Transactions that impact on moving average price

➤ Transaction MIGO with movement type 101,102

➤ Transaction MIGO with movement type 105,106

➤ Whenever clear/ Post GR/ IR clearing account

➤ Invoice, Subsequent debit, subsequent credit and credit memos notes

➤ Transaction MR21 price change of material master

➤ MB1C/ 561 and 562

➤ Goods Issue Reversal 262

➤ MB1B Transaction with movement type 415, 416, 915 and 916

➤ Price control V and S

7.6.2.5.   Transactions not Impact on MAP

➤ MIGO with 103,104 movement types

➤ Goods issue 261 movement type

➤ MI07 with 701 and 702 movement types

Copyrighted© Material

7.7. Variances in GR IR account

Variances in GR IR means there are discrepancies between Purchase order price and quantity, goods receipts quantity and invoice receipt amount and quantity. There are following types of variances accrue in GR IR account,

- Price Variance
- Quantity Variance
- Price quantity Variance

7.7.1. Price Variance

If there are discrepancies between purchase order price and invoice price then price variance accrues e.g.

PO Price 10 and Quantity 15

GR Price 10 and Quantity 15

Invoice Price 12 and quantity 15

7.7.2. Quantity Variance

If there are discrepancies between Purchase order quantities, goods received quantity and quantity invoiced, and then it is eliminate e.g.

PO Price 10 and Quantity 15

Goods Receipt price 10 and Quantity 15

Invoice price 10 and quantity 18

Copyrighted© Material

7.7.3. Price Quantity Variance

Difference between purchase order price and quantity in invoice and goods receipts quantity is called price quantity variance.

PO Price 10 and Quantity 15

Goods receipts Price 10 and quantity 10

Invoice price 12 and quantity 8

Note: in case of standard price of material, difference goes to price difference account. In case of moving average price difference goes to stock account as discuss earlier in previous topics.

Copyrighted© Material

7.8. Reservations and Goods issue

7.8.1. Reservations

It is request to store or warehouse department to preserve desire material ready for issue at certain date for specific purpose. Sometime stock can be block in SAP system and main aim of preserve material is to ensure whenever you need for production or plant maintenance etc. It is immediately available. A material reservation is create in SAP against cost center, plant maintenance order, internal order, and project or may be against asset etc. In simple words, reservation of material is create by user department for reserve a material in store for future use and send a notification to store or warehouse department.

You can create reservation with following Manu path, go to SAP easy access

Logistics> Materials Management>Inventory Management> Reservation> Create/ Change/ Display or Transaction code MB21, MB22 and MB23 respectively.

Note: To view reservation list use transaction code MB25

7.8.1.1. Configuration aspects

SPRO> IMG> Materials Management> Inventory Management and Physical Inventory> Reservation

Here you can configure

7.8.1.1.1. Define default values

Here you define goods movement allowed against movement type for click indicator as well as decide storage location data automatically create or not.

Plnt	Name 1	Mvt	Days m	Rete	M	
0001	Werk 0001	☑	0	30	☑	▲

Figure 7-11 (Default Values For Goods Movement)

Copyrighted© Material

7.8.1.1.2. Maintain copy rules for reservation documents

Transaction Code	Transaction Text	Proposed preselec.	
MB21	Create Reservation	✓	▲

Figure 7-12 (Maintain Copy Rules For Reservation Documents)

Proposed item preselect indicator shows and indicate that the item of reference document appear pre-selected as default value in the item selection list. This indicator is used for all functions that involve referencing a document, e.g.

- Cancelation of material document
- Goods receipts with reference to purchase order
- Goods movement with reference to a reservation
- Release material from GR block stock as reference with material document
- Return delivery with reference to material document

7.8.1.1.3.   Set dynamic availability check

It shows against movement type whenever goods issue material stock in hand or not and accordingly set error or warning message for concern material is available or not available.

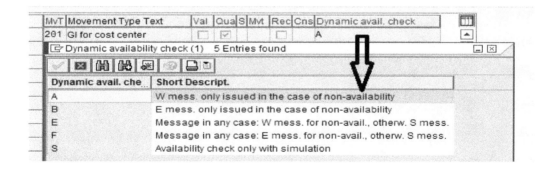

Figure 7-13 (Dynamic Availability Check)

Copyrighted© Material

Reservation includes header section and item section. Header section consists of movement type creator and account assignment etc. and item section includes material, quantity goods recipient and requirement date etc.

There are two ways of creation of reservation. First one is manual creation and second is automatically create reservation. Manual reservation creates and enters directly by user through MB21 transaction code. Automatic reservation indirectly create with some other transaction for example

- Reservation for orders, networks and WBS elements
- Stock Transfer reservations when in reorder point planning stock is short fall from mention point of inventory.
- Plant maintenance order

There are various types of goods issuance in SAP for consumption or transfer of stock. Goods issues can be against production order, reservation, project, work breakdown structure elements (WBS Element) or against cost center. It may be issues to customer for sale or sampling or scraping or wastage. Goods with drawl to customer are responsibility of sales and distribution department. Each goods issue in above mention types will be known movement type. E.g. goods issue to customer having movement type 601, goods issue to cost center and internal orders movement types 201 and 261 respectively.

Here following are some scenarios of issuance of goods against different process flows, for example

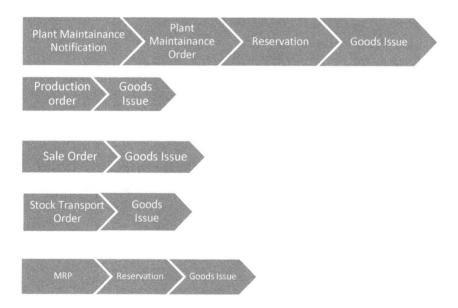

Figure 7-14 (Goods Issuance Scenarios)

It is also possible to goods issue without references. For doing this it is compulsory in issuance document must be mention account assignment. Account assignment can be specifies against cost center, project or can be order.

In SAP system it is function to automatically goods issue with backflush option. Backflush option allows you to automatic goods issue when production order is save or confirm the operations in production planning. System checks stock availability in system and goods issue accordingly. In this case you have no need to check material and perform extra entry in SAP system. For backflush enabling you must set always backflush option in material master MRP 2 as mention

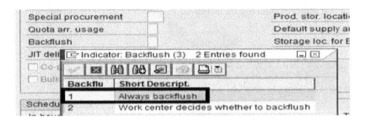

Figure 7-15 (BackFlush Indicator)

Note: You must assure there is backward material availability of all concern materials that are mention in BOM of production operations. If you can enable backflush, material issue automatically with movement type 261.

Copyrighted© Material

7.9. Automatic Create Purchase Order at the Time of Goods Receipt

In SAP system there is option available create purchase order automatically with goods receipts entry. There is single transaction (MIGO) where you have advantage. These are following pre requisite for create automatic purchase order via goods receipts

➢ Check Automatic PO indicator at Material Master Change transaction, Purchasing view

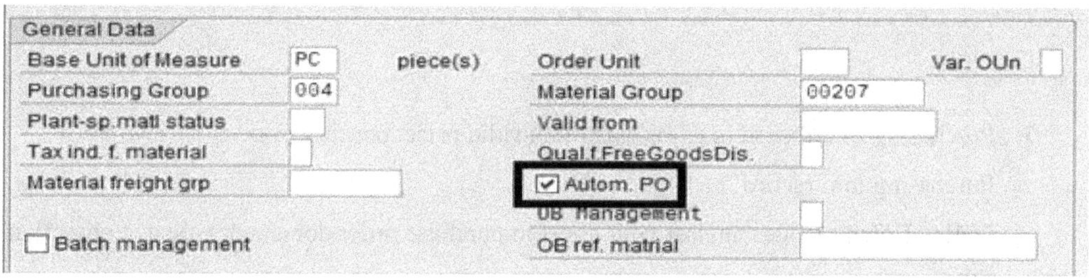

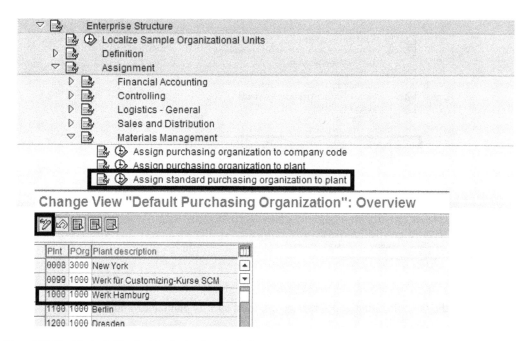

Figure 7-16 (Automatic Purchase Order Indicator)

➢ In customizing, Plant must be assign to your standard purchasing organization

Figure 7-17 (Plant Assign to Standard Purchasing Organization)

Copyrighted© Material

> In vendor master recorder, must be check indicator of Automatic PO

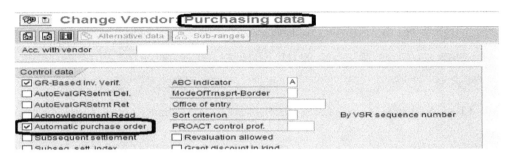

Figure 7-18 (Automatic Purchase Order Indicator in Vendor Master)

> Purchasing Info record must be exist with valid price, because price is retrieve from Purchasing info record
> Define Default values against your concern purchase order document type as transection MB01
> Check Automatic Purchase order creation indicator against movement type (e.g. 101 & 161) in Change View of Automatic Purchase order creation indicator against movement type

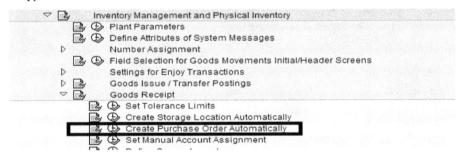

Figure 7-19 (Change View of Automatic Purchase order creation indicator against movement type)

> At the time of crating goods receipt you must specify plant and vendor in MIGO transaction

Copyrighted© Material

7.10. Consignment Stock

In consignment, Vendor stores its material on customer premises or warehouse. When customer with drawls goods concern premises, immediately liability will be generates accordingly. Vendor legally responsible and owner of his stock until it would not be withdrawal from warehouse. In another words, goods are store on customer's location. Payment of consignment stock would be paid by vendor on predefine terms and conditions. It may be at the time of withdrawal of stock or may be on monthly basis. You must manage consignment stock separately from other stock as well as manage its vendor separately basis accordingly. Consignment stock is a type falls in special stock in materials management. To manage consignment stock, you must maintain following master data in your SAP system,

➤ Materials Master Record
➤ Vendor Master Record
➤ Purchasing info record of consignment

In consignment process, you create PO with consignment PO parameters. Goods receipts would be made reference to consignment purchase order. Goods receipts will be non-valuated and will be a part of non-valuated stock. When goods withdraw from consignment stock then liability will be generate. Withdraw price of material is predefine terms and conditions and also maintain in consignment info record of purchasing master data. In SAP system, there are special reports that manage settlement of withdraw of consignment stock.

Note: System not valuate the consignment stock at the time goods receipts from vendor.

In consignment info record you must maintain price of vendor as preliminary negotiating terms and conditions. In your consignment info record, consignment price can be maintained in foreign currency as well as period base and unit of measure. If you procure same consignment material from different vendors, you must maintain consignment info record for all vendors.

Copyrighted© Material

Consignment Material Process Flow

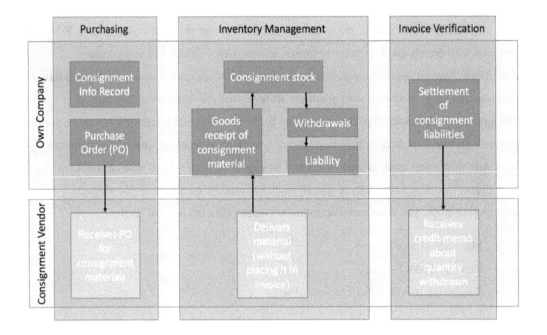

Figure 7-20 (Vendor Consignment Process)

7.10.1. Consignment Purchase Order

Consignment purchase order consist of

- Item category should must be K
- Enter a material number
- Cannot enter price of purchase order and conditions
- Required a goods receipts from consignment PO
- Goods receipts is posted in vendor consignment stock and will be non-valuated
- Cannot enter invoice of consignment item
- Liability generate when goods withdrawal from consignment stock

Copyrighted© Material

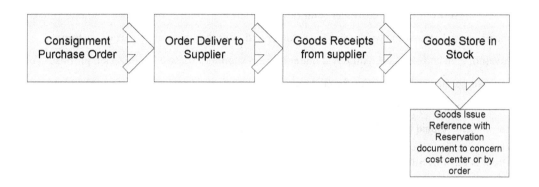

Figure 7-21 (Consignment Process Flow with Reservation)

For consignment stock settlement goes to SAP easy access

Materials Management> Inventory Management> Environment> Consignment> Consignment from Vendor> Liability MRKO

You can view all activates related to settlement and non-settlement consignments withdrawals with this report. You can search by following criteria by plant, by company code, by vendor, by posting date, by document number or by material number.

Consignment entries in automatic account determination

    BSX (Debit) KON

    KON (Credit)

    During (Liability) MRKO,

    KBS (Debit)

    KBS (Credit)

Copyrighted© Material

7.11. Subcontracting

In subcontracting, customer send raw materials to vendor, subcontractor adding values in materials and after some work send to customer and after that material is part of customer inventory. In another case, you buy a material from supplier. Some customization purposes you issue some materials to vendor for customization of semi-finished or finished goods. Vendor adding work and process on these components and send back these components to you. In response, you paid to vendor for his/ her services according to negotiating terms and conditions.

Process Flow of Subcontracting in SAP as

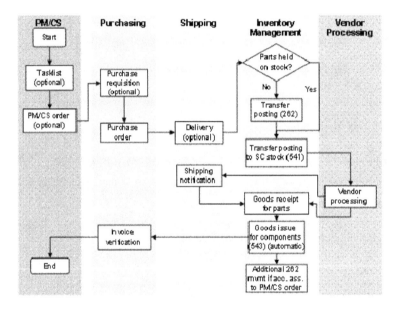

Figure 7-22 (Process Flow of Subcontracting)

Copyrighted© Material

7.11.1. SAP Process in Subcontracting

- Maintain master data of semi-finished or finished good (Transaction MM01)
- If necessary create bills of material of concern semi-finished or finished good (Transaction CS01)
- Create purchase order with item category L
- Issue goods to subcontractor using movement type 541 (Transaction MB1B)
- Goods will be receipts against purchase order via movement type 101 (Transaction MIGO)
- Logistics invoice verification with reference to Purchase order (MIRO)

It is your non valuated stock and also takes into account in material requirement planning. You can run material requirement planning on subcontracting stock. SAP allows you to run MRP on separate area of subcontracting. Two stocks are falls in subcontracting (Quality inspection and unrestricted stock). Subcontracting stock manage at your plant level.

7.11.1.1. *Financial Accounting impact*

At the time of goods Issue to subcontractor

Debit	Credit
Consumption Account	
	Stock account

Figure 7-23 (Accounting impact at the Time of Goods Issuance)

At the time of goods receipts

Debit	Credit
Stock Account	
	Change in stock account

Figure 7-24 (Accounting impact at the Time of Goods Receipts)

Copyrighted© Material

Logistics invoice verification

Debit	Credit
GR IR Account	
	Vendor account

Figure 7-25 (Accounting impact at the Time of Invoice Verification)

Sometimes company companies treat subcontracting work as services. For doing this, customer create service purchase order with item category D. Service entry sheet perform with reference to service purchase order. It is perform according to the work or value addition or services addition. Service entry sheet can be accepted fully or partially in SAP system. Logistics invoice verification performs by customer with reference to purchase order or via service entry sheet.

For configuration aspects in automatic account determination

If material having moving average price

Transaction event key	Particulars Entry description
BSX	Stock account
BSV	Change in Stock (Sub-Contracting)
FRL	Subcontracting charges
WRX	GR IR Clearing account
GBB > VBO	Consumption account

Table 7-15 (Transaction Event Keys at the Time Automatic Account Determination)

Copyrighted© Material

7.12. Tolerances in Goods receipts

You can define tolerance limits for goods receipts. When you perform goods receipts, system check whether goods receipts quantity according to Purchase order or not. Is there any variance falls in quantity? This variance takes into account in SAP with the help of tolerance keys. These tolerances can be defined at company code level. For tolerances there are two keys provided by SAP

7.12.1. Tolerance key B1 (Error Message)

B1 is set for maximum tolerance acceptable percentage variance in goods receipts. In this case, when quantity exceeded from upper and lower limit of tolerances then system create error message. Upper and lower Tolerance percentage define in customizing under tolerance key B1.

7.12.2. Tolerance key B2 (Warning message)

B2 is set for minimum tolerance acceptable percentage variance in goods receipts. In this case if quantity shortfall from upper and lower limit of tolerances, system create warning message. Upper and lower limits of warning message will be creating under B2 tolerance key.

Copyrighted© Material

7.12.3. Configuration aspects of tolerances

For configure tolerances, you can go to SAP easy access under

SPRO> IMG> Materials Management> Inventory Management and Physical Inventory> Goods Receipts> Set Tolerance Limits

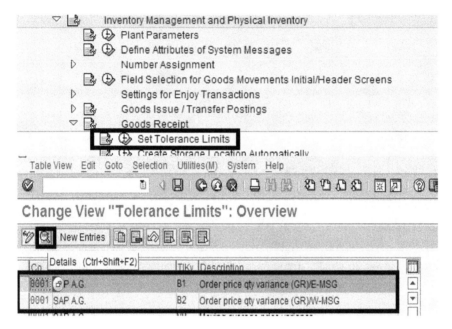

Figure 7-26 (Tolerance Limits)

Here you can view existing setting of tolerances against company code 0001 for both tolerance keys B1 and B2. For viewing tolerances, you can select concern line and press detail button as mention below.

You can configure new tolerances as per against your required company code, for doing this click on new entries button mention below on

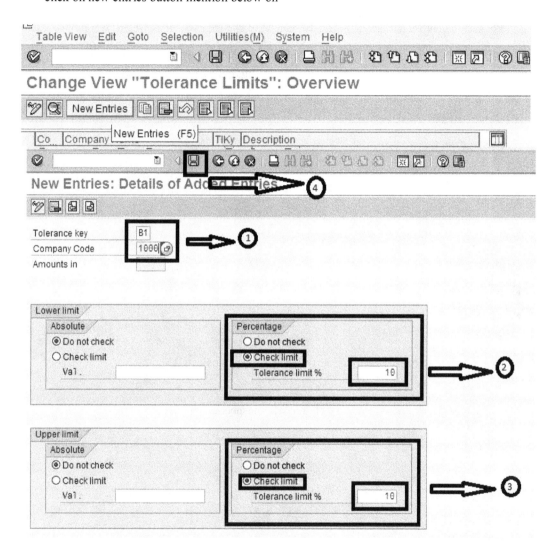

Figure 7-27 (Change View Tolerance Limit Overview Screen)

Note: Follow these steps and similarly create for warning message B2.

7.13. Physical Inventory in SAP Materials Management

Physical inventory has an important part of materials management as well as warehouse management. By legal laws, inventory is an important part of financial statement of your company. It is important for material requirement planning, excess of inventory in stock, stock out risk (shortage) as well capacity planning etc. Accurate supply and demand inventory forecast also directly related to physical inventory.

7.13.1. Inventory Stock Management Unit

Stock management units in SAP are

- Plant
- Storage Location
- Material
- Batch stock
- Special stock (returnable packaging and consignment stock etc.)
- Batches
- Stock types (unrestricted stock, stock in quality inspection and block stock)

7.13.2. Reasons of Accurate Physical Inventory

- Financial statement requirement (balance sheet current assets)
- Material requirement planning
- Excess inventory or stock out risk minimize

Copyrighted© Material

1. Periodic inventory procedure
2. Continuous inventory procedure
3. Cycle counting
4. Inventory sampling

7.13.3.1.   Periodic Inventory Procedure

Physical inventory count on periodic basis according to balance sheet required date

7.13.3.2.   Continuous Inventory Procedure

Inventory will be count on continuous basis during all concern financial physical year

7.13.3.3.   Cycle Count Procedure

In cycle count inventory stock take into account at regular interval basis

7.13.3.4.   Inventory sampling procedure

In inventory sampling procedure, randomly selected stock take into account on required date of your balance sheet.

Copyrighted© Material

There are three phases of physical inventory process

1. Create physical inventory document
2. Enter physical inventory count
3. Post differences

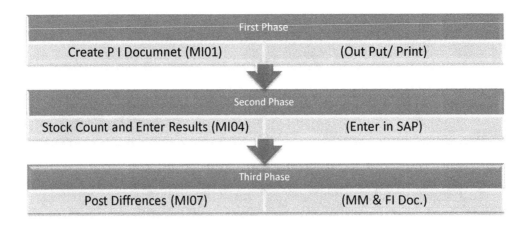

First Phase
| Create P I Documnet (MI01) | (Out Put/ Print) |

Second Phase
| Stock Count and Enter Results (MI04) | (Enter in SAP) |

Third Phase
| Post Diffrences (MI07) | (MM & FI Doc.) |

Table 7-16 (Three Phases of Physical Inventory Process)

7.13.4.1. Create Physical Inventory document

Create physical inventory document is the first phase of inventory audit. Here you create document with large quantity via batch input. When you create document, its print will be execute for physical inventory count in warehouse and selected team will process inventory count at warehouse. You can create/ change and display physical inventory document via respectively transaction codes MI01, MI02 and MI03. Or follow the Manu path under

Logistics > Materials Management > Physical Inventory > Physical Inventory Document > Create, Change or Display

Physical inventory document contain header section and item section. Header section includes Plant, Storage location, Document date, Count Date and indicators of freeze and block inventory indicators (Discuss latterly in detail). You can also create physical inventory document as per selected criteria in document header of physical inventory as

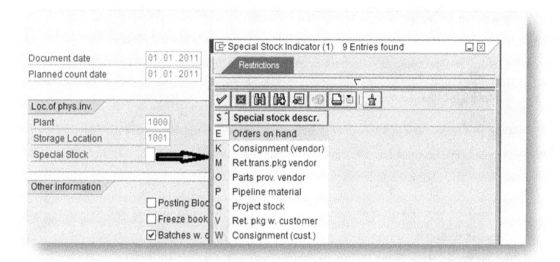

Figure 7-28 (Physical Inventory Document Selection Screen)

In physical inventory document, item section includes material, quantity, stock type, status and batches etc. the status of an item represent whether item will be counted, recounted process or posted.

Note: After post the document you can change following on Physical inventory document header, set or unset posting block, freeze indicator, enter or change physical inventory number, change count date, stock type, delete the document or set deletion indicator as well as enter new item in document.

Copyrighted© Material

7.13.4.2.   Enter Physical Inventory Count

In this phase you enter physical inventory count in the system with reference to physical inventory document (just created for this audit). In physical inventory document, count status of the item is set to count and also updated count date at header level of the document. It is possible there are differences fall in materials (differences accrue in count inventory and system inventory). You can enter count in system via transaction code MI04 or go to SAP easy access

Logistics> Materials Management> Physical Inventory> Inventory Count> Enter

When you enter count in SAP system you can see differences via differences list, here you can view information regarding book inventory, counted inventory, difference quantity and its amount. You can perform the following function with the differences list

- Change, Display or enter count
- Change or display document
- Recount document or item
- Differences can be post

7.13.4.3.   Post Differences

In this phase, you post differences of physical inventory and system inventory. For doing this, you directly access via transaction code MI07 or via Manu path go to SAP easy access

Logistics> Materials Management> Physical Inventory> Differences> Post

When you post the differences in system, then there are two documents will be generate

- Material Document
- Accounting Document

Copyrighted© Material

It is also possible to determine tolerances for difference posting of inventory. These tolerances are defining on users groups in customizing. For doing this, go to SAP essay access screen under

SPRO > IMG> Inventory Management and Physical Inventory> Physical Inventory >Define Tolerances for Inventory Differences or Transaction code OMJ2

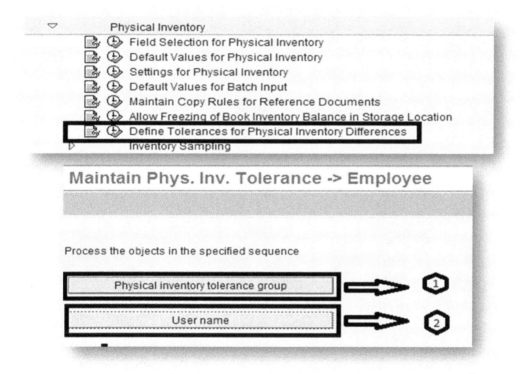

Figure 7-29 (Tolerances for Inventory Differences)

Here you create user group in which you specify tolerance amount and this user group assign to particular user that are authorize for posting differences of inventory.

Copyrighted© Material

Copyrighted© Material

Chapter 8:

Logistics Invoice Verification

Copyrighted© Material

8. Chapter: Logistics Invoice verification

8.1.   What is Logistics invoice verification?

8.2.   Subsequent Debit, Subsequent Credit and Credit Memos

  8.2.1.   Subsequent Debit

  8.2.2.   Subsequent Credit

  8.2.3.   Credit Memo

  8.3.   Planned and Unplanned delivery Cost in logistics invoice verification

  8.3.1.   Standard and Moving Average Price Impact (unplanned delivery cost)

8.4.   Logistics invoicing plan

  8.4.1.   Partial Invoicing Plan

  8.4.2.   Periodic Invoicing Plan

  8.4.3.   Pre-Requisite for invoicing plan

8.5.   Park and Hold Logistics Invoice document

  8.5.1.   Hold Invoice Document

  8.5.2.   Park Invoice Document

8.6.   Invoice in foreign currency

8.7.   Stochastic Block and Manual Block of Invoice

8.8.   Invoice Reduction

8.9.   Cancelations in Materials Management

  8.9.1.   Cancelation of logistics Invoice verification document

  8.9.2.   Cancelation of Inventory Management Document

8.10.   Difference between Cancelations and Rejections (Movement types)

  8.10.1.   Cancelation:

  8.10.2.   Rejections:

  8.11.   Delivery completion indicator in PO

Copyrighted© Material

8.1.   What is Logistics invoice verification?

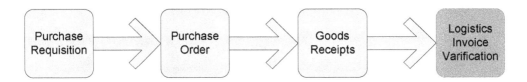

Figure 8-1 (Logistics Invoice Verification)

Logistics invoice verification is the last portion of procurement process. In logistics invoice verification, incoming invoices are comparing with purchase order, goods receipts as well as service entry sheet contents like price and quantity etc. and post them. When posting these invoices, notification sent to financial department for further process. When you post incoming invoices, there are two documents generates i.e. Materials Management and Financial Accounting. Materials management document is used in materials management and financial accounting document used to send notification to financial accounting department for payment.

When posting an invoice there are following impacts accrue in SAP

- Update purchase order history
- MM and FI documents
- Relevant accounts update after posting or parking
- Update material master Accounting 1view (Materials Price)

For posting of logistics invoice you can go SAP Easy access screen under

Logistics> Materials Management> Logistics Invoice Verification> Document Entry> Enter Invoice or directly access via transaction code MIRO

Copyrighted© Material

8.2. Subsequent Debit, Subsequent Credit and Credit Memos

A subsequent debit or subsequent credit arises when logistics invoice already been settled and you receive or send a credit memo from or to supplier respectively. These are directly impact on purchasing value but not relevant to quantity. Total invoice quantity will be not changeable.

Followings are truths about subsequent debit and subsequent credit

- It will show on purchase order history tab
- Value will be update, no quantity base update
- Subsequent debit or credit must be posted after posting of logistics invoice verification
- There are separate transaction in logistics invoice verification screen (MIRO) for both subsequent debit, subsequent credit and credit memo
- If you use tolerance limits in logistics invoice verification and you want to post subsequent debit or subsequent credit, if the concern value exceeded or below the tolerance limits then system will block the logistics invoice
- At one time only you can post one of following subsequent debit, subsequent credit and credit memo
- After posting above documents in system, there is no option to change above documents instead of you cancelation the document, correct it with desire changes and post it.
- You can see subsequent debit, subsequent credit separately in purchase order item detail in purchase order history tab.

8.2.1. Subsequent Debit

Subsequent debit accrue when you already post logistics invoice against purchase order and further cost incurred in concern procurement. A vendor wrongly sent invoice to much low price as actual and after that he/ she sent another invoice, resultant you post subsequent debit.

8.2.2. Subsequent Credit

If a purchase order invoice already been posted with high amount, then you post subsequent credit or credit memo. For example, a vendor sent an invoice high price as actual and after

Copyrighted© Material

verification sent credit memo to buyer for difference amount then you must post it as subsequent credit.

Figure 8-2 (Logistics Invoice Verification Initial Screen)

8.2.3. Credit Memo

Credit memo receive from supplier if you have charge larger amount as actual. When you post credit memo then total invoice quantity in purchase order history is reduce by the credit memo quantity. The maximum quantity you can make a credit for is the quantity that has already been invoiced.

Copyrighted© Material

8.3.   Planned and Unplanned delivery Cost in logistics invoice verification

Delivery cost is known as incidental cost in procurement. There are two types of delivery cost in logistics invoice verification called planned delivery cost and unplanned delivery cost. Planned cost in logistics invoice verification is predefined in purchase order contents or in terms and conditions. Planned cost is predefined with vendor upon custom clearing, freight forwarding or loading unloading etc.

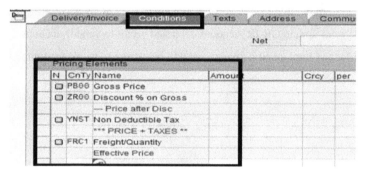

Figure 8-3 (Purchase Order Screen, Conditions Tab)

Delivery cost that is not planned in purchase order and insert at the time of posting of an invoice called unplanned delivery cost. You must enter unplanned delivery cost at invoice document of logistics invoice verification (materials management). Unplanned delivery cost are split among all items of an invoice and posted to separate G/L accounts. There are vendor account, stock Account, GR/IR Account, price difference account and tax accounts are updated when it posting. Below screen shoot shows you unplanned delivery cost. It is enter in MIRO transaction under detail tab.

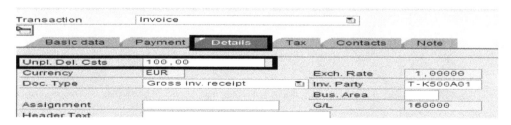

Figure 8-4 (Unplanned Delivery Cost in LIV)

Copyrighted© Material

8.3.1. Standard and Moving Average Price Impact (unplanned delivery cost)

If material having standard price and unplanned cost accrue, then at the time of goods receipts system update stock account debit and credit to GR IR account. At the time of posting an invoice system update the GR IR account, vendor account and difference between order and unplanned cost will be update at price difference account.

If a material having moving average price and unplanned delivery cost accrue, then at the time of goods receipts system debit the stock account and credit the GR IR account. At the time of posting an invoice system update GR IR Account debit and credit to vendor account. Difference between order and unplanned delivery cost will be charge to stock account.

Copyrighted© Material

8.4.   Logistics invoicing plan

The invoice plan is helpful tool in SAP MM in which you can use for post invoice entry on predefine dates and amounts. Invoice plan is independent from goods receipts or service entry sheets. In invoice plans, invoices are created automatically with predefine mention time on PO. In this scenario invoices will generates without receiving vendor invoices with schedule dates and once release the invoice payment will be made done.

It is mostly use for non-stock material and helpful to user department because user did not wait each and every time for vendor invoice against its work (goods or services) and will be proactively payment schedule. The invoicing plans are also reduce the data entry efforts where large number invoices consist of rent of buildings, houses, offices or leasing, utility bills. It is also use for project where company will negotiate with vendor payments on predefine dates.

There are two types of invoicing plans,

- Partial Invoicing plans
- Periodic invoicing plans

8.4.1.   Partial Invoicing Plan

In partial invoicing plan, total purchase order amount divide into individual dates of logistics invoicing. It is use for high value material as well as projects includes procurement of external services. For example you want to construct a (project) building or offices. Total value of construction of building is USD 50000 $. You have agreement with your vendor 20% payment after each stage. There are five stages of project. You can plan invoices accordingly.

8.4.2.   Periodic Invoicing Plan

In periodic invoicing plan the total amount of purchase order is invoice on due dates. It is use for periodic logistics invoices transactions. For example, your company buys a Trailer for material transportation on lease as total worth US 50000 $. Your company pay lease installments on each month or particular due date. So you can plan invoices accordingly.

Copyrighted© Material

8.4.3. Pre-Requisite for invoicing plan

1. In vendor Master data AutoEvalGRSetmt Del. Indicator must be set
2. Tax code and payment terms predefine in PO
3. ERS and IR check box enable in PO invoice tab.
4. Account assignment is mandatory
5. Goods Receipts and GR non-valuated check box enable or not in PO delivery Tab
6. Suggested PO type as Framework Order

For more detail you can consider following detail

In vendor master, vendor purchasing data must be set following indicators

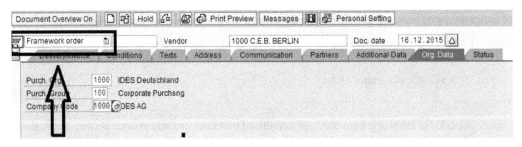

Figure 8-5 (Pre-requisite for Invoicing Plan)

Enter PO document types as Framework order

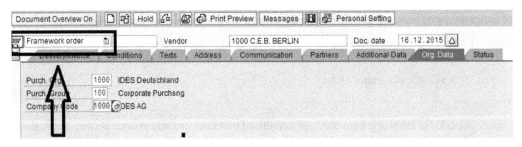

Figure 8-6 (Document Type Framework Order, Initial Screen of Purchase Order)

Enter the validity start and validity end period in PO additional data tab

225
Copyrighted© Material

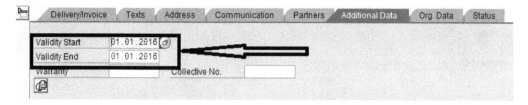

Figure 8-7 (Validity Start and End Period, Additional Data Tab)

Insert account assignment K as cost center or relevant as requires

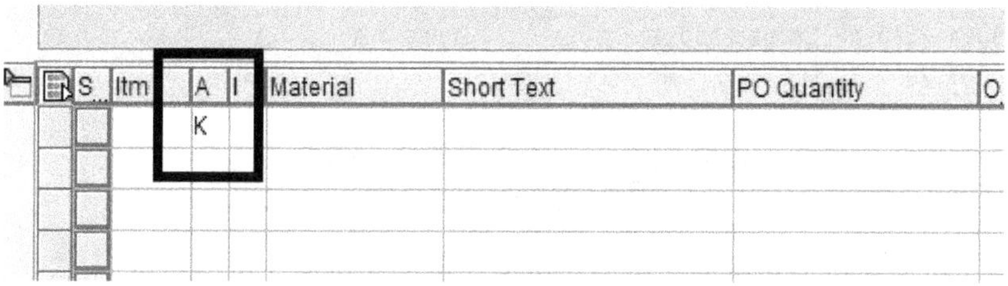

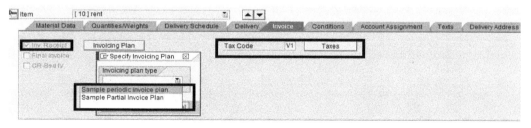

Figure 8-8 (Account Assignment Category)

Goods Receipts and *GR non-valuated* check box enable or not in PO delivery Tab

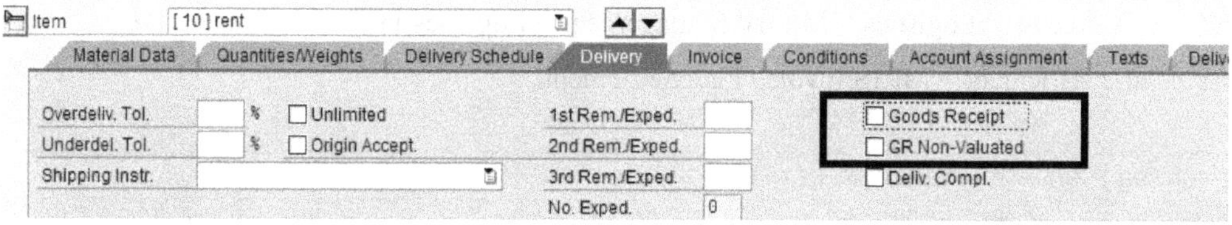

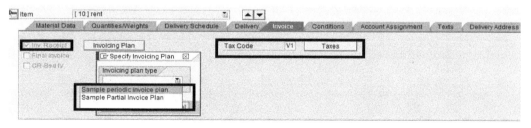

Figure 8-9 (Goods Receipts and GR Non-valuated Check Box)

Tax code and payment terms predefine in PO invoice tab

Figure 8-10 (Specific Invoicing Plan)

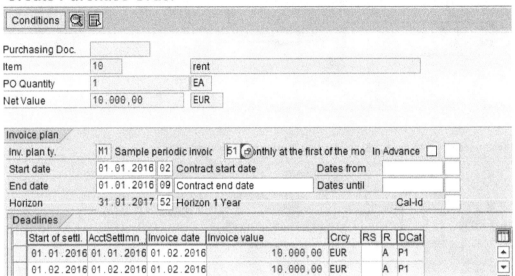

Create Purchase Order

Conditions

Purchasing Doc.		
Item	10	rent
PO Quantity	1	EA
Net Value	10.000,00	EUR

Invoice plan

Inv. plan ty.	M1 Sample periodic invoic	51 Monthly at the first of the mo In Advance ☐
Start date	01.01.2016 02 Contract start date	Dates from
End date	01.01.2016 09 Contract end date	Dates until
Horizon	31.01.2017 52 Horizon 1 Year	Cal-Id

Deadlines

Start of settl.	AcctSettlmn	Invoice date	Invoice value	Crcy	RS	R	DCat
01.01.2016	01.01.2016	01.02.2016	10.000,00	EUR		A	P1
01.02.2016	01.02.2016	01.02.2016	10.000,00	EUR		A	P1

Figure 8-11 (Create Purchase Order Screen, Invoicing Plan)

In logistics invoice verification, the automatic receipts settlements will be made on MRIS transaction code or by SAP Manu path

SAP Easy Access > Logistics > Martial Management > Logistics invoice verification > Automatic settlement > MRIS Invoice Plan Settlement

Invoicing Plan Settlement with Logistics Invoice Verification

Document Selection

Company Code	1000	to		
Plant	1000	to		
Vendor		to		
Purchasing Document	4500012345	to		
Item		to		

Figure 8-12 (Invoicing Plan Settlement)

Copyrighted© Material

8.5. Park and Hold Logistics Invoice document

8.5.1. Hold Invoice Document

At the time of posting logistics invoice verification, SAP system creates two documents. First document will be relevant to materials management and second document will be created on Financial accounting relevant. You can hold invoice data on temporary basis only in Material Management document. When you hold document in current status only MM document will be created.

There will be no impact on financial accounting transaction. Latterly when you complete rest of information in hold document, then you will post hold document. At the time of hold of logistics invoice document system only checks some parameters like vendor and company code. With holding of invoice document there will be no updating in purchase order history. You can check purchase order history in PO screen item detail under purchase order history tab.

8.5.2. Park Invoice Document

At the time of creating logistics invoice document, if you have missing some information regarding document amount, currency, date, tax information or balance data etc. you use park function. In logistics invoice verification you can also park subsequent debit, subsequent credit and credit memo documents as well.

You can park invoice documents in following situations like some time information not complete, sometime junior operator park an invoice document but latterly senior person check concern park document, make necessary changes in it if required then post invoice document. It will be beneficial for senior for reduce burden of data entry. Some time there is major amount differences accrue in balance of invoice document and you wait to get complete information of amount.

When you park the invoice document system create two documents, first is relevant to materials management and second document relevant to financial accounting. Another words,

Copyrighted© Material

accounting transaction will be made and accounts will be update. There are also update purchase order history. You can also change the hold document status with park document.

For Document Parking, you can follow the Manu path

SAP Easy Access Logistics > Materials Management > Logistics Invoice Verification >Document Entry > Park invoice or Transaction code MIR7

You can also go to transaction MIRO Logistics invoice verification screen by choose edit and switch to document parking for directly access document parking screen. You can fill up complete information in park document and click on save as completed document button.

Figure 8-13 (Change Park Invoicing Document)

Save as completed option will be use when balance will be zero and all necessary and mandatory information fill up in invoice screen. There will be update in the purchase order history, accounting and controlling documents, open vendor item in park document as well as index for duplicate invoice checking. As previously discuss logistics invoice document having header data and item data. When we delete park document, system remain save information of header data for evidence but delete item detail data from data base.

There is moreover utility of work list in logistics invoice verification (MIRO) screen. In utility function you can call your hold, park and save documents for further process.

Copyrighted© Material

Figure 8-14 (Worklist Button)

After clicking the show work list button, you can view the following

Figure 8-15 (Worklist)

Copyrighted© Material

8.6. Invoice in foreign currency

Some time you procure a material or services from another country which currency is differ from your local currency for your company code. If you want to enter invoice in foreign currency, then following settings must be take into account

- Configure invoice currency if not in your system
- Configure Exchange rates in customizing for that currency for different time frames

Sometime during creation of purchase order your purchaser know about the currency and exchange rate differences may be accrue, for this scenario you can check the box exchange rate differences on purchase order header screen delivery/invoice tab.

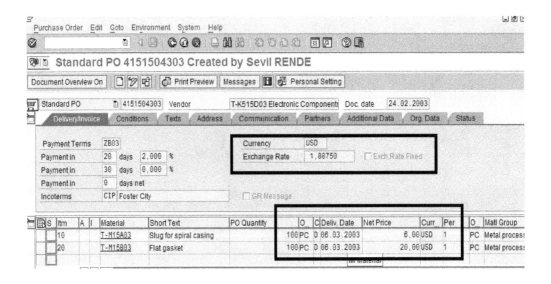

Figure 8-16(Invoice in foreign currency)

In above scenario your company code currency is Euro (EUR). You procure material from another country which currency is USD. Under the delivery/invoice tab you mention currency and exchange rate of current period. The buyer of material also decides exchange rate is fix or not and accordingly check the indicator of Exchange Rate Fixed mention above. If it is fixed, then goods receipts and invoice receipts will be post accordingly.

Copyrighted© Material

If you don't check the Exchange Rate Fixed indicator mention above, system creates accounting transaction in goods receipts and invoice receipts with current exchange rate. During Logistics invoice verification, system also suggest current exchange rate so you can also change it accordingly.

Copyrighted© Material

8.7. Stochastic Block and Manual Block of Invoice

In your live production environment, if you want to check logistics invoices on random basis as well as on sample basis then you have option to enable settings of stochastic block of invoices. For doing this there are some necessary settings will be required in SAP customizing for example,

- *Stochastic block indicator must be set in customizing*

  For active stochastic block indicator go to customizing under SPRP > Materials Management > Logistics Invoice Verification > invoice block > Stochastic block > Active Stochastic Block

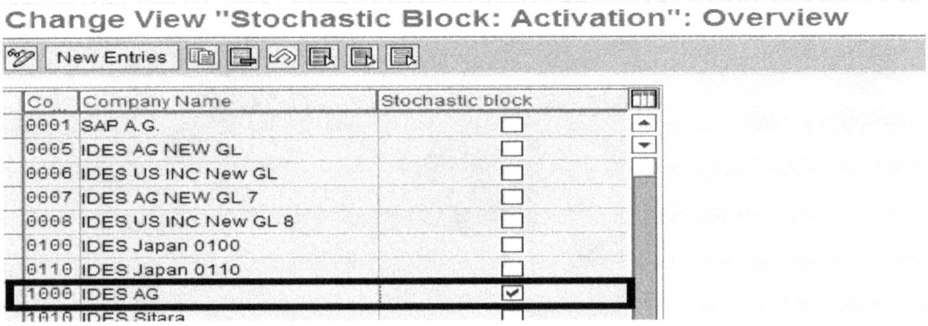

Figure 8-17 (Active Stochastic Block Indicator)

Copyrighted© Material

- *There should must be enable threshold value as well as percentage for invoice*

  For enable threshold value and percentage go to customizing under SPRP > Materials Management > Logistics Invoice Verification > Invoice block > Stochastic block > Set Stochastic Block

Change View ""Stochastic Block: Values"": Overview

Co	Company Name	Threshold value	Currency	Percentage	
0001	SAP A.G.		EUR		
0005	IDES AG NEW GL	3.067,75	EUR	50,00	
0006	IDES US INC New GL	6.000,00	USD	50,00	
0007	IDES AG NEW GL 7	3.067,75	EUR	50,00	
0008	IDES US INC New GL 8	6.000,00	USD	50,00	
0100	IDES Japan 0100		JPY		
0110	IDES Japan 0110		JPY		
1000	IDES AG	50000	EUR	50,00	
1010	IDES Sitara		PKR		
1974	imran butt		PKR		

Figure 8-18 (Enable Threshold Value and Percentage)

As per above customizing settings shows threshold value of company code 1000 is 50,000 (EUR) and percentage of against threshold value is 50%. It allow you invoices are grated than 50000 having probability to blocks 50%. If you set zero as threshold value then degree of probability will be same for all invoices. If you set zero as threshold value and percentage is 99.99% result will be all invoices blocked.

You can also block manually of an invoices both at header level as well as item level in logistics invoice verification screen (MIRO). For header level blocking, go to the payment tab at header of an invoice and set block for payment. It will be block total invoice.

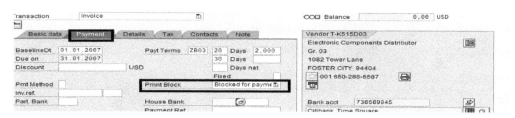

Figure 8-19 (Manually Block for Payment)

Copyrighted© Material

For blocking of invoice at item level you can go to item detail section and set MA indicator.

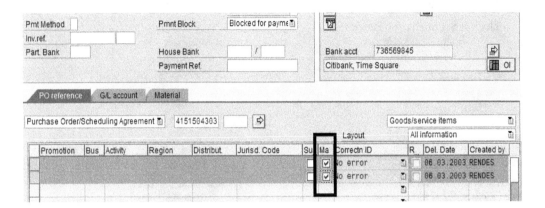

Figure 8-20 (Blocking of Invoice at Item Level)

Copyrighted© Material

8.8. Invoice Reduction

Invoice reduction is used to correct errors. Error related to price variance and quantity variance in vendor invoice. For doing this, you use layout of invoice reduction for posting logistics invoice. In logistics invoice verification screen (MIRO Transaction) item level, you must use tool vendor error: invoice reduction.

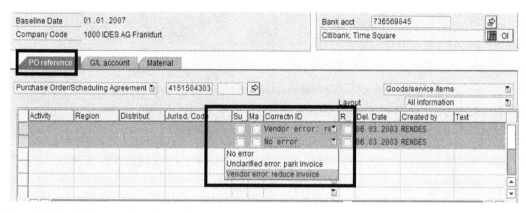

Figure 8-21 (Vendor Error: Invoice Reduction)

At the time of posting of logistics invoice there will be two documents post, first document is relevant to accounting and second document will be relevant to difference amount and quantity as credit memo. In SAP there is a clearing account for invoice reduction so entry of difference is hit on this account. For viewing, go to OBYC Transaction and see

Maintain FI Configuration: Automatic Posting - Procedures

Group   RMK   Materials Management postings (MM)

Procedures

Description	Transaction	Account determ.
Cost (price) differences (mater.ledger)	PRY	☑
Expense/revenue from revaluation	RAP	☑
Inv.reductions from log.inv.verification	RKA	☑
Neutral provisions	RUE	☑

Figure 8-22 (Transaction Key in Automatic Account Determination)

Copyrighted© Material

Here you can view GL account or configure or change as per requirement

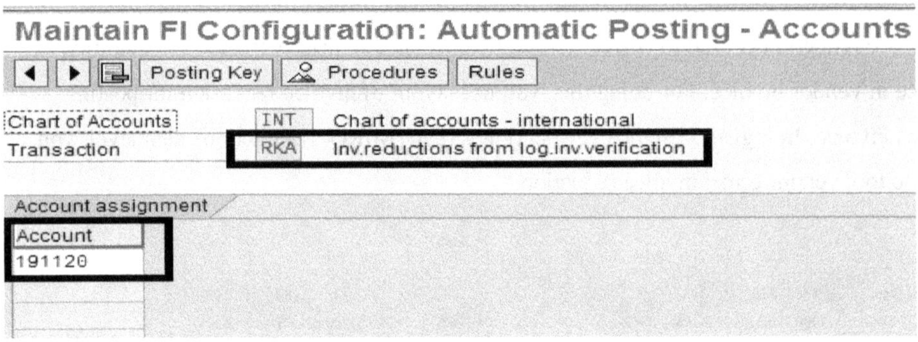

Maintain FI Configuration: Automatic Posting - Accounts

◀ ▶ 🖳 | Posting Key | 👤 Procedures | Rules

| Chart of Accounts | INT | Chart of accounts - international |
| Transaction | RKA | Inv.reductions from log.inv.verification |

Account assignment
Account
191120

Figure 8-23 (GL Account for Difference Posting)

In purchase order history, there is also update with all documents after posting e.g. goods receipts documents, invoice documents as well as credit memos. Clearing account of Invoice reduction clear with credit memo and its offsetting entry will hit on vendor account. Tax of the document is as per your process and you decide whether it is posting in original document or not. The credit memo also corrects the tax posting.

For decision, go to SAP Easy Access Screen

SPRO > Materials Management > Logistics Invoice Verification > Incoming Invoice > Tax Treatment in Invoice reduction

Change View "Tax Treatment in Invoice Reduction": Overview

✏️ | New Entries | 🗐 🗐 🗐 🗐 🗐 🗐

Tax Treatment in Invoice Reduction

Co	Name	Tax for invoice reduction	
0001	SAP A.G.	Tax reduction in complaint dc	▲
0005	IDES AG NEW GL	Tax reduction in complaint dc	▼
0006	IDES US INC New GL	Tax reduction in complaint dc	
0007	IDES AG NEW GL 7	Tax reduction in complaint dc	
0008	IDES US INC New GL 8	Tax reduction in complaint dc	
0100	IDES Japan 0100	Tax reduction in complaint dc	
0110	IDES Japan 0110	Tax reduction in complaint dc	
1000	IDES AG	Tax reduction in complaint dc	
1010	IDES Sitara	Tax reduction in complaint document	
1974	imran butt	Tax reduction in original document	
2000	IDES UK		

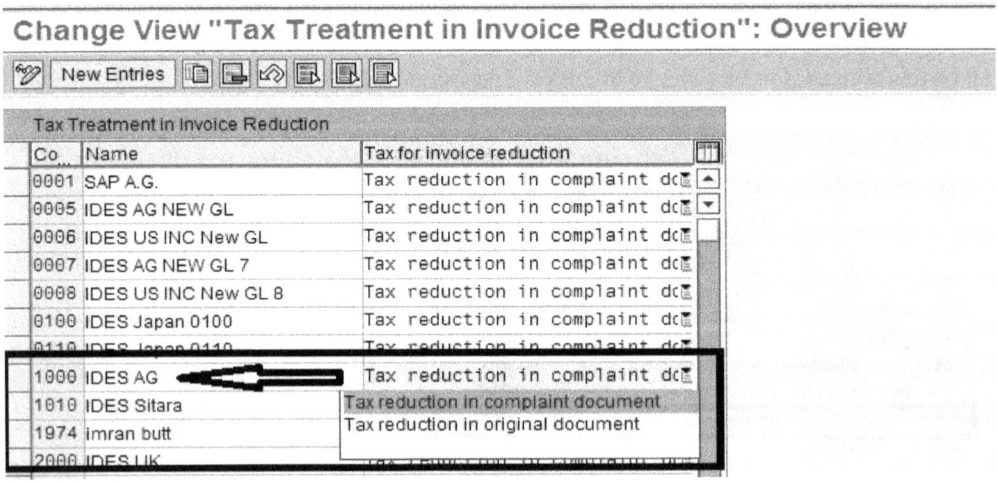

Figure 8-24 (Tax Treatment in Invoice Reduction)

Copyrighted© Material

- *Tax reduction in complement document:* the tax amount of the invoice reduction credit in complement document.

- *Tax reduction in original document:* in this case the complement document does not contain any tax posting.

For more understanding, we have example

We have Purchase Order 10 Pcs at 1 Rs/pc

Goods Receipt against PO is 7 Pcs

Invoice 10 Pcs @ 1.2 Rs/ Pc =12

Tax @ = 1 Rs

So at the time of goods receipts

Debit (Rs)	Credit (Rs)
Stock A/C 7	
	GR/IR A/C 7

Table 8-1 (Tax Treatment During Goods Receipts)

At the time of Invoice

Debit (Rs)	Credit (Rs)
GR/IR A/C @ 7	
Stock Account @ 1.4	
Tax Account @ 1.2	
Clearing Account for Invoice Reduction @ 3.6	
	Vendor Account @ (13.20)

Table 8-2 (Tax Treatment during Invoice)

System create credit memo simultaneously and entries will be

Debit (Rs)	Credit (Rs)
Vendor Account @ 3.96	
	Clearing account for invoice reduction @ (3.6)
	Tax account @ (0.36)

Table 8-3 (Credit Memo Entry)

Copyrighted© Material

8.9.   Cancelations in Materials Management

In your company, Sometime SAP users perform wrong entries in system. Wrong entries may be at the time of creation of Purchase requisition, Request for quotation, Purchase order, and goods receipts or may be at the time of goods issuance (against cost center, against project or internal order) or logistics invoice verifications. Wrong entries may because of wrong materials insert in document, wrong date, wrong amount in document, wrong conditions or may be wrong document types etc.

Most of the companies start their procurement process from Purchase requisition, then create request for quotation with reference to purchase requisition, then purchase order with reference to Purchase requisition or can be directly with Request for quotation (according to their process), then goods receipts (with 101 movement type or may be with 103 or 105 movement type etc.). Then goods issuance or logistics invoice verification. So documents cancelation is depend upon procurement process.

If your procurement process till end up to logistics invoice verification and you find that PR is wrongly create with any mistake (may be consist of PR Date, Wrong Material etc.). Mistake may be at the time creation of purchase order (wrong vendor, wrong plant, wrong purchase organization or may be document type etc.). So at this scenario if your procurement process till end with logistics invoices verification, you required cancelation of documents.

First you cancel that document which is created at the end of process. For example, first cancelation will be consist of logistics invoice verification, then goods receipts documents (101 Mvt or 105 and 103), then corrections of purchase order if mistake is happen at this stage, if not then delete the purchase order, then correct the purchase requisition.

Note: *PO date, PO vendor and Purchase order document type cannot be change; because of the SAP standard system did not allow change of following three after saving the document.*

Copyrighted© Material

Let's suppose, you have mistakenly/wrong enter material at the time of creation of purchase requisition, suppose your procurement process till end up to logistics invoice verification and followings documents create with in this process

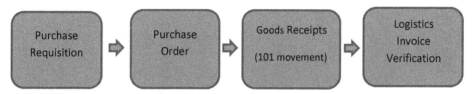

Figure 8-25 (Procurement Process Flow)

You want to cancel all documents that are entering wrongly in SAP system. So cancelation sequence will be as follows

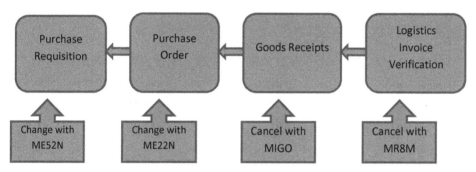

Figure 8-26 (Cancelation Process Flow)

Copyrighted© Material

8.9.1. Cancelation of logistics Invoice verification document

For cancelation of logistics invoice verification document, follow the Manu path

Go to SAP Easy Access > Logistics > Materials Management > Logistics Invoice Verification > Further Processing > Cancel Invoice Document or directly go to transaction code MR8M.

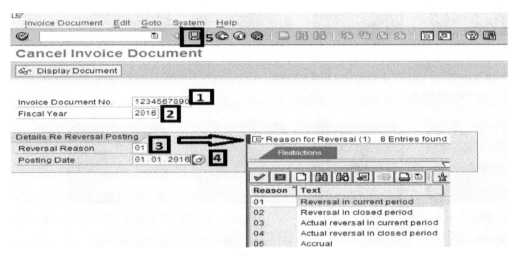

Figure 8-27 (Cancel Invoice Document)

When you cancel the logistics invoice document, system reverses the entry that was just create against this document number e.g. at the time of posting of invoice. System perform entries as

Debit	Credit
GR IR Account	
	Vendor Account

Figure 8-28 (Accounting Entries during Invoice)

At the time of cancelation, system perform following entries

Debit	Credit
Vendor Account	
	GR IR Account

Figure 8-29 (Accounting Entries during Reversal of Invoice)

Copyrighted© Material

8.9.2. Cancelation of Inventory Management Document

For cancelation of inventory management document follow the Manu path

Go to SAP Easy Access > Logistics > Materials Management > Inventory Management >Goods Movement > MIGO - Goods Movement (MIGO)

In MIGO screen select transactions' as cancelation and reference document as Material document number and click on execute button after giving reason in header text field. Insert document and posting date, check box of concern items and then click on post button.

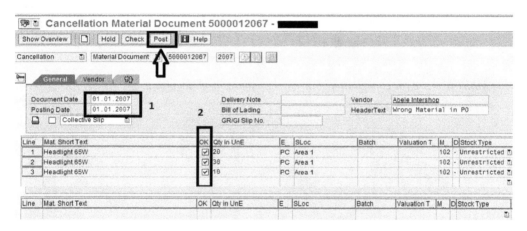

Figure 8-30 (Cancelation of Material Document)

Copyrighted© Material

When you cancel the inventory management document, system reverses the entry that was just create against this document number e.g. at the time of posting of inventory management document. System perform entries as

Debit	Credit
Material/ Stock Account	
	GR/IR Account

Table 8-4 (Accounting Entries during Goods Receipts)

At the time of reversal of inventory management document, system will act as follows

Debit	Credit
GR/IR Account	
	Material/ Stock Account

Table 8-5 (Accounting Entries during Goods Receipts Reversal)

Note: MBST also use for cancelation of inventory management document

Copyrighted© Material

8.10. Difference between Cancelations and Rejections (Movement types)

8.10.1. Cancelation:

Cancelation of document will be perform due to wrong material, document date, document type, wrong plant, wrong purchasing organization etc. insert in purchasing document. Cancelations are fully different with rejections. At the time of cancelation of inventory management documents (e.g. Goods Issuance, Goods Receipts and Transfer posting documents etc.) you select transaction as cancelation and reference document as material document which is you want to cancel (MIGO transaction).

Every goods movement consists of movement type. Movement type shows where the goods are moved (block stock, quality inspection or unrestricted stock etc.). As earlier mention movement type consist of 3 digits key. For example, 261 movement type shows goods issue against order, 201 shows goods issue against cost center 101 shows goods receipts against purchase order etc. when you cancel any document system will reverse document with next movement type. For example, 101 inventory management document cancel with 102, 201 documents cancel with 202 movement type, similarly transfer posting material to material will be post 309 movement type and its cancelation with 310 etc. system automatically select reversal movement type at the time of cancelation.

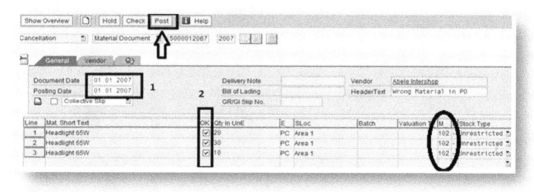

Figure 8-31 (Cancelation of Material Document)

Copyrighted© Material

Usually rejection in inventory management document because of vendor send wrong material, wrong quality, wrong quantity or wrong material characteristics etc. or may be any other reason. If u wants to reject the material with any reason you need a reference document. You can go to MIGO transaction and insert transition as Return delivery and reference document as material document. Following figure shows material rejections against movement types.

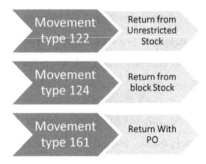

Figure 8-32 (Rejection Movement Types)

8.11. Delivery completion indicator in PO

If you select delivery completion indicator in purchase order, system consider all open quantity of concern PO mark zero (whether all quantity of PO is open or partial quantity is open) or concern item consider as closed. System will consider all deliveries related to this purchase order have been completed or no more goods receipts are expected. You can manually select this

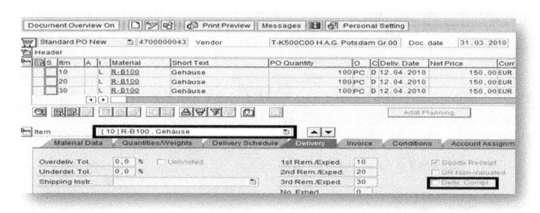

Figure 8-33 (Delivery Completion Indicator in PO)

indicator in PO screen in item detail under the delivery tab, at the time of goods receipts in MIGO transaction as well as SAP system automatically mark this indicator when all deliveries arrive and completed of concern purchase order according to SAP system.

It is possible, there are under and over delivery tolerances set in purchase order. A customizing in SAP can be maintained in the following section to control what scenario the delivery completion indicator is set. For settings go to

Copyrighted© Material

SPRO > Materials Management > Inventory Management and Physical Inventory > Goods Receipts > Set Delivery Completed Indicator

Change View "Default: "Delivery-Completed" Indicator": Overview

Plant	Name 1	Del. compl. default	
0001	🔲rk 0001	☑	▲
0005	Hamburg	☑	▼
0006	New York	☐	
0007	Werk Hamburg	☑	
0008	New York	☐	
1000	Werk Hamburg	☑	
1100	Berlin	☑	

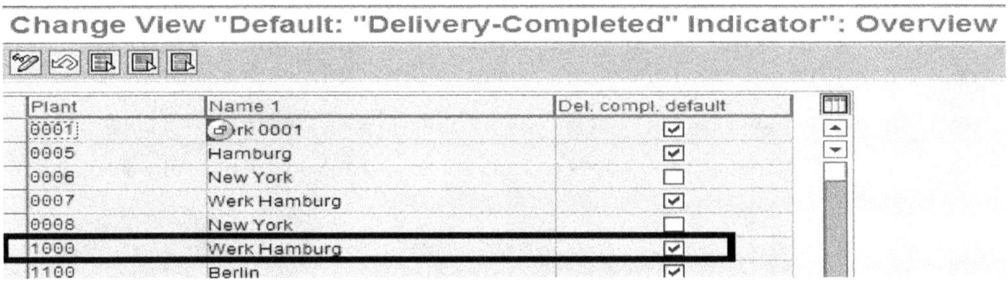

Figure 8-34 (Delivery Completed Indicator at Plant)

Delivery completion indicator is set in customizing at each plant level. If this indicator is set at plant level in customizing as seen above, SAP system automatically suggest inward delivery completion indicator for goods receipts if the deliver quantity fall within the over delivery tolerances. For further detail we have example,

PO = 1000 Units

Plant = 1000

Over Delivery tolerances = 5%

      a. If the flag is not set in customizing setting for plant 1000, Delivery completion indicator will be set when deliver quantity reaches the tolerances (e.g. 1050 quantity)

      b. If flag is set in customizing setting for plant 1000, delivery completion indicator will be set when the total quantity reaches the order quantity (e.g. 1000)

Copyrighted© Material

Copyrighted© Material

Chapter 9:

Release Strategies in Procurement Documents

Copyrighted© Material

9. Chapter: Release Strategies in Procurement Documents

9.1.   Release Strategies in Procurement Documents

9.2.   Preparation of required objects for Release Strategy in SAP

   9.2.1.   Configuration of Characteristics and Class for Release strategy

   9.2.2.   Define Release Strategy for Purchase Order

Copyrighted© Material

9.1. Release Strategies in Procurement Documents

The release strategies in (SAP MM) procurement documents are approval hierarchy of both internal (Purchase requisition e.g.) and external documents (Purchase order). Your company consists of large number of people who are responsible for buying goods and services from market from different suppliers. These buyers are creating number of purchase orders on daily basis and their Supervisors and Managers are supervising this procurement on daily basis. As already discuss purchase order is a legal and external document of your company that send to suppliers for particular procurement. So it is necessary to control this document because lots of cost errors and frauds may be accruing in this document. For control of purchase order as well as internal documents like purchase requisition recommends you release strategies in procurement. You can implement release strategies on Request for quotation, purchase requisition, contracts and purchase orders. All are having same basis concept of configuration. In this lesson you will learn and implement only the release strategy in purchase order.

The configuration of release strategies in purchase order consist of

Release Characteristics
Release Class
Assign Characteristics to Class
Release Group
Release Code
Release indicators
Setting Release strategies
Work flow assignment or assign release code to respective user

Release strategies can be with classification and without classification. Release strategy with classification will be implementing on header level of purchasing document e.g. document type, total value of purchase order etc. Release strategy without classification is implementing on item level e.g. value of line item etc.

Copyrighted© Material

When release strategy with classification will implement in PO at header level, the new release strategy tab will appear on header and similarly when release strategy implement at item level, release strategy tab will be showing on item detail section of PO for approvals.

After implementation of release strategy in procurement, process will be

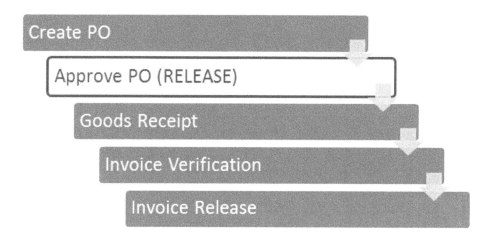

Figure 9-1 (Approval of Purchase Order)

Let's suppose in purchase order, approval hierarchy of your company is

- If the PO value is less than USD 100, buyer will approval authority

- If the PO value is 100 or greater, Manager/Director will approval authority

Note: In SAP Standard system, you can define release strategy up to maximum 8 levels. Above mention are only two levels.

9.2. Preparation of required objects for Release Strategy in SAP

Before are going to start configuring release strategy in system, we need to define the combination of parameters to trigger the release strategy. This criterion can be combination of the document type of purchase order, purchase order value, plant, purchasing organization, valuation type or purchase group etc. In SAP system we have run time structure with name CEKKO (communication release strategy determination purchasing document) which is provide

Copyrighted© Material

you all the maximum field using which release strategy can be configured with combinations and necessary requirements. You can view these fields of structure by using transaction SE12. Here you put your structure name CEKKO and click on display button. You can see more detail in below mention image screen

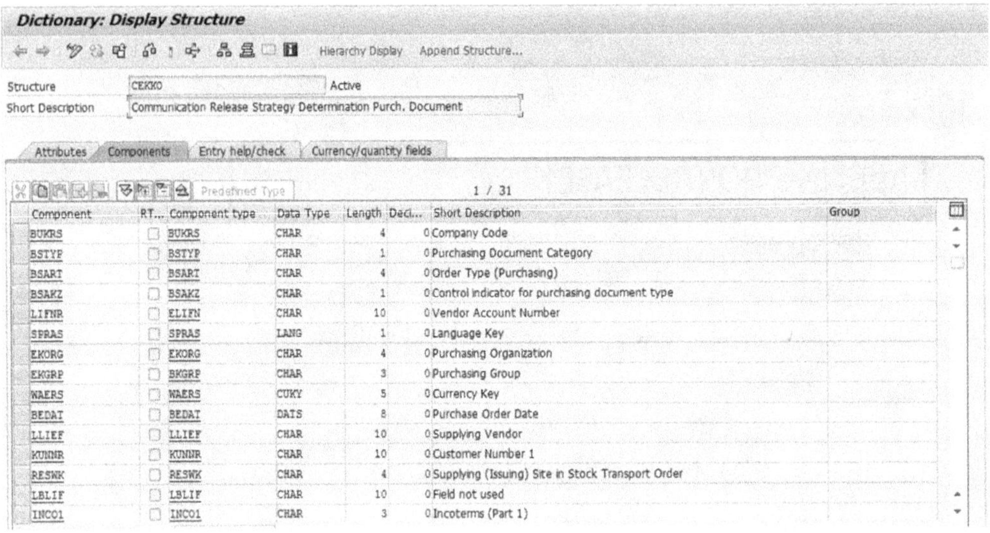

Figure 9-2 (Communication Release Strategy Determination Purchasing Document)

9.2.1. Configuration of Characteristics and Class for Release strategy

9.2.1.1. Creating Characteristics of each selected attributes

Let's assume we are configuring release strategy with the combination of three fields. The selected fields are document type (CEKKO - BSART), purchasing organization (CEKKO - EKORG) and total value of purchase order (CEKKO - GNETW). After that we need to create individual characteristics for each mention field. For doing this directly go to transaction code CT04 or under customizing SPRO-IMG > Material Management > Purchasing > Purchase Order > Release Procedure for Purchase Order

Here provide the name of characteristic and click on create characteristic button mention on screen. Here you give the name relevant to your characteristic that latterly identify easily for further configuration.

Copyrighted© Material

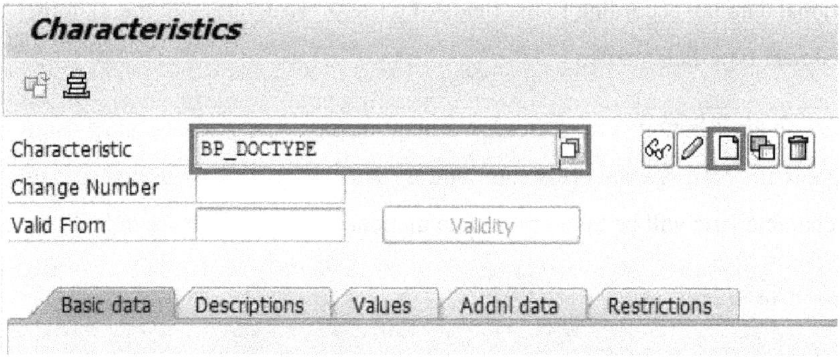

Figure 9-3 (Initial Data Screen of Characteristic)

In basic data screen, mention description of characteristic. In value tab, mention the technical name and description of document type. For document type characteristic, click on radio button of single value that is mention on value assignment area. If there are multiple document types, you must click on multiple value radio button on value assignment area.

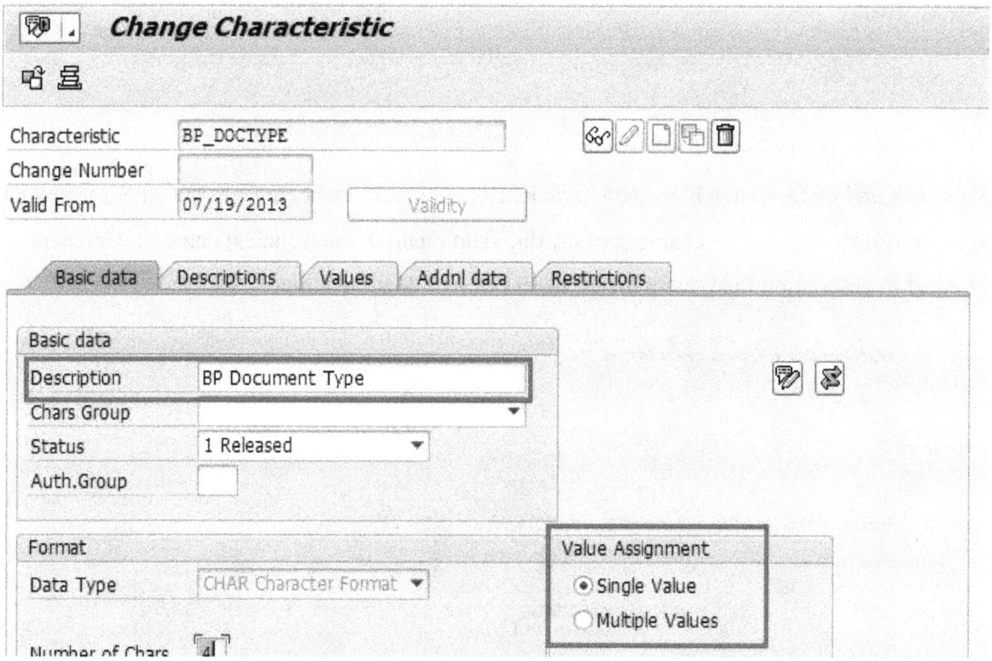

Figure 9-4 (Basic Data Tab Screen of Characteristic)

Copyrighted© Material

Now click on additional data tab according to the fields of CEKKO structure, you mention the table name and document type field name.

Note: when you click on enter button system create warning message "format data taken from data dictionary". Ignore the message and press enter button. The warning message specifies due to the data type of characteristic will be taken from data dictionary of this structure in SAP.

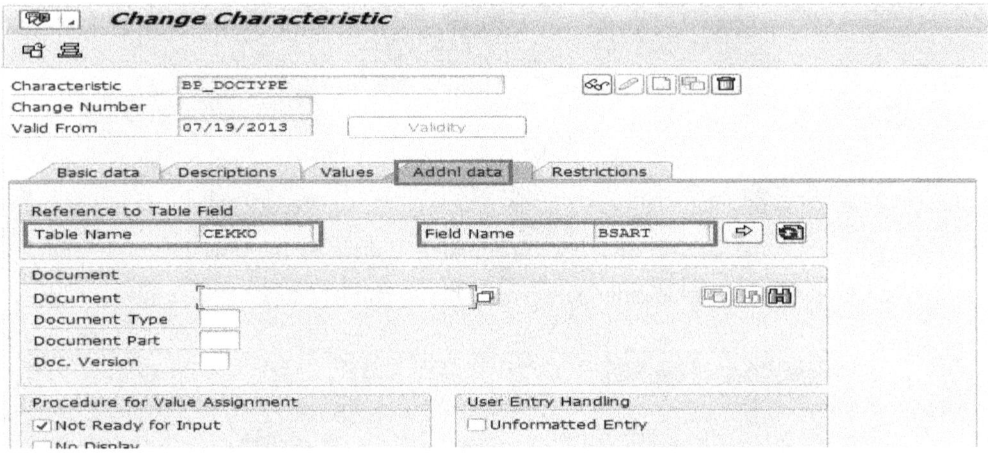

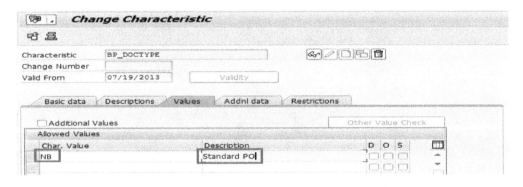

Figure 9-5 (Additional Data Tab Screen of Characteristic)

Now click and go to value tab in characteristic. Here mention the document type which you want to use in release strategy. In characteristic value field mention the technical name of document type and in description field, mention the description of document type.

Figure 9-6 (Values Data Tab Screen of Characteristic)

Copyrighted© Material

You make sure characteristic are used in release strategy class, for this purpose navigate to restrictions tab, here mention the class type 032 for release strategy and save the document type characteristic

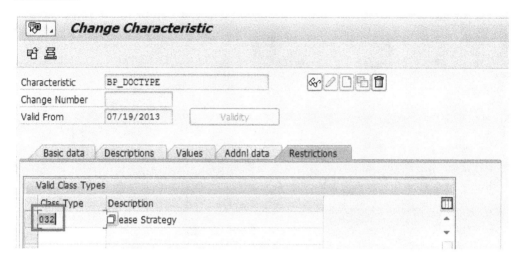

Figure 9-7 (Restriction Tab Screen of Characteristic)

Note: A same method is used for characteristic for purchasing organization.

In third characteristic purchase order net value, we need to follow the same steps except below mention

- In Additional Data tab structure name CEKKO and field name will be GNETW use for purchase order net value.
- Mention USD or relative currency for the characteristic.
- If you have multiple criteria for different range of values, the same has to be provided in value tab with a multiple value radio button tick in basic data tab screen.
- Since there is interval in the purchase order values, you must have to configure the characteristic to allow the values in intervals. For doing this you must tick on check box "Interval Vals allowed" in value assignment area mention in basic data screen tab. For example

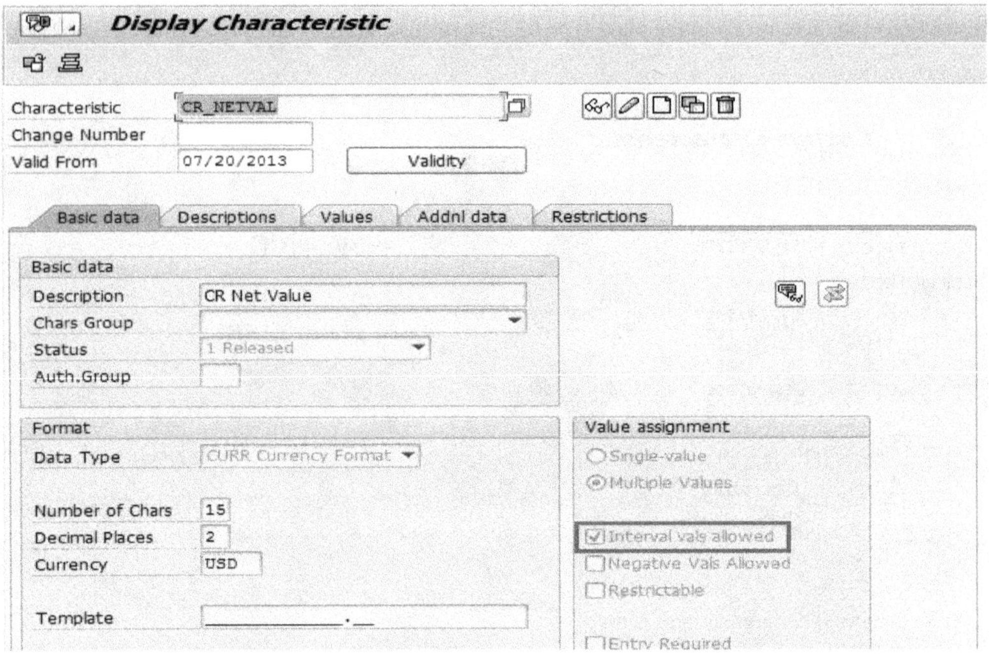

Characteristic	CR_NETVAL
Change Number	
Valid From	07/20/2013

Validity

Basic data | Descriptions | Values | Addnl data | Restrictions

Basic data

Description	CR Net Value
Chars Group	
Status	1 Released
Auth.Group	

Format

Data Type	CURR Currency Format
Number of Chars	15
Decimal Places	2
Currency	USD
Template	.

Value assignment

○ Single-value
◉ Multiple Values

☑ Interval vals allowed
☐ Negative Vals Allowed
☐ Restrictable

☐ Entry Required

Figure 9-8 (Characteristic Purchase Order Net Value Basic Tab Screen)

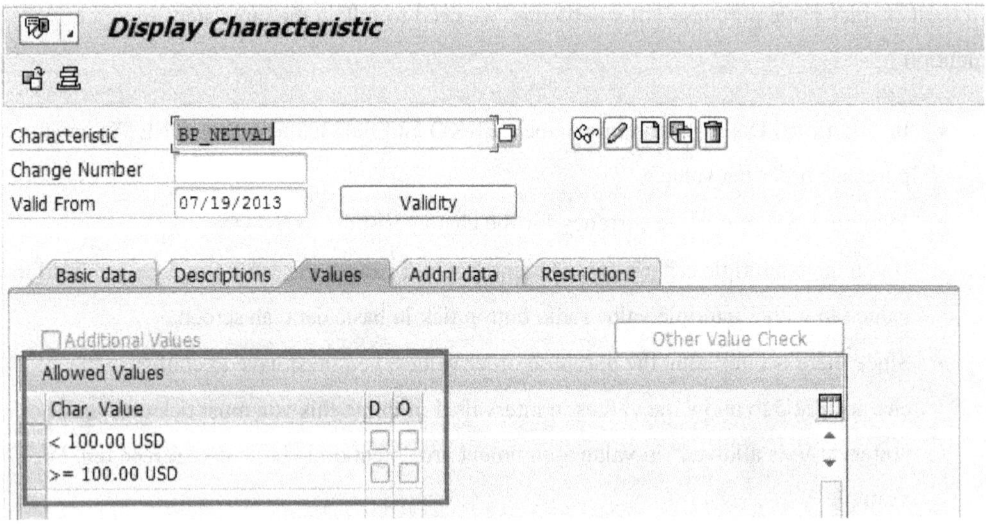

Display Characteristic

Characteristic	BP_NETVAL
Change Number	
Valid From	07/19/2013

Validity

Basic data | Descriptions | **Values** | Addnl data | Restrictions

☐ Additional Values

Other Value Check

Allowed Values

Char. Value	D	O
< 100.00 USD	☐	☐
>= 100.00 USD	☐	☐

Figure 9-9 (Allowed Values in Characteristic)

Now, you have created the following characteristic for release strategy

257
Copyrighted© Material

- BP_DOCTYPE for document type NB as standard purchase order

- BP_PURORG for purchasing organization BP01

- BP_NETVAL for net value below 100 USD and above 100 USD

9.2.1.2.   Creating Class for Purchase Order Release Strategy

For creating class for purchase order release strategy, go to transaction code CL02 or go to customizing SPRO-IMG > Material Management > Purchasing > Purchase Order > Release Procedures for Purchase Orders > Edit Class

In main screen of Class, provide appropriate name of class, mention class type 032 and click on create class button mention on below screen

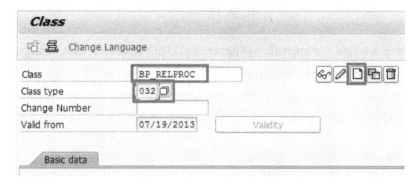

Figure 9-10 (Initial Screen of Class)

On new screen, provide the appropriate description of class used for release strategy and click on radio button *do ne check* mention on below screen

Copyrighted© Material

Change Class:

Change Language

Class	BP_RELPROC
Class type	032 Release Strategy
Change Number	
Valid from	07/19/2013 Validity

Basic data Keywords Char. Texts

Basic data

Description	BP Release Procedure for Purchase Order
Status	1 Released
Class group	
Organizational area	☐ Local class
Valid From	07/19/2013	Valid to	12/31/9999

Same classification		Authorizations	
⦿ Do not check		Class maintenance	
○ Warning message		Classification	
○ Check with error		Find object	

Figure 9-11 (Basic Data Screen of Class)

Now the next step is assign characteristic you just created to this class for release strategy. These characteristic are only restricted to class type 032 was mention at the time of creation of characteristic. For assignment, navigate to Char. Tab screen and insert characteristic names on different lines and press save button.

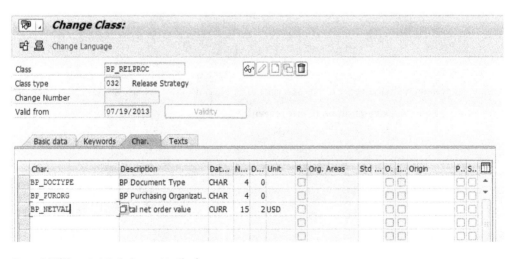

Change Class:

Change Language

Class	BP_RELPROC
Class type	032 Release Strategy
Change Number	
Valid from	07/19/2013 Validity

Basic data Keywords **Char.** Texts

Char.	Description	Dat...	N...	D...	Unit	R..	Org. Areas	Std ...	O.	I..	Origin	P..	S..
BP_DOCTYPE	BP Document Type	CHAR	4	0		☐			☐	☐		☐	☐
BP_PURORG	BP Purchasing Organizati...	CHAR	4	0		☐			☐	☐		☐	☐
BP_NETVAL	Total net order value	CURR	15	2	USD	☐			☐	☐		☐	☐
						☐			☐	☐		☐	☐
						☐			☐	☐		☐	☐

Figure 9-12 (Characteristic Assignment to Class)

Copyrighted© Material

9.2.2. Define Release Strategy for Purchase Order

After creating of characteristics, class and their assignments, the next step is to configure

- Release Groups

- Release Codes

- Release Indicator

- Release Strategy

9.2.2.1. Configuration of Release Groups

For configuration of release groups, go to customizing SPRO-IMG > Material Management > Purchasing > Purchase Order > Release Procedures for Purchase Orders > Click on Release Groups

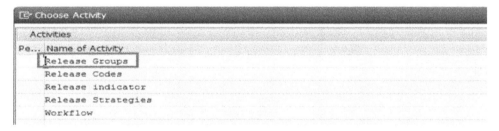

Figure 9-13 (Activates in Defining Release Strategy)

By double clicking on release groups, new screen will be appearing. Here you mention the release group name e.g. BP, mention class name you just created and press save button.

Change View "Release Groups: External Purchasing Document": Overview

New Entries   BC Set: Change Field Values

Rel.Grp	Rel.Obj.	Class	Description
BP	2	BP_RELPROC	Rel. Strategy for PO

Figure 9-14 (Combine Release Group and Release Class)

Copyrighted© Material

9.2.2.2.   Configuration of Release Codes

You can configure new release codes in customizing SPRO-IMG > Material Management > Purchasing > Purchase Order > Release Procedures for Purchase Orders > Click on Release Codes

By double clicking on release codes option, new screen will appear. Here you maintain your release codes. These codes will be configuring according to level of your release strategy. Release codes are for example,

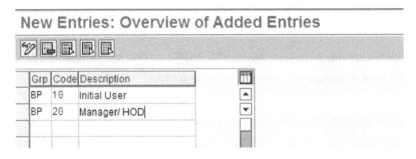

Figure 9-15 (Release Codes)

Copyrighted© Material

9.2.2.3. *Configuration of Release Indicator*

You can configure release indicator in customizing SPRO-IMG > Material Management > Purchasing > Purchase Order > Release Procedures for Purchase Orders > Click on Release Indicator

Release indicator specify whether purchasing document (purchase order or purchase requisition) can be process or blocked for follow on functions.

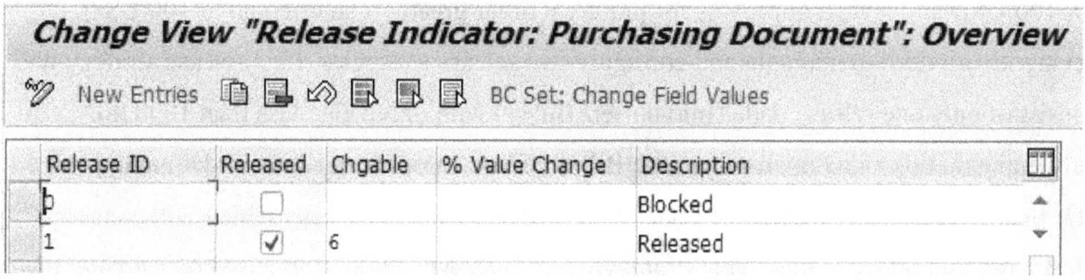

Figure 9-16 (Release Indicator)

Above mention screen specify release ID for initial status and release. Release ID 0 indicates status blocked and release ID 1 specify status released. The field changeable contain the parameter which will define how will system response if a procurement document is changed after the start of the release procedure. It means if your purchase order is release, you can also change its values that lead to change in new release status. If you allow changing in document, you have option to define the percentage of changes allowed.

9.2.2.4. *Configure Release Strategies*

You can configure new release strategy in customizing SPRO-IMG > Material Management > Purchasing > Purchase Order > Release Procedures for Purchase Orders > Click on Release Strategies

By clicking on release strategies option, system will propose you sub options to proceed further. Click on new entries button and specify the release group, key for release strategy and description of release strategy.

Copyrighted© Material

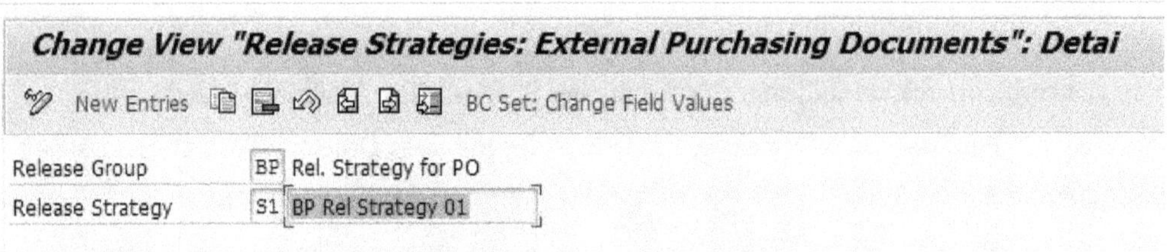

Figure 9-17 (Release Strategy Technical Name and Description)

Now suppose you want to carry on release strategy on one level only for your purchase order below 100 USD and level 2 approvals for purchase order greater than or equal to 100 USD. For achieving it, you need to maintain and configure two release strategies. First release strategy will be consist of only one release code (Initial user/ Buyer) with only value less than 100 USD. You already maintain this value in characteristic BP_NETVAL. For the purchase order having value greater than or equal to 100 USD, you need to create new release strategy which will consist of two level and two release codes. This strategy will trigger when your purchase order greater than or equal to 100 USD. Let's suppose we configure two-level release strategy which includes approvals from initial user/ buyer and Manager/ HOD.

On the change view of release strategy select release group, specify release strategy key and description. In release code area, mention your release codes as follows

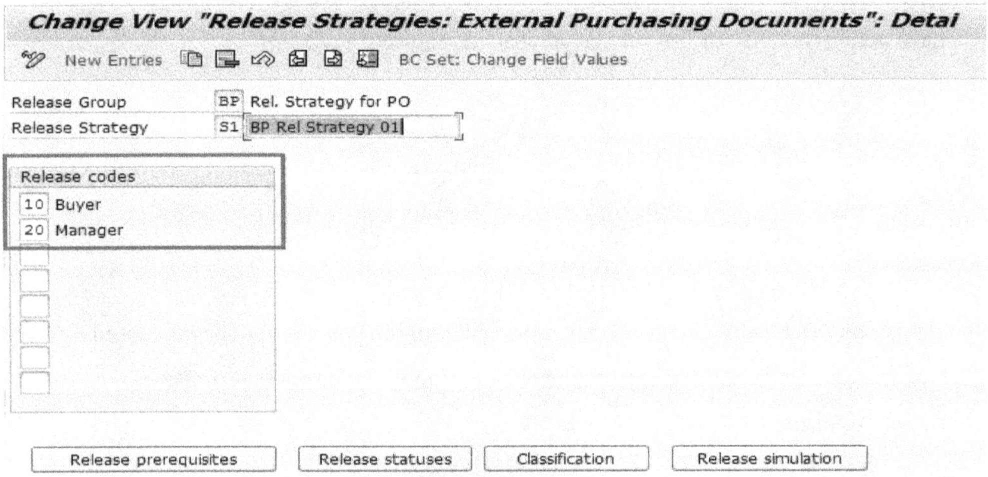

Figure 9-18 (Release Code Assignment)

Copyrighted© Material

After specifying the release codes, click on release prerequisites button for each release code. In below mention screen indicate that there is no pre requisite of release code 10 (Buyer) and 10 is pre requisite for release code 20 (Manager). By specifying it click on continue button.

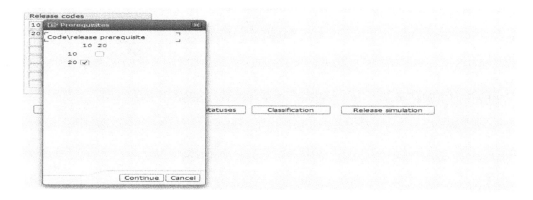

Figure 9-19 (Release Pre-Requisites)

The next step is to set release statuses, click on release statuses button mention below on screen. Here you can see release IDs for each. It specifies when the document is created and when both the release statuses are at initial condition.

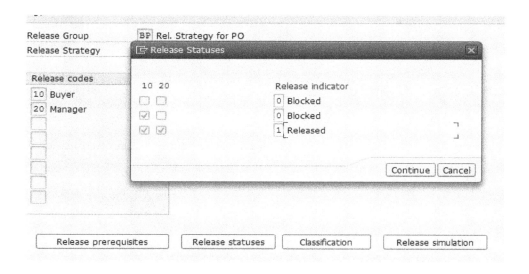

Figure 9-20 (Release Statuses)

Copyrighted© Material

When the first level of release of purchase order is carried out, it means when purchase order is released by initial user (Release code 10) than the overall status is still blocked for procurement. When the document is release by Manager (Release Code 20) than document overall status will be released. After this configuration, click on continue button.

Next step is to assignment of values of classification to release strategy. For doing this click on classification button

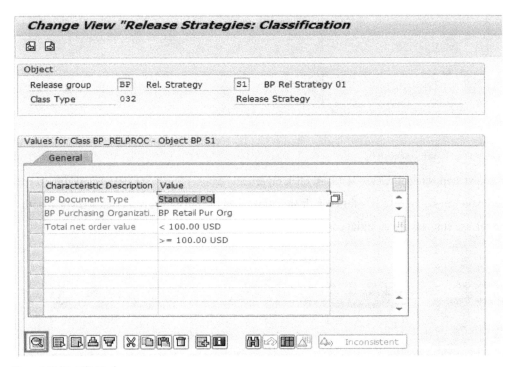

Figure 9-21 (Classification)

Here you need to mention required or necessary suitable values from all the characteristics. If you have multiple values in your characteristics, you select appropriate value which you want to consider in your release strategy. Select the characteristics row and click on choose button from bottom. It is also possible to directly mention characteristics values here provided additional values option is enable in your characteristic.

Copyrighted© Material

9.2.2.5. Configure your Work-Flow

You can configuration of work-low in customizing SPRO-IMG > Material Management > Purchasing > Purchase Order > Release Procedures for Purchase Orders > Click on work flow button

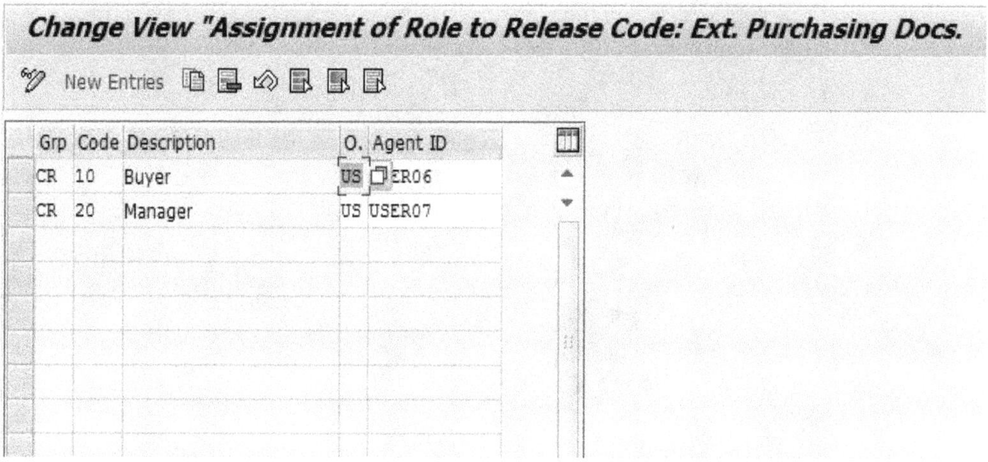

Figure 9-22 (Release Strategy Workflow)

Click on new entries button to create records for user involved in release strategy. Here you specify the release group, appropriate release codes and respective user IDs mention on agent ID column. Please make sure user IDs are specified in with agent type US which indicated that mention agent name is user ID of your SAP system. You must create each line for each user ID who are part of release procedure and should be attach to each release code.

Note: You have another option of authorization of release codes to user. For doing this, go to SU01 user maintenance screen and mention/ assign release code to appropriate role of that user under the material management section release codes.

Copyrighted© Material

Copyrighted© Material

Copyrighted© Material

Chapter 10:
Material Requirement Planning

Copyrighted© Material

10. Chapter 10: Material Requirement Planning

10.1.   Material Requirement Planning

   10.1.1.   MRP Profile

   10.1.2.   Consumption based planning

   10.1.3.   Planning calendar

   10.1.4.   Planning Processes

   10.1.5.   Planning Evaluation

   10.1.6.   Lot Size Calculation

   10.1.7.   Pre-requisites of Consumption Based Planning

   10.1.8.   Material Requirement planning procedures

   10.1.9.   Reorder Point Planning

   10.1.10.   Forecast Based Planning

   10.1.11.   Time Phase Planning

Copyrighted© Material

10.1. Material Requirement Planning (MRP)

The basic function of Material requirement planning is to ensure that raw material is always available for production and final product is complete for delivery. MRP monitor the stock of materials and generate procurement proposals for procurement as well production.

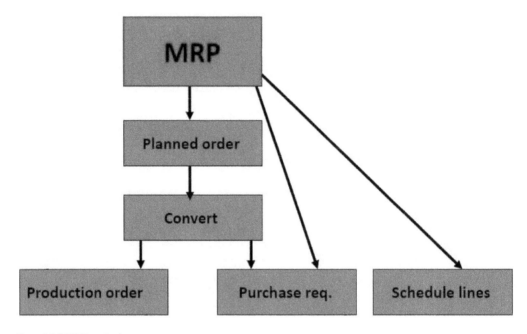

Figure 0-1 (MRP Overview)

MRP results suggest which material required for which quantity, which date, from what supplier and for which time. It is consider shortage conditions of stocks and generate procurement proposals/ elements. Likely procurement proposals are purchase requisitions, planned orders and scheduling agreements schedule lines. Planned orders and requisitions are internal proposals and we can change as per requirements and for in-house production system generates planned orders for production.

Copyrighted© Material

For external procurement you have option weather you create planned order or purchase requisition for external purchase quantities on the basis of creation indicator or MRP group in material master record. You can view it by transaction MD02 single item multilevel planning screen. For more detail you can see below mention image

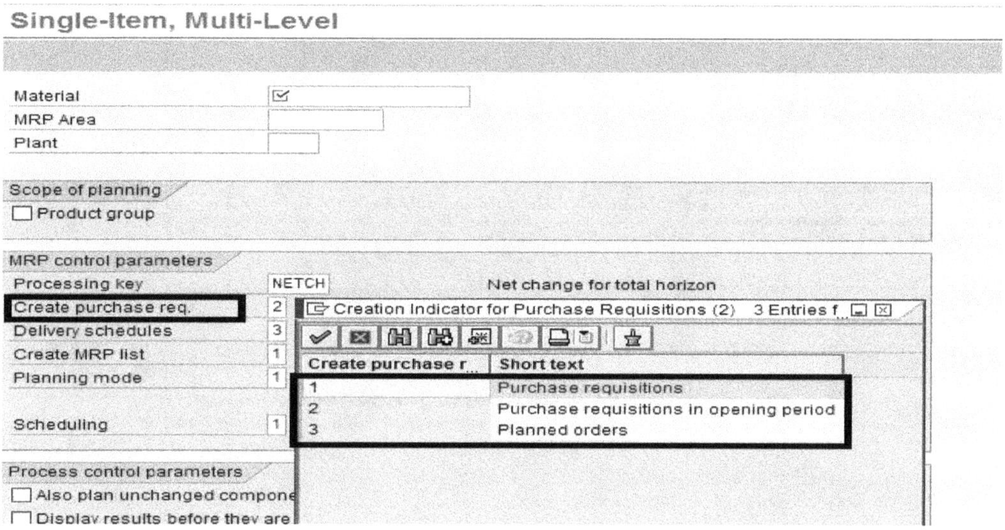

Figure 0-2 (MRP Run, Single Item Multilevel)

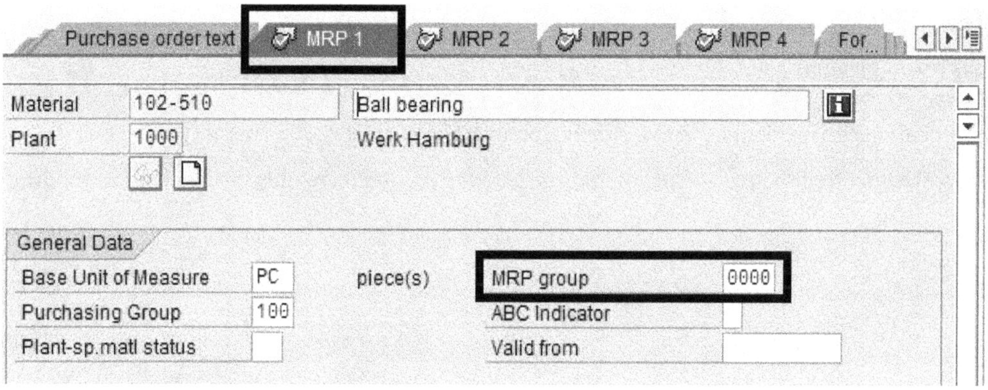

Figure 0-3 (MRP Group)

For change/display MRP group you can use transaction MM02/MM03 respectively.

Copyrighted© Material

When you have finished MRP planning, you must convert planned order into purchase requisition and for further processing these requisitions are converting into purchase orders. The creation indicators of schedule lines are select the initial screen of planning run as follows

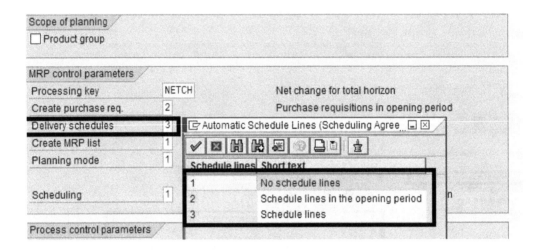

Figure 0-4 (Initial Screen of Planning Run, Delivery Schedules)

Plant parameters or a MRP groups control whether or not created schedule agreement schedule lines. If scheduling agreements exist for a material and it is indicated as MRP relevant in source list then it is also possible to create scheduling agreement schedule lines directly during material requirement planning run.

The procurement type defines in customizing on material attributes of material types. You can decide, whether to in-house production only or external procurement only or uses both as follows in customizing.

Copyrighted© Material

In MRP profile you can create your own predefine parameters or record for your MRP. Parameters may be MRP type, MRP controller, ABC Indicator, scheduling margin key, safety stock, reorder point, lot size and rounding values etc. It reduces the time efforts, error rate as well as data entry errors. In MRP profile you define which fields are filled with predefine values when MRP record is enter in master data, which values these fields have and which of these values can be overwritten and which one are not. You can give the name (4 digits) and description as per your own choice. You can create MRP Profile by transaction code MMD1 and assign the concern material in material master record of concern material. MRP profile creation screen mention below

Create MRP Profile: Selection Screen

ZMRP   Name of Profile   Test MRP for IDES

Checkboxes for MRP Profile
Selected fields will be   Write-protected   Only default value
copied to the profile   in matl maintenance   in matl maintenance

Field	Fixed val.	Default value
MRP Type	☐	☑
MRP Controller (Materials Plan	☐	☑
ABC Indicator	☑	☐
Planned Delivery Time in Days	☑	☐
In-house production time	☐	☑
Scheduling Margin Key for Floa	☐	☑
Dependent requirements ind. fo	☐	☑
Indicator for Requirements Gro	☑	☐
Safety Stock	☑	☐
Reorder Point	☑	☐
Lot size (materials planning)	☐	☑

Figure 0-5 (MRP Profile Initial Screen)

Go to Data Screen 1 button and put your default values for your MRP profile and save the profile. After creation of MRP Profile next step is assignment of your profile to material master record in MRP 2 screen by clicking on go to Main Menu > Edit > MRP Profile. Here you can assign the MRP profile to material master record.

Copyrighted© Material

10.1.2. Consumption based planning

In your company materials are consumed in daily productions, daily operations, on daily services or plant maintenances etc. for continuous replenishment of stock of materials you can follows the consumption based planning for future requirements. Consumption based planning is a planning method which is based on past consumption of material and using enter or log of forecast to determine future material requirements. Consumption based planning is not link with dependent or independent requirement which is found in production scheduling. Requirement planning takes place at plant level. All the stock that is relevant to plant is consider in planning. You can also exclude stock of individual's storage locations from MRP. You can define MRP areas for your planning. Multiple storage locations can be considered in one MRP area. You can also requirement planning without MRP area.

There are three types of MRP areas,

1. Plant MRP areas
2. Storage location MRP areas
3. Subcontracting MRP areas

10.1.3. Planning calendar

The planning calendar is used to describe the length of total period for consumption based planning. You can access it by transaction MD25 or by using Manu path SAP Easy access under logistics > Materials Management > MRP > MRP > Master Data > Planning Calendar > Create Periods.

The Planning calendar is creating for each plant in system for MRP. Whenever creating a new planning calendar in system, a three character code for the new calendar can be created for MRP. After creating a planning calendar in system, it is possible to define variables where the calendar has been flagged to start a period as a week day. The planning calendar will ascertain whether a day is working day or a holiday by referencing the relevant factory calendar configuration in IMG of your company.

Copyrighted© Material

10.1.4. Planning Processes

10.1.4.1.   Planning at Plant Level

In SAP system planning is carried out at plant level. You can also planning at storage location level. The following processes are take into account when you want to use consumption based planning,

First of all check the planning file entry in system. System will check whether a material change and relevant to MRP and also check need for include in planning or not. System will perform net calculations for every planned material for MRP. System check the stock availability in warehouse, fixed receipts from production or purchasing to make sure the requirement quantity is covered and system create procurement proposals accordingly. After that lot size calculation performs as per selected lot size in material master records. Scheduling is executed to determine the start and finish date of procurement proposals. As per selection parameters planned orders, purchase requisitions or schedule line scheduling agreements are created in system for procurement. At the end SAP system calculate the actual days and receipts days for the delivery of the material.

10.1.4.2.   Planning at storage location level

Most of companies planning run carried out at plant level with including all storage locations exist in that plant. Sometime client required MRP run at storage location level. Client with storage location remote from the associated plant may want to perform planning at lower level of enterprise structure. Some time you plan your storage locations as per planned material types or unique type of materials take place on particular storage location or a certain types of spare parts for your plant. So in SAP system you can select specific storage locations for MRP or exclude specific storage locations from MRP.

Copyrighted© Material

10.1.5. Planning Evaluation

Your planning can be evaluate on following basis, first one with the MRP list and second one is stock requirement list.

10.1.5.1.   MRP list

MRP list represent the planning results of planned material for MRP. The MRP list is initially working document for MRP controller to work from. MRP list is a static list and MRP changes not shown on list until next planning run carried out. The MRP list can be display for individual material by using the transaction code MD05 or by using SAP easy access under the logistics Materials Management > MRP > MRP > Evaluations > MRP list- Material

10.1.5.2.   Stock Requirement List

The stock requirement list represents the current up to date stock requirement situations of material. As compare with MRP list, Stock requirement list is dynamic and updated. You can view it by transaction code MD04 or by using SAP easy access under the logistics Materials Management > MRP > MRP > Evaluations > Stock requirement list- Material

Note: In planning run if you create planned orders. Planned orders can be converting into PRs individually or collectively by transaction MD14 and by collectively MD15.

Copyrighted© Material

For Material requirement planning it is a prerequisite that MRP views must maintain in material master record. In MRP 1 view it is mandatory for planning for you to maintain lot size and MRP type in system. System determine shortage situation of material for requirement date in the net requirement calculation. As already discuss, it is consider as receipts of materials. Receipt quantity is calculated by system in the lot size calculation. In SAP system, three lot size procedures available for calculating the lot size. These are followings

10.1.6.1. *Lot size procedures*

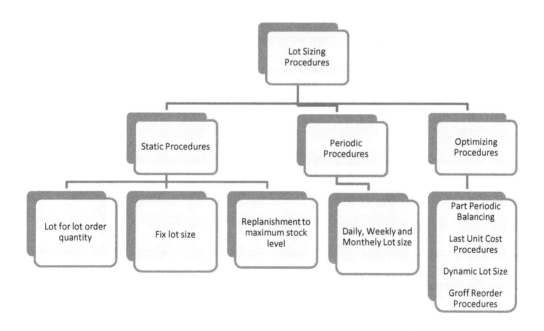

Figure 0-6 (Lot Size Procedures)

You can define lot size procedures in customizing SAP IMG- SPRO Materials Management > Consumption Based Planning > Planning > Lot Size Calculation > Define lot size procedure

10.1.6.1.1.1.   Static Lot Size

MRP calculation quantity is calculate that quantity which is enters and specified in SAP material master record. Static procedures include, lot for lot order quantity, fixed lot size and replenishment to maximum stock level.

10.1.6.1.1.2.   *Lot for lot order quantity*

When you procure the exact lot size again and again you use the lot for lot order quantity. You have chosen the selection EX for lot-for-lot order quantity in lot size field mention in material master data MRP1 view. Exact lot size mean the difference to the reorder point is proposed to the reorder point planning. In certain cases the method is only suitable for e.g. spare components

General Data				
Base Unit of Measure	PC	piece(s)	MRP group	
Purchasing Group			ABC Indicator	
Plant-sp.matl status			Valid from	

MRP procedure				
MRP Type	PD	MRP		
Reorder Point			Planning time fence	
Planning cycle			MRP Controller	001

Lot size data				
Lot size	EX	Lot-for-lot order quantity		
Minimum Lot Size			Maximum Lot Size	

Figure 0-7 (Lot Size Indicator)

10.1.6.1.1.3.   *Fixed lot size*

In fixed lot size the system calculate the procurement proposed only the shortage quantity. If fixed lot size not sufficient for covering the shortage quantity then system creates several procurement proposals in the same date until material shortage is cover for planning and eliminated. It is useful to select a fixed lot size, if it is only delivering in pallet of a certain quantity or tank of a certain sizes of materials. Indicator FX and fixed lot size quantity in the lot size field mention in material master record MRP 1 view for that material.

Copyrighted© Material

10.1.6.1.1.4. Replenishment to maximum stock level

If you want your stock replenish or fill the highest possible level or you can only store a specific quantity due to limitation of storage facilities than you can use lot sizing procedure replenishment up to maximum stock level. You can use the replenishment lot size procedure with MRP "MRP type" and with reorder point planning where system creates the stock bringing up to maximum level mention in material master data. You must have set indicator HB in the lot size field and put maximum quantity in maximum stock level field in MRP1 view material master record. System can create lot size with and without considering external requirements in reorder point planning, system calculate the MRP in case of not considering external requirements such as follows

Lot Size = Maximum stock level – Plant Stock (Current) – Fixed receipts

In case of considering external requirement where external requirement take into account in MRP calculations consider all requirement of MRP must be covered and once they are covered then defined maximum stock level must not be exceeded but also does not have to be reached. System create calculations by using two formulas

Lot size = + Reorder point + Total Requirement of stock including lead time – Plant stock (Current) – Fixed receipts

&

Lot Size = Maximum stock level – Plant Stock (Current) – Fixed receipts

Example:

Suppose maximum stock = 10

Reorder point = 4

Current plant stock = 2

Fixed receipts = 0

Total Requirements = 8

Copyrighted© Material

10.1.6.2.   Lot size calculations

Reorder point planning without considering external requirements: 10 – 2 = 8

Reorder point planning with consider external requirement (Formula 1): 4 + 8 -2 = 10

Reorder point planning with consider external requirement (Formula 2): 10 – 2 = 8

10.1.6.2.1.   Periodic Lot Size

In periodic lot size system combine together several requirements quantities with in a time frame together to form a lot. The length of a time period can be a day or a week or month or according to the posting period etc. System takes to mean period start of the planning calendar as the availability date or as delivery date of stock.

10.1.6.2.2.   Optimize lot size

In static and periodic lot size procedures costs are not consider and take into account during planning. In optimize lot size procedures, system take into account. It is group together shortage in that way which showing cost is minimizing. Cost includes in optimizing lot size are setup cost, ordering cost and storage cost. Optimizing lot size procedures includes

- Part Periodic Balancing
- Last Unit Cost Procedures
- Dynamic Lot Size
- Groff Reorder Procedures

Copyrighted© Material

10.1.7. Pre-requisites of Consumption Based Planning

The followings are the prerequisites for consumption based planning

10.1.7.1.   *Activate material requirement planning*

Requirement planning must be activate for the relevant plant in customizing, for doing this you can follows as SAP IMG – SPRO

Materials Management > Consumption based planning > Planning > Activate material requirement planning

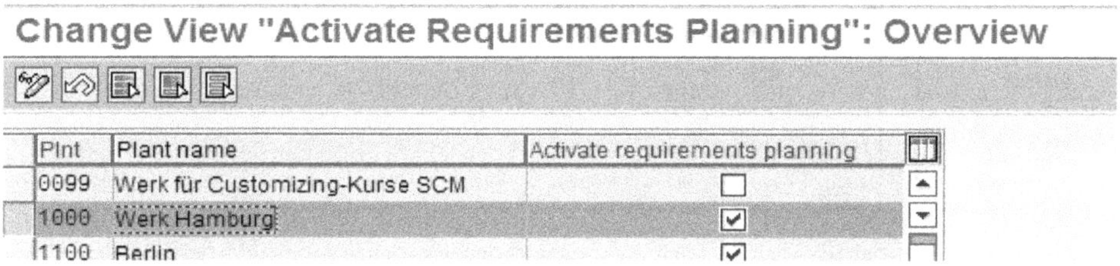

Figure 0-8 (Activate Material Requirement Planning)

10.1.7.2.   *Maintain plant parameters*

You must maintain plant parameters must be activated for relevant plant in customizing, for doing this you can follows as SAP IMG –SPRO

Materials Management > Consumption based planning > Plant parameters > carry out overall maintenance of plant parameters

Figure 0-9 (Plant Parameters Create, Maintain, Delete and Copy)

Copyrighted© Material

Here you can also create, delete and copy of plant parameters for material requirements planning. For maintaining of plant parameters you can adopt planning parameters from any existing plant which are using MRP enable instead of create new plant parameters. For adopt/maintain plant parameters you can click on copy button mention above and copy parameters from existing plant such as follows

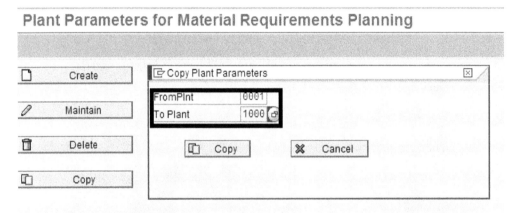

Figure 0-10 (Copy Plant Parameter)

You can also maintain new parameters by clicking on maintain button such as above mention screen

Figure 0-11 (Maintain Plant Parameters)

Copyrighted© Material

10.1.7.3.   MRP Settings in Material Master Record

You must have maintain MRP data in material master records by using transition create material MM01 or via change material MM02 such as follows

Figure 0-12 (MRP Views Material Master)

Copyrighted© Material

10.1.8. Material Requirement Planning Procedures

Consumption based planning (CBP) consider requirement quantity on the basis of previous/ historical consumption. External requirements like sales order, reservations and planned independent requirements are not consider and relevant to consumption based planning. Consumption based planning is good option to calculate require quantity with minimum planning efforts. The CBP is use for materials that are not produces in house. MRP Based planning uses mostly for semi-finished goods, finished goods and important assembly components. Sales order, reservations and planned independent requirements etc. are consider in MRP.

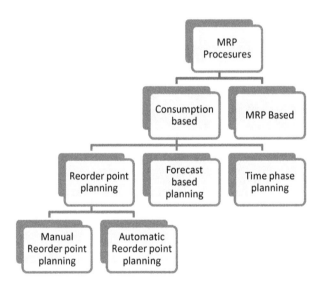

Figure 0-13 (Material Requirement Planning Procedures)

Following above mention are the procedures of MRP. Consumption based planning includes reorder point planning; forecast based planning and time phase planning.

Copyrighted© Material

10.1.9. Reorder Point Planning

In reorder point planning system check reorder point in master data of material. When the stock fall below the reorder point system generate and trigger procurement proposals. Reorder point should also take into account replenishment lead time. Lead time is a difference between order giving and order receiving of particular material. Reorder point planning consists of manual reorder point planning and automatic reorder point planning.

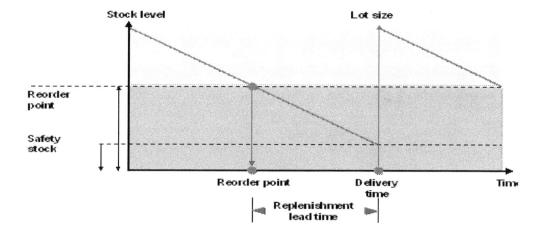

Figure 0-14 (Reorder Point Planning)

Copyrighted© Material

10.1.9.1.   Manual Reorder Point

In manual reorder point planning safety stock and reorder level manually maintain in material master record. Select MRP type manual reorder point planning as VB. MRP type said whether material is plan and consider for requirement planning or not. Reorder point said when stock level consume up to 100 kg system generate procurement proposals according to lot size. Lot size tells us how the material will be procuring or procured with a lot. Maximum stock is 400 mentions in master data. System proposes procurement proposals 300 qty for replenishment to maximum stock level as per selected lot size in master data.

Create Material 102-511 (Trading goods)

| 🖃 | ⇒ Additional data | 🖳 Organizational levels | 🖧 Check screen data | 🔒 |

| Purchase order text | ⊙ MRP 1 | ⊙ MRP 2 | ⊙ MRP 3 | ⊙ MRP 4 | For... | ◀ ▶ |

| Material | 102-511 | Ball bearing MRP | 🖬 |
| Plant | 1000 | Werk Hamburg |

General Data

Base Unit of Measure	PC	piece(s)	MRP group	0000
Purchasing Group	100		ABC Indicator	
Plant-sp.matl status			Valid from	

MRP procedure

MRP Type	VB	Manual reorder point planning
Reorder Point	100		Planning time fence	
Planning cycle			MRP Controller	101

Lot size data

Lot size	HB	Replenish to maximum stock level
Minimum Lot Size			Maximum Lot Size	
Fixed lot size			Maximum stock level	400
Ordering costs			Storage costs ind.	

Figure 0-15 (Manual Reorder Point Planning)

Copyrighted© Material

In MD04 stock requirement list you can see stock is zero of planned material

Stock/Requirements List as of 12:39 Hrs

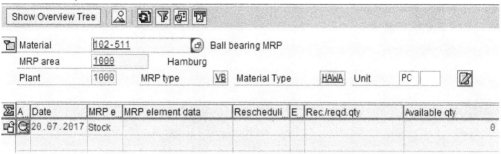

Show Overview Tree									

Material	102-511		Ball bearing MRP						
MRP area	1000	Hamburg							
Plant	1000	MRP type	VB	Material Type	HAWA	Unit	PC		

	A	Date	MRP e	MRP element data	Rescheduli	E	Rec./reqd.qty	Available qty
		20.07.2017	Stock					0

Figure 0-16 (Stock/Requirement List)

Manual reorder point planning execute as follows by transaction MD03

Single-Item, Single-Level

Material	102-511
MRP Area	1000
Plant	1000

MRP control parameters

Processing key	NETCH	Net change for total horizon
Create purchase req.	1	Purchase requisitions in opening period
Delivery schedules	3	Schedule lines
Create MRP list	1	MRP list
Planning mode	1	Adapt planning data (normal mode)
Scheduling	1	Basic dates will be determined for plann

Figure 0-17 (Planning Run Initial Screen)

Copyrighted© Material

Stock requirement list after MRP run (MD04)

You can see below screen system generate procurement proposal of respective material. Since stock was less than 100 system generate proposal 400 as per selected lot size.

Figure 0-18 (Stock Requirement List)

Note: in planning run if you create planned orders. Than convert planned orders into PRs individually by transaction MD14 and by collectively MD15

Copyrighted© Material

10.1.9.2.   Automatic reorder point planning

In automatic reorder point planning safety stock and reorder level are determined by integrated forecast program. System use historical values for forecast future requirements. On the bases of past data system suggests safety stock and reorders level and also takes into account replenishment lead time. Since the forecast carried out system put these values in material master data. System always checks warehouse stock and compare with reorder point. If the stock less than the reorder point, than system generate procurement proposals as per mention lot size in material master record. The reorder point consider the following points

- Safety stock
- Future Requirements or previous consumption values
- Replenishment lead time

The integrated forecast program suggests you to safety stock as well reorder point. System calculate reorder point as follows

*Reorder point = Safety stock +Daily Requirements * Replenishment lead time*

MRP warehouse stock will be

Warehouse stock + on order stock

On order stock is consider purchase requisitions, purchase orders and planned orders.

Copyrighted© Material

10.1.10. Forecast Based Planning

Most likely reorder point planning, forecast based planning also considers historical material consumption. Same likely reorder level planning, forecast based planning take into account historical values of consumption. Forecast program of system suggest forecast values. The forecast values are used in MRP as the future forecast requirement of materials. Forecast based planning use MRP type VV which is said forecast based planning.

For further detail let's consider forecast based planning uses past one year (12 months) historical values of consumption and calculate on monthly basis

10.1.10.1.1.1. Configuration settings:

For lot size setting go to transaction OMI4 or follow the Manu path under customizing IMG – SPRO

Materials Management > Consumption Based Planning > Planning > Lot-size calculations > Defining Lot-sizing procedures

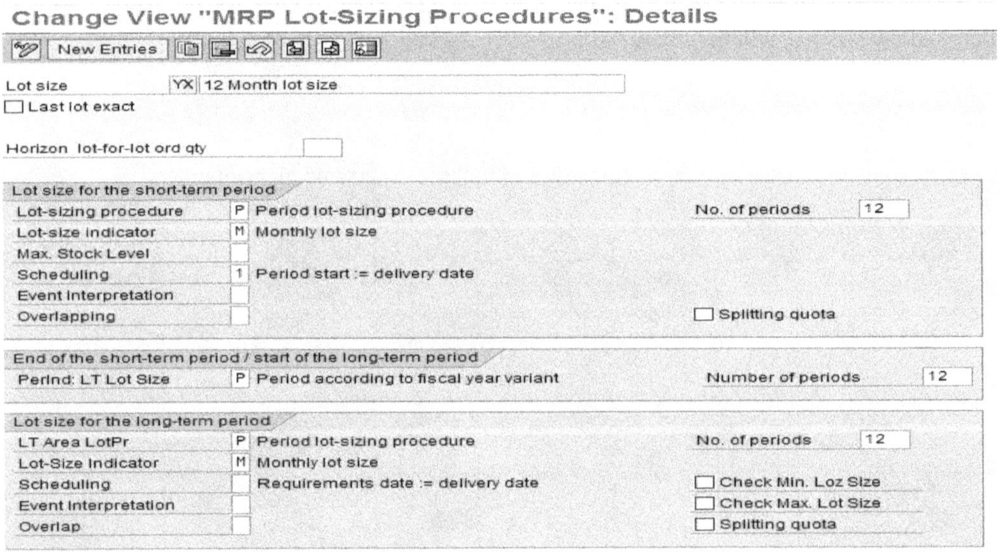

Figure 0-19 (Change View MRP Lot Sizing Procedures)

Copyrighted© Material

10.1.10.1.1.2. Master Data Settings:

Change master data of concern material with lot size YX (12 month lot size) and change MRP type as VV forecast based planning in MRP1 view such as follows

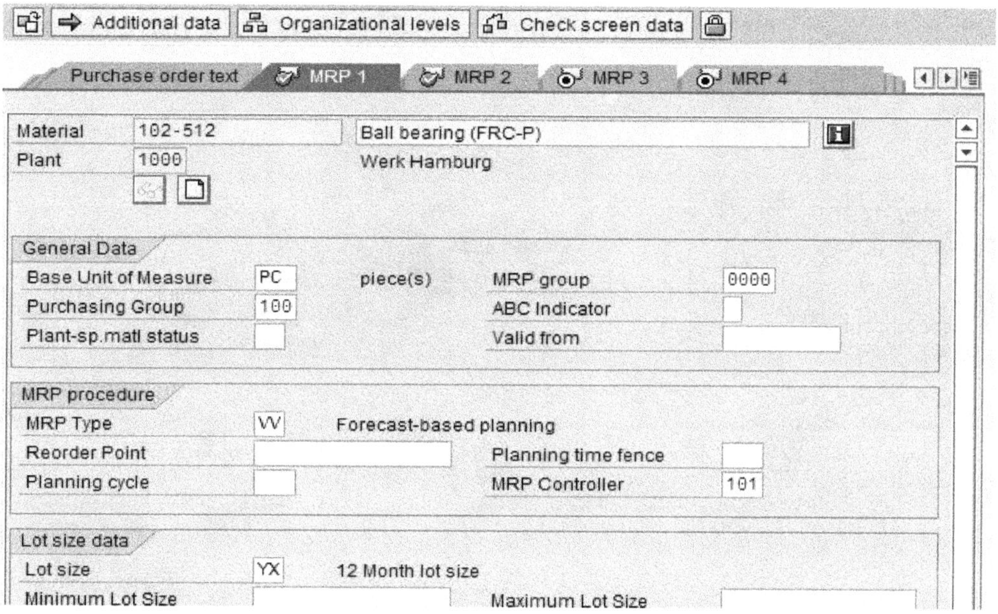

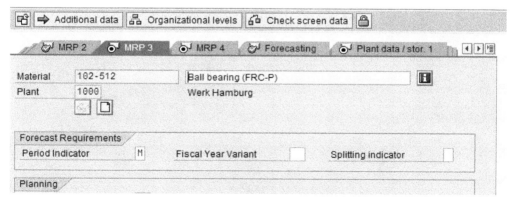

Figure 0-20 (MRP 1 View Parameters for Forecast Based Planning)

In MRP3 view change as follows

Figure 0-21 (MRP 3 View Parameters for Forecast Based Planning)

Copyrighted© Material

In master data, forecast view setting as follows

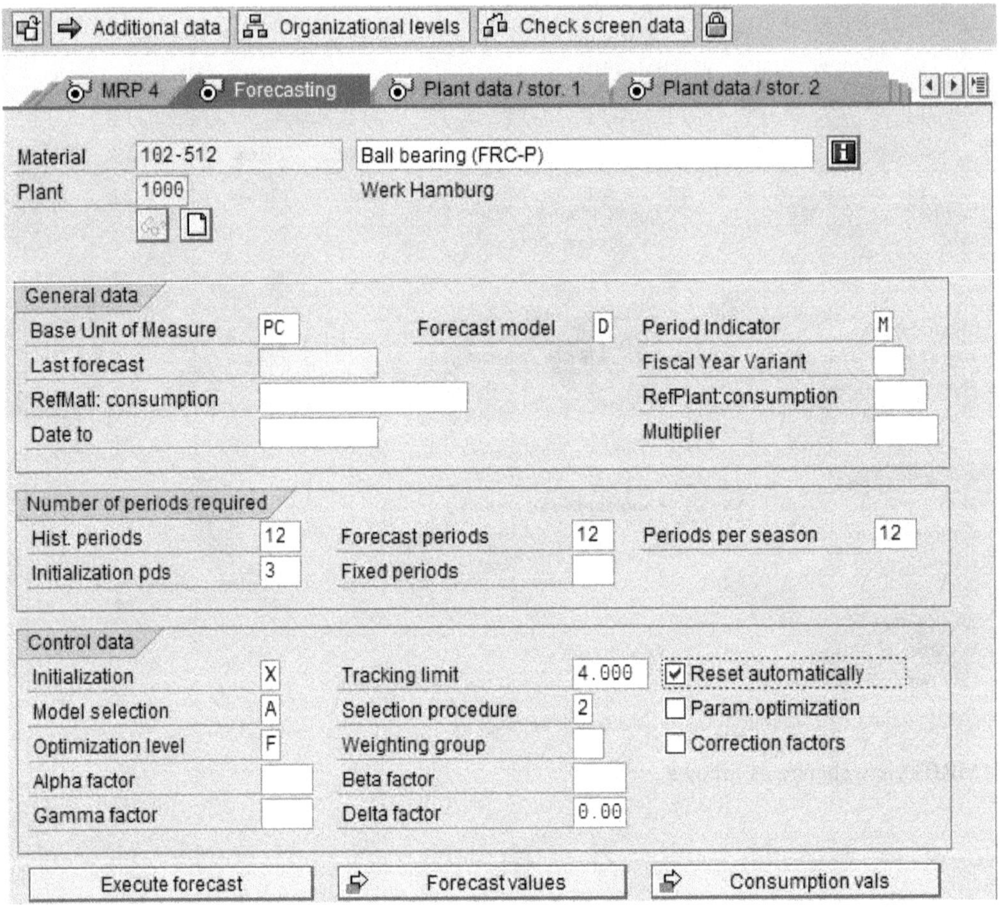

Figure 0-22 (Forecasting View Parameters for Forecast Based Planning)

Copyrighted© Material

Maintain Consumption in Material Master such as follows

Period	Total consumption	Corrected value	Qutnt
07.2017	100	100	1.00
06.2017	100	100	1.00
05.2017	100	100	1.00
04.2017	100	100	1.00
03.2017	100	100	1.00
02.2017	100	100	1.00
01.2017	100	100	1.00
12.2016	100	100	1.00
11.2016	100	100	1.00
10.2016	100	100	1.00
09.2016	100	100	1.00

Material 102-512 Ball bearing (FRC-P)
Plant 1000 Werk Hamburg

Base Unit of Measure PC   Period Indicator M   Fiscal Year Variant

Consumption values

Unpind consumption

Figure 0-23 (Consumption Values)

10.1.10.1.1.3.   Execute Forecast Based Planning

Execute forecast planning by transaction code MP30 on specific plant. You can see also historical values by clicking on button "Historical values"

Click on the execute button for execute the forecast planning

Forecast values   Historical values   Execute

Material 102-512 Ball bearing (FRC-P)
MRP Area 1000 Hamburg
Plant 1000 Werk Hamburg

Basic data
Last forecast		Base Unit of Measure	PC
Forecast model	D	Service level (%)	0.0
Period Indicator	M	Safety Stock	0
Forecast profile		Reorder Point	0
Basic value	0	Trend value	0

Control data
Initialization	X	Tracking limit	4.000
Model selection	A	Selection procedure	2
☐ Param optimization		Optimization level	F

Number of values
Historical periods	12	Forecast periods	12
Initialization pds	3	Fixed periods	0
Periods per season	12		

294
Copyrighted© Material

Material	102-512	Ball bearing (FRC-P)
MRP Area	1000	Hamburg
Plant	1000	Werk Hamburg

Basic data		Enter Forecast Date	☒
Last forecast			
Forecast model		⊙ M 07.2017	0
Period Indicator		○ M 08.2017	
Forecast profile			
Basic value		✓ ✗	

Figure 0-24 (Forecast Run)

Click enter button. You can see the executed forecast values of 12 months listed below

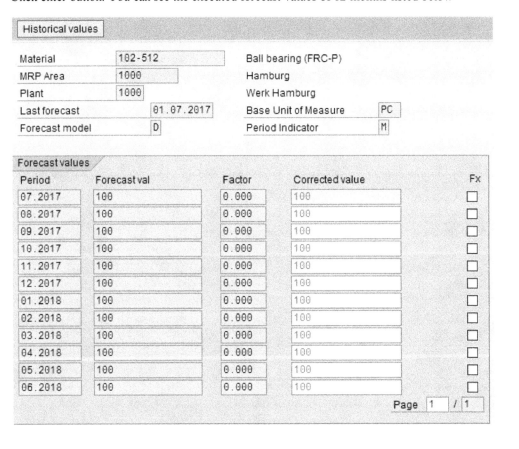

Historical values			

Material	102-512	Ball bearing (FRC-P)	
MRP Area	1000	Hamburg	
Plant	1000	Werk Hamburg	
Last forecast	01.07.2017	Base Unit of Measure	PC
Forecast model	D	Period Indicator	M

Forecast values

Period	Forecast val	Factor	Corrected value	Fx
07.2017	100	0.000	100	☐
08.2017	100	0.000	100	☐
09.2017	100	0.000	100	☐
10.2017	100	0.000	100	☐
11.2017	100	0.000	100	☐
12.2017	100	0.000	100	☐
01.2018	100	0.000	100	☐
02.2018	100	0.000	100	☐
03.2018	100	0.000	100	☐
04.2018	100	0.000	100	☐
05.2018	100	0.000	100	☐
06.2018	100	0.000	100	☐

Page 1 / 1

Figure 0-25 (Forecast Run)

Copyrighted© Material

Check stock requirement list by transaction MD04

Show Overview Tree					

Material   102-512   Ball bearing (FRC-P)

MRP area   1000   Hamburg

Plant   1000   MRP type   VV   Material Type   HAWA   Unit   PC

A	Date	MRP e	MRP element data	Rescheduli	E	Rec./reqd.qty	Available qty
	21.07.2017	Stock					0
	01.08.2017	ForReq	M 08/2017			100-	100-
	01.09.2017	ForReq	M 09/2017			100-	200-
	02.10.2017	ForReq	M 10/2017			100-	300-
	02.11.2017	ForReq	M 11/2017			100-	400-
	01.12.2017	ForReq	M 12/2017			100-	500-
	02.01.2018	ForReq	M 01/2018			100-	600-
	01.02.2018	ForReq	M 02/2018			100-	700-
	01.03.2018	ForReq	M 03/2018			100-	800-
	03.04.2018	ForReq	M 04/2018			100-	900-
	02.05.2018	ForReq	M 05/2018			100-	1,000-
	01.06.2018	ForReq	M 06/2018			100-	1,100-

Figure 0-26 (Stock Requirement List)

Now you can execute MRP by transaction MD03 for creating of purchase requisitions of material with following parameters

Single-Item, Single-Level

Material   102-512   Ball bearing (FRC-P)

MRP Area   1000   Hamburg

Plant   1000   Werk Hamburg

MRP control parameters

Processing key	NETCH	Net change for total horizon
Create purchase req.	1	Purchase requisitions
Delivery schedules	3	Schedule lines
Create MRP list	1	MRP list
Planning mode	3	Delete and recreate planning data
Scheduling	2	Lead time scheduling and capacity planni
Planning date	21.07.2017	

Figure 0-27 (Planning Run Initial Screen)

Copyrighted© Material

Now again view stock Requirement list by transaction MD04 after executing MRP. System generate PR as consider forecast values

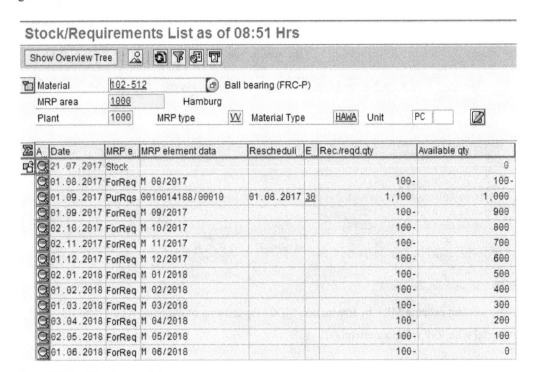

Stock/Requirements List as of 08:51 Hrs

Show Overview Tree

Material 102-512 Ball bearing (FRC-P)
MRP area 1000 Hamburg
Plant 1000 MRP type VV Material Type HAWA Unit PC

A	Date	MRP e	MRP element data	Rescheduli	E	Rec./reqd.qty	Available qty
	21.07.2017	Stock					0
	01.08.2017	ForReq	M 08/2017			100-	100-
	01.09.2017	PurRqs	0010014188/00010	01.08.2017	30	1,100	1,000
	01.09.2017	ForReq	M 09/2017			100-	900
	02.10.2017	ForReq	M 10/2017			100-	800
	02.11.2017	ForReq	M 11/2017			100-	700
	01.12.2017	ForReq	M 12/2017			100-	600
	02.01.2018	ForReq	M 01/2018			100-	500
	01.02.2018	ForReq	M 02/2018			100-	400
	01.03.2018	ForReq	M 03/2018			100-	300
	03.04.2018	ForReq	M 04/2018			100-	200
	02.05.2018	ForReq	M 05/2018			100-	100
	01.06.2018	ForReq	M 06/2018			100-	0

Figure 0-28 (Stock Requirement List)

Copyrighted© Material

10.1.10.1.2. Forecast Models

Forecast models are used to calculate the material requirement. Before you run forecast you must select model for calculate forecasting values. Forecasting models with examples are shown below charts

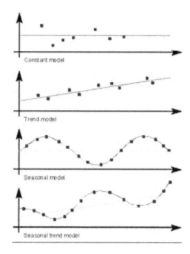

Figure 0-29 (Forecast Models)

You can select model manually or system has also capability to select automatically. For manual selection of forecast model, it is mandatory to choose according to historical or consumption values as well as consumption trends'.

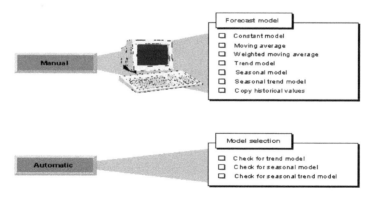

Figure 0-30 (Model Selection)

Copyrighted© Material

You can define your forecasting model with following

Pattern	Forecast model
Constant	Constant model
	Constant model with smoothing factor adaptation
	Moving average model
	Weighted moving average model
Trend	Trend model (1st-order exponential smoothing)
	Trend model (2nd-order exponential smoothing model, with and without parameter optimization)
Seasonal	Seasonal model (Winters' method)
Seasonal trend	Seasonal trend model (1st-order exponential smoothing model)
Irregular	No forecast
	Moving average model
	Weighted moving average model

Table 0-1 (Pattern vs. Forecast Model)

SAP system can automatically select a forecast model on the basis of past consumption values. For doing this system carried out statistical tests and check whether seasonal requirement pattern or trend pattern applies. In seasonal test system clear the historical values of any possible trends and carries out auto correlation test. In trend test system subjects the historical values to regression analysis. System also checks whether trend patterns are exist in system or not. In automatically model selection, system also select model with the help of using combination of Alpha, Beta and Gamma. The smoothing factor is also varied between 0.2 to 0.8 in interval of 0.2. System will chose lowest mean absolute deviation model.

Copyrighted© Material

10.1.11.   Time Phase Planning

If a vendor delivers material on certain date of a week or month etc. on regular basis, you can use time phase planning. It is understood material is plan accordingly that delivery cycle. Time phase planning uses historical values to calculate MRP. Planning run is must be executed with predefine intervals in a specific rhythm.

Copyrighted© Material

Copyrighted© Material

Copyrighted© Material

Chapter 11:

Automatic Account

Determination

Copyrighted© Material

11. Chapter 11: Automatic account determination

11.1.   Automatic account determination

    11.1.1.   Valuation Area

    11.1.2.   Chart of accounts

    11.1.3.   Valuation class

    11.1.4.   Transaction key

    11.1.5.   Material and Material Type

    11.1.6.   Movement Type

    11.1.7.   Valuation Grouping Code

    11.1.8.   Account Category Reference

    11.1.9.   Value String

    11.1.10.   Process Steps for Automatic Account Determination

    11.1.11.   Account determination with wizard

    11.1.12.   Account determination without wizard

11.2.   Split Valuation

    11.2.1.   Procurement Type

    11.2.2.   Country of Origin

    11.2.3.   Quality of material

    11.2.4.   Valuation category and valuation types

    11.2.5.   Configuration of split valuation

11.3.   Material Ledger in SAP

    11.3.1.   Material Price Analysis

    11.3.2.   Material Price Determination

11.4.   Additional Topic

Copyrighted© Material

11.1. Automatic account determination

Goods receipts, goods issue and logistics invoice verifications etc. are integrated with financials and materials management. In posting of these documents system create both material management and financial accounting documents. Amount of financial documents are posted in relevant G/L account. These G/L accounts are determined by system automatically during posting of documents. It is all about automatic account determination.

Your company procures materials with purchase order. Inventory clerk post goods receipts in SAP system with reference to that purchase order. Simultaneously account clerk post logistics invoice with reference to that purchase order. You can see system automatically determine accounts which are used to posting financial documents. System suggests relevant G/L account with automatic account determination. Automatic account determination reduces the data entry error, efforts and time. It's all about your configuration which determine which amount is debit and which credit is. Some concepts are very important before your understanding of automatic account determination at the of inventory posting. Automatic account determination is used in following cases

Figure 0-1 (Material Management Operations)

Copyrighted© Material

11.1.1. Valuation Area

Valuation area is use to evaluate the stock of material. It is the organizational unit that subdivides an enterprise for the purpose of valuation. Valuation area can be at plant level or can be at company code level. If a valuation area mark as plant level, all the stock valuated at plant level. If a valuation area set or assign to company code level, all the stock valuated at company code level. Once you configure valuation area after that it is unchangeable in system.

Note: if you want to run product cost, PP and MRP, it is mandatory that valuation area assign to plant level.

11.1.2. Chart of accounts

Chart of accounts are define at client level. The master chart of account is assign to each respective several company code. It is a 4 digit code. Several company code use list of G/L accounts. It is used for daily posting of your company. You can use one chart of account in many company codes. For each GL account the chart of account contain the account number, account name and technical information. Operating chart of account, country specific chart of account and group chart of accounts are the types of chart of accounts.

11.1.3. Valuation class

For determination of stock account of material, valuation class use and plays an important role. In automatic account determination it is mandatory to create material type and after that valuation class. Valuation class is assign to material type. When you create a material master data, you need to assign a valuation class in master record in Account1 view screen. Valuation class is classified as per according to material type and assign to it accordingly. For example in standard SAP system configuration material type ROH as Raw material is used valuation class 3000, 3001 and 3002 or for ERSA (Spare parts) use 3040 valuation class.

Copyrighted© Material

11.1.4. Transaction key

Transaction keys are used to determine accounts or posting keys for line items that are automatically created by the system. Once these are defining in SAP system, these are unchangeable after that. These are predefining in SAP system and determine posting in materials management and financial accounting. E.g. BSX for inventory posting, GBB for consumption and WRX used in GR/IR clearing posting. It is automatically determine whether a posting made in stock account, consumption account or price difference account etc.

11.1.5. Material and Material Type

We have already discussed in details about material and material type. Material type is always assigned with the material at the time of creation of master data. Material and material type directly link with automatic account determination and influencing factors for inventory posting. Valuation class, material type and account category reference are link together in configuration that helps inventory posting in respective GL account.

11.1.6. Movement Type

Movement type tells us where the stock actually takes place or move on. E.g. movement type 261 describe for consumption against order, 201 consumption against cost center, 561 initial entry of stock balance etc. e.g. for these consumption posting you need to different expense accounts etc. It is your choices you have configure setting to post all consumption in one account or post in different accounts. In automatic account determination, different account use for different material types, e.g. trading goods, raw material, spare parts and packaging materials entries post with their respective GL accounts which are differentiating each other's.

11.1.7. Valuation Grouping Code

Valuation grouping code use to differentiation GL account assignment based on valuation area within chart of account. GL account assign automatically with the help of valuation area. We have option for grouping to gather valuation areas with the same chart of account or we can change chart of account for each valuation area. As already mention, chart of accounts is the

Copyrighted© Material

complete list of GL accounts. There are two types of account determination according to valuation area. Further example for your consideration

Company Code	Valuation Area	Valuation Grouping code
1000	1000	0001
1000	1100	0001
1000	1200	0002
1000	1300	0002
1000	1400	0002
1000	1500	0002

Table 0-1 (Valuation Grouping Code)

In above mention example, valuation area is based on plant. 1000, 1100, 1200 etc. are plants. You can see same valuation area 0001 is used for plant 1000 and 1100. Similarly 0002 valuation is used for other plants. GL accounts in automatic account determination are based on accordingly in above assignment.

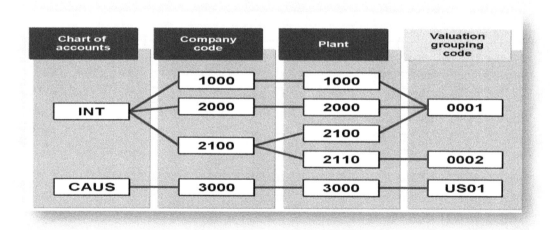

Figure 0-2 (Valuation Grouping Code)   Source: www.help.sap.com

If you active valuation grouping code in configuration than you must assign the valuation code to valuation area. If your valuation grouping code is active and valuation area at plant level and you want to differentiate GL account for different plants with in same chart of account and business

Copyrighted© Material

process, you can assign different valuation grouping code for the plants within that chart of account. In mention example for plant 2110 which use 0002 valuation grouping code, you can use different GL accounts for same business processes. For example in consumption posting scenario with above mention example,

For Plant 2100

Plant 2100 (GL Account 3000000)	
Consumption account (Dr)	
	Stock account (Cr)

Table 0-2 (Consumption Posting at Plant 2100)

For plant 2110

Plant 2110 (GL Account 3000001)	
Consumption account (Dr)	
	Stock account (Cr)

Table 0-3 (Consumption Posting at Plant 2110)

Note:

For activating valuation grouping code you can go code under customizing IMG SPRO > Materials Management > Valuation and Account Assignment > Account Determination without Wizard > Define Valuation Control

You can assign valuation grouping code under customizing IMG SPRO > Materials Management > Valuation and Account Assignment > Account Determination without Wizard > Group Together Valuation Areas

11.1.8. Account Category Reference

Account category reference is used to link the valuation class and material type. Many valuation classes can be assigning to account category references. For automatic account determination you must check on attributes of material types whether check button quantity and value base updating on. It should must be check on both quantity and value base. When you create material

Copyrighted© Material

master data, you must maintain accounting views, where you assign relevant valuation class to material. In back end configuration, material type assign with account category reference. Valuation class also link with account category reference. Behind valuation class, specific GL account is linked for account posting.

11.1.9. Value String

Movement type and GL accounts are connected with value string e.g. WE01, WE06 and WE14. String means way or sequence of processes. Here, system finds the correct path by which valuation data to be hutted according to respective transaction. Value string decides which of posting transactions lead to GL account postings in individual cases. These value strings are predefine in SAP system and you cannot define it by own. If there is quantity and value updating setting exist in attributes of material types, system always find a right value string for inventory document posting.

Value string WE01, for the goods receipts against a purchase order contain transaction/ event keys BSX and offsetting entry in GR IR clearing account. If there is any price difference accrue, then it goes to PRD. WE01 includes BSX, WRX, PRD, KDM, EIN, EKG, BSV, FRN, FRL and UMB. WA14 use for free of charge delivery with movement type 511 and includes BSX, PRD, UMB and WA01 is used for issuance of goods or goods receipts other and includes event keys BSX, GBB, PRD and UMB.

Copyrighted© Material

11.1.10. Process Steps for Automatic Account Determination

You have two options in automatic account determination. First one is automatic account determination with wizard and second one in account determination without wizard. Account determination with wizard includes following steps

11.1.11. Account determination with wizard

- Prerequisites
- Select material type used
- Active purchase account management
- Active purchase account management for company codes
- Assign chart of accounts
- Assign plants to groups
- Different inventory accounts
- Examine different material types
- Select account posting
- Maintain valuation classes
- Maintain inventory accounts
- Maintain debit credit rules
- Maintain MM transaction
- Final screen

Copyrighted© Material

11.1.12. Account determination without wizard

Second one is automatic account determination without wizard. Here we see only without wizard process which includes,

11.1.12.1. Define valuation control

As already mention you must need to active valuation grouping code. You can active it by transaction OMWM or go to under customizing IMG SPRO > Materials Management > Valuation and Account Assignment > Account Determination without Wizard > Define valuation control

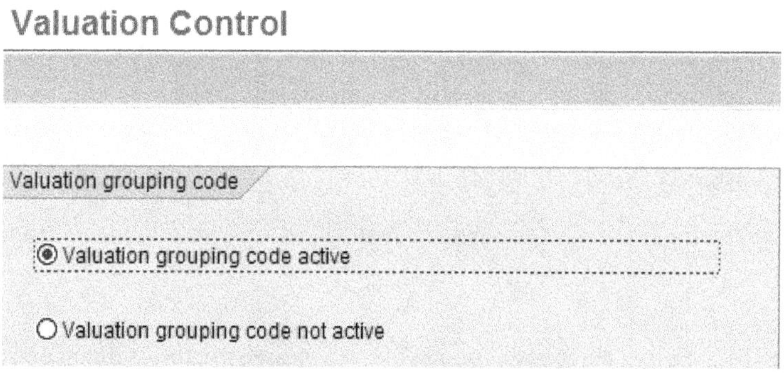

Figure 0-3 (Active Valuation Grouping Code)

Copyrighted© Material

11.1.12.2. Group together Valuation Area

It make easier to determine automatic account determination. In this step you assign valuation area to valuation grouping code. Valuation grouping code already discuss in detail. You can configure it by transaction code OMWD or go to under customizing IMG SPRO > Materials Management > Valuation and Account Assignment > Account Determination without Wizard > Group together Valuation Area

Val. Area	CoCode	Company Name	Chrt/Accts	Val.Grpg Code
0001	0001	SAP A.G.	INT	0001
0005	0001	SAP A.G.	INT	0001
0006	0006	IDES US INC New GL	CAUS	US01
0007	0007	IDES AG NEW GL 7	INT	0001
0008	0008	IDES US INC New GL 8	CAUS	US01
0099	1000	IDES AG	INT	0001
1000	1000	IDES AG	INT	0001

Figure 0-4 (Group together Valuation Area)

Note: Before assignment of valuation grouping code to valuation area following settings are mandatory

- Plant must be assign to company code in your enterprise structure assignments
- Valuation level must be define in your enterprise structure
- Valuation grouping code must be active

Copyrighted© Material

11.1.12.3. Define Material Types, Valuation Classes and Account Category References

As we already discuss material types, valuation classes and account category references. Here first you need to define attribute of material types and after that define account category references (ACR). For doing this, go to transaction code OMSK

Or

Go to under customizing IMG SPRO > Materials Management > Valuation and Account Assignment > Account Determination without Wizard > Define Valuation Classes

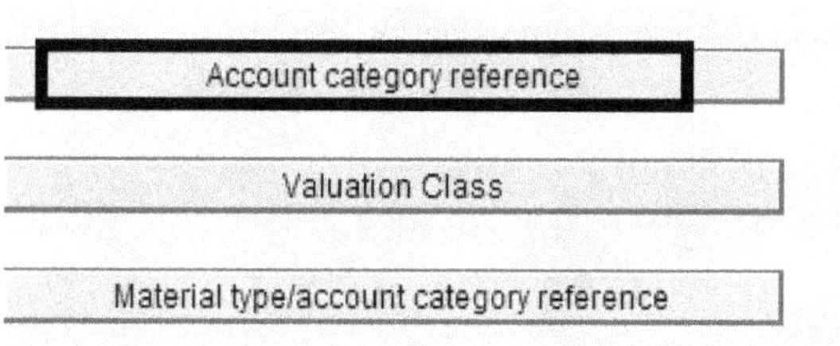

Figure 0-5 (Account Category Reference)

Click on account category reference (ACR) button, here you can maintain account category reference by clicking on New Entry button mention in screen. You create one reference as per material type

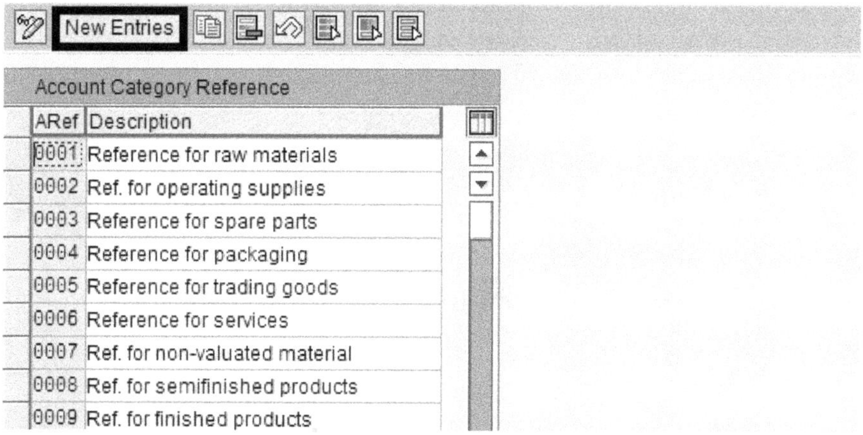

Figure 0-6 (Account Category Reference Entries)

Copyrighted© Material

After creating and saving account category reference, click on go back button than click on valuation class option

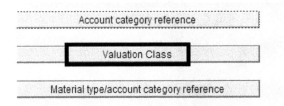

Figure 0-7 (Valuation Class Configuration)

Here you can maintain valuation class and assign valuation class to account category reference by clicking on new entry button

ValCl	ARef	Description	Description
3000	0001	Raw materials 1	
3000	0001	Raw materials 1	Reference for raw materials
3001	0001	Raw materials 2	Reference for raw materials
3002	0001	Raw materials 3	Reference for raw materials
3003	0001	Raw materials 4	Reference for raw materials
3030	0002	Operating supplies	Ref. for operating supplies
3040	0003	Spare parts	Reference for spare parts
3050	0004	(Returnable) packaging	Reference for packaging

Figure 0-8 (Valuation Class Configuration)

Copyrighted© Material

After creating and saving click on go back button and go to option Material type/account category reference.

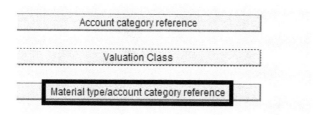

Figure 0-9 (Material type/account category reference Button)

Here you must assign the account category reference to a respective material type as follows mention in screen

NLAG	Non-stock material	0010	Ref. for NLAG
NOF1	Nonfoods	0005	Reference for trading goods
PIPE	Pipeline material	0001	Reference for raw materials
PLAN	Trading goods (planned)	0005	Reference for trading goods
PLM	PLM Minimal Material Type		
PROC	Process material	0009	Ref. for finished products
PROD	Product group	0008	Ref. for semifinished products
ROH	Raw material	0001	Reference for raw materials
TROH	Textile Raw Material	0001	Reference for raw materials
UNBW	Non-valuated material	0007	Ref. for non-valuated material

Figure 0-10 (Assignment of Relevant Material Class with Account Category Reference)

Copyrighted© Material

11.1.12.4. Define Account Grouping for Movement types

Here you assign the account grouping to movement types. The account grouping is a finer subdivision of the transaction key/ event keys for automatic account determination. For defining account grouping for movement type go to transaction code OMWN

Or

Go to under customizing IMG SPRO > Materials Management > Valuation and Account Assignment > Account Determination without Wizard > Define Account Grouping for Movement types

MvT	S	Val.Update	Qty update	Mvt	Cns	Val.strng	Cn	TEKey	Acct modif	C
101		☐	☐	B	A	WE06	1	KBS		☑
101		☐	☐	B	E	WE06	1	KBS		☑
101		☐	☐	B	P	WE06	1	KBS		☑
101		☐	☐	B	V	WE06	1	KBS		☑
101	E	☐	☐	B		WE01	3	PRD		☐
101	E	☐	☐	B	E	WE06	1	KBS		☑
101	E	☐	☐	B	P	WE06	1	KBS		☑
101	Q	☐	☐	B		WE01	3	PRD		☐
101	Q	☐	☐	B	P	WE06	1	KBS		☑
101		☐	☑	B	A	WE06	1	KBS		☑
101		☐	☑	B	V	WE06	1	KBS		☑
101	E	☐	☑	B		WE01	3	PRD		☐
101	E	☐	☑	B	E	WE06	1	KBS		☑
101	E	☐	☑	B	P	WE06	1	KBS		☑
101	0	☐	☑	B	V	WE06	1	KBS		☑
101	Q	☐	☑	B		WE01	3	PRD		☐
101	Q	☐	☑	B	P	WE06	1	KBS		☑
101		☑	☐	B	A	WE06	1	KBS		☑

Figure 0-11 (Account Grouping for Movement types)

Copyrighted© Material

11.1.12.5.   Configure Automatic Posting

In this step you maintain setting of inventory posting and logistics invoice verification transactions for posting automatically with their respective GL accounts. You can configure automatic posting by transaction OBYC or

Go to under customizing IMG SPRO > Materials Management > Valuation and Account Assignment > Account Determination without Wizard > Configure Automatic Posting

Double click on transaction key BSX and insert your chart of account (e.g. INT) and click enter button

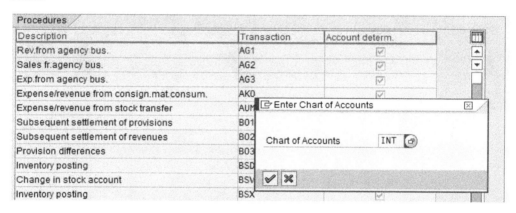

Figure 0-12 (Configure Automatic Posting)

Copyrighted© Material

Here you can maintain respective GL account based on transaction/ event key with the suitable combination of valuation class and account modifier.

Chart of Accounts	INT	Chart of accounts - international
Transaction	BSX	Inventory posting

Account assignment

Valuation cl	Account
3000	300000
3001	300010
3030	303000
3040	304000
3050	305000
3100	310000
7900	790000
7910	790010
7920	792000

Figure 0-13 (GL Account for Automatic Posting)

Copyrighted© Material

Step	Transaction	Details
1	OMWM	Active valuation grouping code
2	OMWD	Group together valuation area (Valuation grouping code + Company code + Chart of account + Valuation area)
3	OMSK	Account category reference (Material type + Account category reference + Valuation class)
4	OMWN	Account grouping for movement type (Value string + Valuation class + Movement Type + Value update indicator + Quantity update indicator)
5	OBYC	Configure automatic posting (Value String + Valuation class + Chart of account + GL account

Table 0-4 (Automatic Posting Details with Transaction)

For more understanding

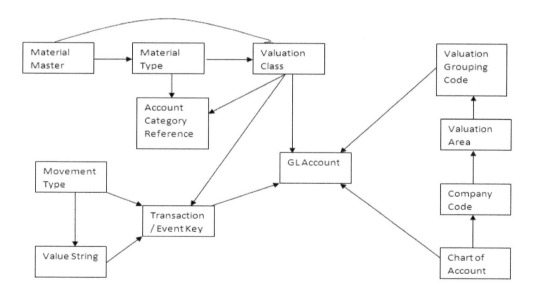

Figure 0-14 (More Detail of Automatic Posting)

Copyrighted© Material

11.2. Split Valuation

Material valuation can be at company code level or can be at plant level. You can maintain two or three prices of single material master data. These materials are necessary to valuate in particular valuation area separately in system. For split valuation price control indicator must be v (moving average price). It can also be evaluated at below mention examples

11.2.1. Procurement Type

In your organization the one particular "AAA" material procure via different types of procurement. It may be procure from in-house or may be procurement from externally any specific vendor.

11.2.2. Country of Origin

Particular "BBB" material may be procure from different origins, may be one origin is USA another from Canada.

11.2.3. Quality of material

It is also possible your "CCC" material having three different qualities like superior quality A, normal quality B and inferior quality C. Split valuation enable you to evaluate your sub-stock mention in above examples. So you will differentiate material price according to above mention

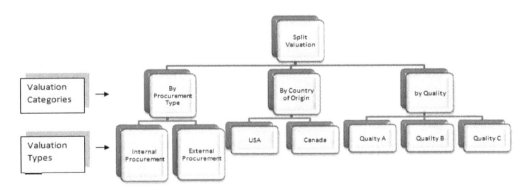

Figure 0-15 (Split Valuation)

Copyrighted© Material

11.2.4. Valuation category and valuation types

11.2.4.1.   *Valuation category*

Valuation category is a criterion in which material is subject to split valuated. For configuration of valuation category you first required to set valuation area in system. In standard SAP system contain several by default valuation categories e.g.

- H for origin
- B for procurement type
- C for quality

11.2.4.2.   *Valuation Type*

Each valuation category having valuation type which tells what individual characteristics has existed in it. Each valuation type is representing sub stock e.g. A quality Stock, B quality stock, foreign vendor stock, local vendor stock etc. After creation of valuation type, you need to assign it to valuation category. Every material which you want to plan for split valuation, you need to assign split valuation category in material master record Accounting1 view. In standard SAP system you can view your stock as per valuation types in different reports e.g. MMBE and MB52.

11.2.5. Configuration of split valuation

For configuration of split valuation you can use following steps

- Global definition of valuation categories independently of the valuation area
- Global definition of valuation types independently of the valuation area
- Assignment of valuation categories and relevant valuation types
- Decide which global valuation category is used which valuation area, this said to be local definition

Copyrighted© Material

You can define valuation category, valuation type and their assignments in customizing under IMGP-SPRO > Materials Management > Valuation and Account Assignment > Split Valuation > Configure Split Valuation

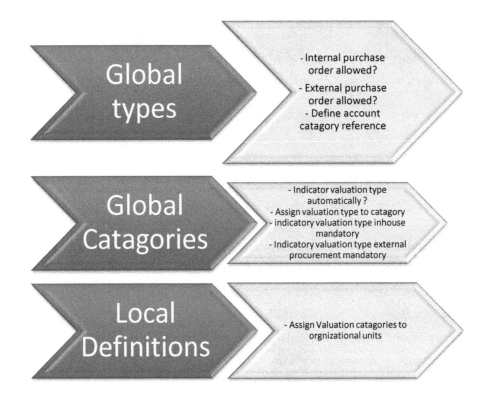

Figure 0-16 (Configure Split Valuation)

11.3. Material Ledger in SAP

The main aim of material ledger is to keeping records of your inventory in three different currencies. Companies having multiple operations in different countries that prefer reporting and valuation of stock in multiple currencies can use material ledger. It also takes into account fluctuation in price, exchange rate differences and factors those impacts on price fluctuation. Material ledger is tightly integrated with materials management, costing as well as production planning modules. The second important function of material ledger is to calculate the actual cost of both productions as well as procurement materials.

All goods movement inside a period is valuated at standard price (S) in actual costing. Price changes and factors that impact on price changes are consider in material ledger. In material ledger, at the end of each period actual cost is calculated for each plan material. Calculated actual cost of material said to be periodic unit price and can be used to reevaluate the inventory for the period to be closed. The calculated unit price will be the standard price for the upcoming period.

For usage of material ledger, it is mandatory that you must active it on back end. For doing this you can go to transaction code OMX1 or find by go to customizing

IMG-SPRO Controlling > Product Cost Controlling > Actual Costing/Material Ledger > Activate Valuation

Valuation Area	Company Code	ML Act.	Price Deter.	Price Det. Binding in Val Area
0001	0001	☐		☐
0005	0001	☐		☐
0006	0006	☐		☐
0007	0007	☐		☐
0008	0008	☐		☐
0099	1000	☐		☐
1000	1000	☑	3	☐
1100	1000	☐		☐
1200	1000	☐		☐

Figure 0-17 (Activate Valuation)

Copyrighted© Material

Several checks must be taking into account before you plan your material in material ledger. First you must check whether material ledger indicator active in material master record or not. It must be in activated status. The indicator found in material master data account 1 screen.

Secondly, relevant valuation class must be assign to material that plan for actual costing/ material ledger in material master record Accounting1 view.

Thirdly, in attributes of material type it is obligatory to check the radio button of valuation updating or the material type can be checked to see, if material valuation can be updated by viewing the configuration transaction in customizing

IMG-SPRO > Controlling > Product Cost Controlling > Actual Costing/ Material Ledger > Actual Costing > Activate

Materials that are considered for material ledger, system automatically pick information regarding the valuation relevance. Information collection sources are e.g. inventory management (Posted inventory document which are relevant for value updating), logistics invoice verifications, order settlements, and initial entry of stock balances, free deliveries, inward inventory movement from consignments and transfer postings. For material ledger/ actual costing, collected data is used doe periodic unit price determination. Variances and differences are taking into account during unit price determination. Possibly, following differences are collected during course

- Difference cause by revaluation
- Price differences
- Exchange rate differences

Copyrighted© Material

11.3.1. Material Price Analysis

The material price analysis can be view by transaction CKM3 for your material or by menu path under

Logistics > Materials Management > Valuation > Actual Costing/ Material Ledger > Material Ledger > Material Price Analysis

It shows the vaulted transaction and display the result of the determination material price for specific plant with considerable price and exchange rate differences. The report shows the opening stock, goods receipts, goods issue and invoices etc.

11.3.2. Material Price Determination

There are three types that determine material periodic unit price

- Single level material price determination
- Multiple level material price determination
- Transaction based material price determination

Copyrighted© Material

11.4. Additional Topic

11.4.1. Reporting in SAP Materials Management

Materials Management Master Data Reports

Transaction Code	Description
MM03	Display Material Master
MK03	Display Vendor – Purchasing
MK04	Purchasing Vendor Changes
XK03	Display Vendor – Central
XK04	Central Vendor Changes
ME1L	Info Records by Vendor
ME1M	Info Records by Material
ME1P	Purchase Order Price History
ME1E	Quotation Price History
ME13	Display Info Record
ME14	Display Info Record Changes
ME03	Display Source List
ME04	Display Source List Changes
MEQ3	Display Quota Arrangement
MEQ4	Display Quota Arrangement Changes
MKVZ	Display Purchasing Vendor List
MKVG	Display Vendor Condition Groups
MSC3N	Display Batch
MEKA	Display Purchasing Conditions
MN03	Display Message Condition – RFQ
MN06	Display Message Condition – Purchase Order
MN09	Display Message Condition – Scheduling Ag.
MN12	Display Message Condition – Delivery Sched.
MM60	Display Materials List

Copyrighted© Material

Logistics Information System Reports

Transaction Code	Description
MCBA	Plant
MCBC	Storage Location
MCBE	Material
MCBR	Batches
MC.9	Material Stock
MC.A	Material Receipts / Issues
MC.B	Inventory Turnover – Material
MC.1	Plant Stock
MC.2	Plant Receipts / Issues
MC.3	Plant Inventory Turnover
MC.5	Stock – Storage Location
MC.6	Storage Location Receipts / Issues
MC.7	Storage Location Inventory Turnover

Purchasing Information System Reports

Transaction Code	Description
MCE1	Purchase Group Analysis
MCE3	Vendor Analysis
MCE5	Material Groups Analysis
MCE7	Material Analysis
MC$G	Material Purchasing Values
MC$I	Material Purchasing Quantities
MC$O	Material Frequencies
MC$4	Vendor Purchasing Values
MC$6	Vendor Purchasing Quantities
MC$:	Vendor Frequencies
MC$0	Purchasing Group Values

Copyrighted© Material

MC$2	Purchasing Group Frequencies
MC$<	Material Group Purchasing Values
MC$>	Material Group Purchasing Quantities
MC$E	Material Group Frequencies

Purchasing Reports

Transaction Code	Description
ME80FN	General Analysis of Purchasing Documents
ME81N	Analysis of Order Values
ME23N	Display Purchase Order
ME53N	Display Purchase Requisition
ME5A	List Display Of Requisitions
ME33L	Display Scheduling Agreement
ME39	Display Delivery Schedule
ME43	Display RFQ
ME4L	List RFQ by Vendor
ME4M	List RFQ by Material
ME4S	List RFQ by Collective Number
ME48	Display Quotation
ME2L	Purchasing Documents per Vendor
ME2M	Purchasing Documents per Material
ME2K	Purchasing Documents by Account Assignment
ME2W	Purchasing Document by Supplying Plant
ME2V	Expected Goods Receipts
MD13	Display Planned Order Single
MD16	Display Planned Order Collective

Copyrighted© Material

Logistics Invoice Verification Reports

Transaction Code	Description
MB5S	List of GR/IR balances
MIR6	Invoice Overview
MIR4	Display Invoice
MIR5	Display Invoice List

Stock Reports

Transaction Code	Description
MMBE	Stock Overview
MB51	Material Document List
MB03	Display Material Document
MB54	Vendor consignment stocks
CO09	Material Availability
MB5C	Batch Where Used Pick Up List

Physical Inventory Reports

Transaction Code	Description
MI22	Physical Inventory Document – material
MI23	Physical Inventory Data – material
MIDO	Physical Inventory Overview
MI03	Display Physical Inventory Document
MI06	Display Count Document

Copyrighted© Material

Material Requirement Planning Reports

Transaction Code	Description
MD21	Display Planning File Entries
MDRE	Planning File Entries Consistency Report
MD04	Stock Requirements List
MD05	MRP List Material Display
MD06	MRP List Collective Display
MD07	Stock Requirements List Collective

Copyrighted© Material

Index

A

ABC Indicator...77, 107, 274
Account Assignment 82, 151, 152, 183, 226, 309, 312, 313, 314, 317, 318, 323, 329
Account category reference . 40, 42, 82, 153, 304, 307, 309, 310, 314, 315, 316
Account determination without wizard 152, 304, 312
Account Grouping...317
Account groups...92, 93
Accounting Data 38, 81
Accounting Information Data 92, 99
Activate material requirement planning 282
Activate Valuation 324
Alpha.. 66, 67, 299
Attributes of material types............................ 38, 40, 188
Authority for Exemption..102
Authorization Group 100
Automatic account determination 17, 152, 153, 304, 305
Automatic Evaluated Receipt settlement 105
Automatic Evaluated Receipt settlement - Return.........105

B

Backflush 80
Basic Data Screen.. 38, 53, 259
Batch Entry..79
Beta... 66, 67, 299
Bills of Material...38, 51
BOM.. 16, 38, 51, 79, 197
Bulk Storage 73
Business Volume Comparison/Agreement Necessary....106

C

Cancelation........................... 194, 218, 240, 241, 242, 244
Cash Management Group..100
Centrally agreed contracts 159
Certification Date for Minority Vendor 101
Change in stock account..204
Characteristics 250, 251, 253
Chart of accounts... 304, 306
Class 250, 251, 253, 258, 259, 260, 316
Classification Data..38, 56
Client ..9, 10, 23, 24, 30, 40, 41, 45, 49, 53, 69, 71, 75, 112, 153, 276, 306

Communication 98, 253
Company code 24, 32, 33, 136, 149, 320
Conditions.... 16, 17, 69, 105, 107, 116, 117, 120, 121, 125, 136, 222, 327
Configure Automatic Posting......................................318
Consignment 17,120, 143, 148, 155, 159, 162, 168, 171, 178, 200, 201, 202, 325
Consumable materials 17, 165, 168, 183, 184
Consumption 13, 64, 70, 77, 78, 79, 80, 175, 183, 184, 204, 205, 270, 275, 278, 282, 285, 291, 294, 309
Consumption based planning.............................. 275, 285
Continuous Inventory Procedure 210
Contract release orders...160
Contracts 17, 147, 157, 158, 159
Copy rules for reservation documents 194
Costing Data 38, 85
Costing Lot Size..87
Costing Overhead Group 86
Credit Memo 218, 221, 238
Critical Part...60
Cross plant material status...55
Cycle Count Procedure..210
Cycle Counting...70

D

Date to..65
Delivery completion indicator in PO..................... 218, 246
Delivery cost 222
Delta Factor...67
Division...55
Document Index Active 106
dynamic availability check...194

E

Enterprise Structure... 17, 21, 22, 23, 24, 25, 28, 30, 31, 32, 33
ERP...2, 3, 4, 5, 9
Error Message.. 168, 206
Exemption Number...102
external procurement............ 41, 47, 80, 127, 133, 272, 273
External Procurement 80, 132, 133

Copyrighted© Material

F

Field selection.............. 38, 45, 47, 92, 93, 94, 95, 146, 151
Financial Accounting 2, 18, 24, 100, 101, 168, 184, 186, 204, 219
Finished goods........................... 76, 83, 169, 185, 203, 285
Fixed lot size 279
Fixed Periods 65
Forecast based planning 77, 285, 291, 292
Forecast models.......................................64, 298, 299
Forecast Models 298
forecast planning... 5, 294
Forecast program 291
Forecast values 65, 290
Forecasting Data..38, 63
Framework Order 132, 155, 165, 225
Future Price 84

G

Gamma.. 66, 67, 299
General Data Screen 92, 98
Good Receipt-Based Invoice Verification 105
Goods Issues... 17, 168, 196, 239
Goods Receipt Processing Time 60
Goods Receipts .29, 105, 134, 154, 155, 172, 183, 186, 189, 204, 207, 225, 226, 238, 243, 244, 247, 329
GR IR Account 186, 187, 189, 205, 223, 241
Group Counter...86

H

Hazardous Material Number 69
Head Office...100
Historical periods 65
Hold Invoice.. 218, 228
Human Capital Management............................... 2, 14, 17

I

Incoterms 104
industry sector....................................... 38, 48
Industry Specific solutions..2, 7
Initialization Indicator 65
Interest Calculation Frequency 101
Interest calculation indicator.......................................101
Inventory audits 17
Inventory management... 17, 169
Inventory sampling procedure....................................210
Invoice in foreign currency 218, 231
Invoice Reduction 218, 236, 237, 238

invoicing plan...218, 224, 225
Item categories.. 159, 160
Item categories M and W 160
Item category 136, 149, 154, 155, 156, 160, 165, 201
Item category M 160
Item category W 160

L

Legacy systems 2, 4
Limits Item Category 155
Logistics invoice verifications 17
Lot for lot order quantity..279
Lot Size................................... 78, 270, 278, 279, 280, 281
Lot Size Calculation 270, 278
Lot size calculations 281
Lot size procedure...79, 278, 280
Lot-sizing procedures...291

M

Managerial Accounting 19
Manual Block.. 218, 233
Manual Reorder Point..287
Mass Maintenance........................38, 49, 50, 92, 93, 112
Master data in Purchasing............................... 116, 117
Material Description 54
Material Ledger 82, 304, 324, 325, 326
Material ledgers...17
Material master17, 38, 39, 40, 42, 45, 47, 48, 49, 52, 53, 54, 55, 59, 60, 62, 65, 69, 70, 71, 77, 81, 83, 88, 112, 117, 123, 126, 150, 152, 162, 163, 174, 183, 185, 188, 189, 190, 197, 219, 272, 274, 276, 278, 279, 280, 284, 287, 290, 306, 310, 321, 322, 325
Material Master Record 38, 52, 284
Material Origin Indicator 86
Material Price Analysis 304, 326
Material Price Determination 304, 326
Material requirement planning...... 17, 62, 76, 209, 271, 278
Material Requirement Planning (MRP) Data.............. 38, 76
Material Type 40, 41, 42, 43, 46, 47, 77, 304, 307, 316, 320
Material types... 17, 38, 40
Materials group 54
Maximum Lot Size..78
Maximum Stock Level 79
Maximum Storage Period 70
Minimum Lot Size...78
Minimum Remaining Shelf Life 71
Minimum Safety Stock 80
Minority Indicator...101
Mode of Transport for Foreign Trade...........................107

Copyrighted© Material

Model Selection 66, 298
Movement type ...29, 80, 168, 172, 173, 174, 175, 176, 180, 181, 182, 190, 193, 194, 195, 196, 197, 199, 204, 218, 239, 244, 307, 310, 317, 320
Moving average price... 41, 82, 83, 168, 183, 185, 188, 189, 190, 192, 205, 218, 223, 321
Moving average price calculation 189
MRP Controller 78
MRP Group 77, 272
MRP list 277
MRP Profile... 270, 274
MRP Settings 284
MRP Type 77
Multiplier..65

N

Name 98, 263
Number of Goods Receipt slips.........................70
Number of period initialization.........................65
Number ranges....................................... 93, 144

O

Office of Entry..107
Old Material Number 55
Operational Significance................................2, 6
Optimize lot size 281
Order Acknowledgement 106
Order Currency 104
Order unit..59
Origin group 86
Outline Agreements 132, 157

P

Park Invoice 218, 228
Partial Invoicing Plan............................... 218, 224
Partner role 92, 93, 108
Partner Schema.................................... 109, 110
Period Indicator 64, 71
Period Indicator for Shelf Life Expiration Date.................71
Periodic Inventory Procedure 210
Periodic Invoicing Plan 218, 224
Periodic Lot Size...281
Personnel Number..102
Physical Inventory...... 29, 70, 168, 173, 193, 207, 209, 210, 211, 212, 213, 214, 247, 330
Physical inventory count 211, 213
Physical inventory document.................. 211, 212, 213
Physical year variant 64

Picking Area..69
Picking Storage Type 73
Planned independent requirements.....................285
Planning at storage location level 276
Planning calendar 270, 275
Planning Cycle..78
Planning Evaluation............................... 270, 277
Planning Processes............................... 270, 276
Plant 2, 14, 16, 22, 24, 25, 26, 27, 28, 32, 33, 38, 47, 50, 51, 59, 65, 68, 94, 117, 118, 120, 121, 123, 137, 142, 143, 178, 180, 181, 198, 199, 209, 212, 247, 275, 276, 280, 282, 283, 309, 313, 328, 329
PO Box Address...98
Post Differences...213
Post to inspection stock indicator 60, 75
Previous Account Number................................102
Price Comparison Statement............................141
Price Control..82
Price Unit..................................... 83, 186, 189
Price Variance 168, 191
Pricing Date Category.......................................105
Procurement Documents 249, 250, 251
Procurement Type 79, 304, 321
Production Planning...............................2, 14, 16, 51
Production Storage Location 79
Project System.. 2, 15, 18
Purchase group 34, 149
Purchase info Record 116, 117
Purchase Order.59, 106, 118, 119, 132, 148, 168, 198, 199, 201, 222, 225, 227, 238, 250, 252, 253, 257, 258, 260, 261, 262, 266, 327, 329
Purchase Requisition132, 142, 143, 144, 145, 146, 147, 329
Purchase requisitions.......................................17
Purchasing Data 38, 58, 92, 103
Purchasing information system........................17
Purchasing organization 22, 30, 33, 136, 149
Purchasing value key...60

Q

Quality Management 2, 14, 18, 38, 75
Quantity Variance 168, 191, 192
Quota arrangement...................... 17, 61, 80, 125, 126, 127
Quota Arrangement Usage................. 61, 62, 80, 126, 127
Quotation 118, 135, 136, 139, 140, 327, 329

R

Reconciliation account 94, 99
Rejections..218, 244, 245
Release Codes..................................... 260, 261

Release Group 100, 251, 260
Release Indicator 260, 262
Release strategies...17, 251, 258
Release with documentation 163
Release without documentation...........................163, 164
Reorder point....................78, 270, 280, 281, 286, 287, 290
Reorder point planning.......77, 78, 195, 279, 280, 285, 286, 287, 288, 290, 291
Reorder Point Planning 270, 286
Replenishment lead time 290
Replenishment to maximum stock level.......................280
Reporting...5, 16, 17, 327
Request for quotations..17
Reservation............................. 17, 168, 193, 194, 195, 202
Reset Forecast Model Automatically...............................66
Restricted stock 168, 170
Return Vendor 106
RFQ 54, 135, 136, 137, 138, 139, 141, 150, 327, 329
Road map of SAP... 2, 8, 10

S

Safety stock 80, 274, 287, 290
Safety Stock..80
Sales and Distribution 2, 16, 38, 55, 57
Sales order...285
SAP Activate 2, 10, 12
SAP CO 14, 19
SAP FI 2, 14, 18
SAP Functional Modules.......................................2, 14, 16
SAP HCM 2, 14, 17
SAP Modules...2, 14
SAP PP 2, 14, 16
SAP PS 2, 18
SAP QM 2, 14, 18
SAP S/4 HANA 2, 9
SAP SD 2, 14, 16
SAP Solution Manager...2, 12
SAP Technical Modules 2, 14
Scheduling Agreement types 163
scheduling agreements 17, 157, 162, 164, 271, 273, 276
Search Term 98
semi finished goods...285
Service-based Invoice Verification 106
Services 7, 12, 15, 16, 38, 88, 148, 155
Services Item Category..155
Sort Key..100
Source list....................17, 39, 60, 116, 117, 122, 123, 273
Source List Indicator..60
Source of Supply 133
Special Procurement Type..79

Split valuations 17
Standard item category..154
Standard price......82, 83, 168, 185, 186, 187, 192, 223, 324
Static Lot Size...279
Stochastic Block...218, 233, 234
Stock Account .183, 186, 187, 188, 189, 204, 222, 238, 243
Stock Management Unit....................................... 168, 209
Stock material..168, 183, 224
Stock Placement 73
Stock Requirement List 277, 289, 296, 297
Stock Transfer....17, 148, 162, 168, 178, 179, 180, 181, 195
Stock Transport order 181
Stock types 17, 209
Storage Bin 69
Storage location 28, 80, 212, 275
Storage Section...73
Storage Type Indicator for Stock Removal.....................73
Street Address 98
Subcontracting..17, 120, 143, 148, 155, 159, 162, 168, 171, 203, 204, 205, 275
Subsequent Credit 218, 220
Subsequent Debit 218, 220
Subsequent Settlement..106
Supply chain management..3, 6

T

Task List Group 86
Task List Type...86
Tax indicator...59
Tax reduction..238
Third Party item category..155
Time Phase Planning 270, 300
Time Unit...71
Title..98
Tolerance key B1.. 168, 206
Tolerance key B2.. 168, 206
Tolerances . 60, 117, 150, 168, 206, 207, 208, 214, 246, 247
Tolerances of Physical Inventory Differences 214
Total Shelf Life...71
Tracking Limit 66
Transaction event key 205
Transaction key.. 304, 307
Transfer posting.................... 17, 168, 178, 179, 180, 244
Two Step Picking...74
Types of contract 159

U

Unit of Measure...54
Unlimited over delivery indicator 60

Unrestricted stock... 168, 170

V

Validity Date of Exemption...102
Valuation Area..................................... 304, 306, 308, 313
Valuation category...82, 304, 322
Valuation Class... 82, 315
Valuation Classes 314
Valuation control 312
Valuation Type...322
Value String 304, 310, 320
Variances in GR IR account 168, 191
Vendor account..205
Vendor master 17, 39, 59, 60, 92, 93, 97, 98, 100, 107, 108, 112, 117, 162, 199, 225

Vendor Master Record........................ 92, 96, 97, 112, 200
Vendor Number Ranges 92, 96
Vendor Recipient Type 102
Vendor Schema Group 105
Vendor Sort Criterion 107

W

Warehouse Management Data................................38, 72
Warning message 168, 206
With Quantity Structure Indicator 86
Withholding Tax Code 101
Withholding tax country key...101
WM Unit..73
Work-Flow..266

Copyrighted© Material

Copyrighted© Material

Copyrighted© Material